CHASING SHADOWS

PARINAYA PRADHAN

CHASING SHADOWS

A Journey of Love, Loss, Pain, Betrayal and Resilience.

PALMETTO
PUBLISHING
Charleston, SC
www.PalmettoPublishing.com

Chasing Shadows
Copyright © 2024 by Parinaya Pradhan

All rights reserved
No portion of this book may be reproduced, stored in a retrieval system, or transmitted in any form by any means–electronic, mechanical, photocopy, recording, or other–except for brief quotations in printed reviews, without prior permission of the author.

First Edition

Paperback ISBN: 979-8-8229-4847-1
eBook ISBN: 979-8-8229-4848-8

CONTENTS

1: The Day 1
2: The Hunch 14
3: There She Goes 19
4: Diya's Arrival 32
5: The Diagnosis 39
6: The Beautiful Call 42
7: The Treatment 46
8: The Superwoman 52
9: Maya's Family 63
10: The Surgery 84
11: Radiation 101
12: The Misunderstandings 117
13: Girls Night Out 140
14: The Cancer Returns 146
15: Trip to Nepal 158
16: Self Blames 168
17: Emotions 175
18: Diya's Revisit 182

19: Trip to Kansas	188
20: Day of the CT scan	195
21: She Leaves for Nepal	198
22: Days after she was gone	205
23: The Fundraiser	211
24: Second Visit to Nepal	224
25: The Divorce	233
26: The Court House	239
27: Visiting Maya before Leaving Nepal	248
28: The Third Visit to Nepal	255
29: Visiting Maya at the Hospital	260
30: Barahi Jungle Lodge	277
31: Maya's House Visit	285
32: Hospital Visit with Kamli	299
33: The Dreaded Day	319
34: The Final Goodbye	331
35: The Revelation	338
About the Author	347

1

THE DAY

JANUARY 25*th*, 2021, unfolded like any normal day. It was frigid but the sun had not forgotten to embrace us with its warmth. Amidst the hustle of meeting deadlines and attending to daily chores, nothing looked out of the ordinary.

As night fell, a peaceful calm settled over the surroundings, replacing the earlier chaos of the day. The crisp breeze carried the enticing scent of nearby meals being prepared as I ventured out to take out the trash. Dinner was done and mom had gone to bed. I lay silently flipping over the TV channels while trying to finish the book, soon due at the library. Little did I know that the seemingly uneventful day held an unexpected twist that would reshape my entire perspective on life.

While absentmindedly flipping through the TV channels, I was disrupted with a text message. I expected it to be a random message from a friend or a spammer, but when I read it, it sent my heart plummeting. It was a text from Diya, Maya's sister, asking me if I had spoken to Maya that day.

For almost two years, Diya and I hadn't exchanged words. She was well aware that Maya and I had distanced ourselves from each other, rarely conversing. Despite our once-close relationship, Diya and I had drifted apart, neglecting to check on each other or say hello the entire time since Maya left two years ago.

"Did di[1] call you?" her message read.

"Call me for what? About what?" I replied anxiously.

There was no response for a while. The unnerving silence got my mind racing. I kept staring at the phone but there was no sign that she had seen my text or any sign to show she was *typing…*

The sound of the television faded into distant chatter and returning to my book seemed irrelevant. My mind refused to focus, indulging instead in flights of imagination. Receiving the text from Diya had stirred up a whirlwind of emotions, and the lack of response only added layers of uncertainty and tension to the already fraught situation.

As I awaited a response, my apprehension grew, and I could feel myself slipping into an emotional void, until Maya's brother, Kiran, called me. Without bothering to greet him, I immediately asked, "Kiran, what's happening? What's wrong with Maya?"

"Oh, you heard?" he asked.

After explaining how I had come across the news, he clarified that Maya had gone for a checkup due to discomfort in her nose.

---

1   Sister

The doctors suspected a tumor, and if confirmed, surgery might be necessary. A wave of numbness engulfed me as he spoke. While he also expressed concern, he lacked further details. Sensing the prevailing uncertainty, I ended the call, promising to reach out again after gathering more information from Maya.

It was already 10 pm when I called her. She answered, sounding worried, and asked, *"Is everything ok?"* She seemed more concerned that I had called so late at night, which was unusual for me to do.

"Forget about me, what's going on? Everything ok with you?" I asked.

"Oh, did da² tell you?" she said casually.

"Not everything, what's going on?" I inquired further.

"I think it's just sinus, but I wanted to get it checked to be on the safer side," she replied casually and mentioned that she was going the next day to find out. She didn't mention anything about the possibility of it being a tumor. I offered to come right away, but she insisted otherwise. Furthermore, she was heading to bed and didn't want her roommate inconvenienced. She assured me that her appointment was the next day and that she would update me further.

"I don't think it's a big deal and you shouldn't worry," she affirmed. I insisted I would come the next day to take her for her appointment. She was hesitant but I was adamant and confirmed I would be there at 7 am.

* * *

It was a challenge to get any rest that night, and the hours seemed never-ending. Emotions ran high and despite my attempts not to worry excessively, I couldn't escape the anxiety. Maya's description of the situation didn't sound too dire, but we needed more information. I also felt a mix of vexation and excitement about seeing her after such a long time—it felt like ages ago!

After numerous moments of tossing and turning, I managed to snatch only a brief amount of sleep. Daylight couldn't come soon enough. Following a quick shower, I set off. I arrived early and waited in the parking lot. About five minutes later, I called her to join me. She responded with a text, mentioning that her roommate would be accompanying us as well.

"*Uh no!*" I uttered. She chuckled and said she would be down in a minute. I was hoping for some quality time alone with her but now I had to deal with someone else. But deep down I was glad to know someone cared for Maya and she didn't have to make that dreadful trip alone.

* * *

When we met, a broad smile adorned her face, mirroring my own. We exchanged warm greetings with a tight hug, the familiar comfort of which I had sorely missed. It seemed she might have missed mine just as much. Our smiles persisted as she introduced me to Jamie. I extended a friendly handshake, but to my surprise, received no shared smile. The day was cold, and Jamie's handshake even colder. As our hands met, she cast a sidelong glance at me, as if harboring disdain—perhaps it was just my imagination. I couldn't help but wonder if Maya had shared details about why she left me. It's natural for me to be cast as the bad guy, especially when compared to someone like Maya.

* * *

The appointment was scheduled in Yale New Haven Hospital, requiring a thirty-minute drive south to Stamford to pick her up, followed by an hour's journey north. Trumbull, where we owned a house, served as a convenient midpoint. Throughout the drive, Jamie remained quietly observant, offering responses only when prompted. Surprisingly, I found myself appreciating her reserved demeanor. Ordinarily, I made a concerted effort to engage with new acquaintances, but on this occasion, I felt indifferent. It seemed like a rare opportunity to share the events of my life, hoping to hear from Maya as well. For the past two years, I had longed for her with every waking moment, and now, I intended to make the most of this chance—a moment to lay bare everything on my mind as I rambled on.

The first thing Maya said when she saw my car was, *"Why did you have to buy this car?"* It felt good hearing this. It had been two long years that someone reprimanded me with concern.

I grinned and asked, *"It's good right?"*

"Hmmmm....," she said.

* * *

I remember the day when our friends, Avi and Ash, visited me, just the day after I had purchased my car. Very typical of them - they loved it, and both expressed great desire to splurge in something similar in the future.

"You guys should. If not now, then when? We only live once bro," I encouraged them.

To which they responded, *"Come on bro, our wives won't let us."*

I chuckled and replied, *"Too bad, my wife left me and that's the only reason I got to buy this or else she would never allow it."*

We had all burst out in laughter and when I told Maya this, she remained quiet and offered no response. Perhaps she did not want to be reminded of her leaving. I understood it was tough for her, and taking such a step wouldn't have been easy, especially when it seemed like we had so much going on for us.

* * *

Unaware that our lives were also destined for harsh actualities such as the cold, bitter New England winter with icy winds churning deep into our bones, we snuck into the car. I had kept the engine running and set the temperature just warm and turned on the seat heater, just the way she would like. I wanted to play some music to add to the ambiance, but my 'new' car's media system froze and wouldn't turn on. *"New car huh?"* she teased.

We conversed throughout the journey, reminiscent of the good old days. Her company never bored me. We could spend hours together, comfortable in silence, without any pressure to say something. It was a beautiful aspect of our relationship—no need for attention-seeking behaviors, no signs of possessiveness, and no acts to display our affection; we just knew. She wasn't demanding, and I'd like to believe I wasn't either. We simply knew that we cared deeply for each other. However, despite all this, there was "something" missing. There was an element of dissatisfaction in her being with me.

It was a bitterly cold day, as if the heavens had conspired to match the gloom of the reality ahead. As I drove, peering through the windshield, the scene outside was grim, reminiscent of the solemnity of hospital visits with looming questions. It weighed heavily on our minds, amplifying the sense of uncertainty that hung in the air. The streets were coated in a dirty slush of salt and snow, churned up by passing tires into an uneven array of skid marks. The windshield wipers swayed back and forth, leaving streaks of white residue behind, adding to the overall sense of gloominess in the surroundings.

Just a day ago it looked beautiful and serene. Now the street signs did not seem clear, and visibility was near zero. I drove at a snail's pace, but we were scheduled to reach on time. Ignoring the weather outside, I did most of the yapping, fearing I may not get the chance again. I condensed my conversation to fit all that had happened in the past two years. I spoke relatively fast and later realized I still had time on our way back to continue my chatter. So, I slowed the pace of my storytelling while she listened in awe. She would smirk and give a sidelong glance, slightly tilting her head to the side, every time I said that I had done something stupid. She was a good listener. Nothing had changed. She still looked the same, acted the same way, smiled the same way, glanced at me the same way, except she did not call me *baba*!

* * *

Nepalese women tend to call their spouses "*baba*" with love. It meant "*babes*," the Nepalese way. When we first got into the relationship, she had asked what she would call me. I thought she would always call me by my nickname, *Hansu*, but she gave it her own tweak and started calling me *Hanchu*. She had rumbled through heaps of cute pet names for me. "*Boo*," "*Bee*," and with many trials and mispronunciations, she settled on "*Baba*." It took me time to adjust to it, but gradually grew into it. I felt loved and hearing it out of her mouth was even more admirable.

* * *

"*Hanchu,*" she said, bringing me back from my brief imagination to rectify her not calling me '*baba.*' "*Do you have water?*"

Things appeared normal as we reached the hospital. I was concerned that Jamie might want to wait in the car with me, leading to unnecessary and forced conversations. When we arrived, I asked Maya if Jamie would accompany her. She confirmed, and Jamie agreed to go. I dropped them off at the main entrance, instructing them to keep me updated while I found parking and waited in the car. Waiting for Maya never bored me; it felt like I was meant to wait for her.

As I waited, time seemed to stretch endlessly. I occupied myself with games on my phone, switching between trading apps and scanning through headline news. Not being familiar with New Haven, I opted to head to the nearest service station, a fifteen-minute drive away. I had requested Jamie to give me a heads up ten to fifteen minutes before they were finished.

After about an hour, Jamie called, stating that it would take more time, possibly all day, and asked if I could take her home. Maya shouldn't have brought her along, I thought. Although it meant a two-hour drive back and forth, I was willing to do it for Jamie as she had been there for Maya. Jamie didn't offer to be dropped off at the train station; instead, she asked me to drop her off in Middletown at her friend's place and pick her up when Maya was done. This added another hour in the opposite direction, and when she noticed my hesitation, she said, *"Don't worry, drop me off in Stamford,"* as if it was my obligation. She seemed indifferent to the inconvenience.

On my way to drop Jamie off, before I could ask for updates on Maya, Maya's mom called. I told her I hadn't received any news, so I asked Jamie. The phone was connected to the car Bluetooth. Jamie reassured her, *"Oh, there is nothing to worry, mamu³."* She further explained that the biopsy was done but did not reveal anything concerning.

I let out a sigh of relief as I was hearing it for the first time too. *"Please do some offering to your Gods,"* Jamie suggested to Maya's mom. Upon hearing this, Maya's mom was overjoyed and sobbed in happiness. When she spoke to me, she instructed me not to leave Maya's side at any cost, all while crying.

After she hung up, I asked Jamie about the quick results. *"Yeah, I'm surprised too,"* she replied. Later, we would find out that it was her inconsideration in understanding the doctor's words. Eager to

---

3   Mother

deliver the good news, she shared it without fully comprehending the situation. Nevertheless, it brought us joy, albeit briefly.

When I did drop her off, she asked if I was taking Maya home to Trumbull that night. I hadn't expected that question. Was that what Maya had told her? Startled, I replied that I didn't know and needed to check with Maya.

Jamie advised, *"Oh please, you should take her there and make her rest for a few days. I can pack all her stuff or even bring it to Trumbull."*

For a while I thought she was very caring and understood the fact that I would take care of Maya better than her, and having my mother around was an added bonus. Or perhaps, Maya's absence for a few days would allow Jamie to enjoy the apartment by herself without having to sleep on the couch, as she did every day. Only she would know.

I returned to New Haven. I parked in the Walgreens parking lot and to kill time, strolled around the store, used the restroom, and finally took my passport photos, a task I had been procrastinating for a long time. After a day of waiting, constantly falling in and out of brief naps, and receiving a few updates from Maya, I finally caught up on my winks.

Maya completed her procedures around 5 pm. The doctors had taken a few blood samples and performed a biopsy to detect any traces of malignant tissues. Maya explained to me that it was a painful experience. It was hard to listen to her vivid description, causing my body to shudder. She shared that the nurse conducting the biopsy was new, working under the doctor's guidance. Maya, unfortunately, became the guinea pig for the inexperienced nurse. Despite Maya's nervousness, the nurse was incapable of alleviating her pain, which otherwise could have been avoided with a more seasoned professional. Nevertheless, everyone needs to start somewhere. I just hoped that the doctors overseeing Maya's treatment were not beginners.

The results wouldn't be out for a few days. We headed back to her apartment. I did ask her if she wanted to spend a few days in Trumbull. She gave me a nod of refusal and smiled. On our way back, we grabbed a Subway sandwich and talked and shared as many more details as we could. There was an aura of certain oddness and uncomfortable chill that ran through my spine, reminding me not to get too comfortable and this was just a brief meeting. We would be soon going our own ways once this was over. I didn't care, at least I got to see her finally after her many attempts of avoiding me.

I initially didn't take these tests too seriously, opting instead to lighten the mood with some witty banter. There was an abundance of topics to discuss, and I constantly felt as though time wasn't on our side to cover everything. I made sure to update her on how I'd embraced activities she always encouraged me to try when we were together – things like yoga, running, gardening, cleaning, and even abstaining from alcohol. Work was going smoothly, and I was eager to share my progress with her.

As we arrived at her apartment, she kindly invited me upstairs. Suddenly, I found myself falling silent, realizing I'd dominated the conversation. It was now Jamie's turn to take the lead. She gracefully brewed tea and delved into topics ranging from her new business venture to her insights on the stock market, her trading strategies, and even her preferences and dislikes when it came to men.

***

Even after our separation, Maya used to come by the house and spend time with me and the dogs. One day, she had planned to stop by after attending a friend's baby shower nearby. She had called me on the way and informed me of her visit. In anticipation, I cooked her favorite meals, knowing she would be yearning for them. However, later, she called to say she wasn't coming and had already decided to head back. Curious, I asked why she had changed her mind. She explained that our friends had advised her against meeting if we were trying to move on from each other, as it would be difficult for both of us.

Maya had now rented herself a one-bedroom apartment, spacious enough for one person. Since she had taken in Jamie, Maya let her use the couch to crash. Both of them worked in the same company, but Jamie had been laid off from work and had nowhere to go. Maya wanted to support her until she was able to get back on her feet. Jamie went on to live with Maya for nearly two years. Maya never requested rent and never asked Jamie to share grocery costs, and Jamie never offered to contribute.

During the thirty minutes I spent in the apartment, I was pleased to see that Jamie did care for Maya. She would ask if Maya wanted tea or coffee, inquired about dinner preferences, and suggested watching a movie or resting. It brought me comfort to know that someone was taking care of Maya, and she wasn't alone.

While Maya and I were in the midst of our conversation, Jamie began watching a show on Netflix, dividing Maya's attention. Recognizing the shift, I decided to call it a night and bid them both goodnights. Maya expressed her gratitude for the day, prompting a stern look from me in return. She responded with a smile and said, *"Alright, no thank you then!"*

Finally, my music system decided to work. Perhaps it too wanted me to talk and not get distracted listening to music while Maya was around. I played some soothing music and drove home, smiling to myself content to have spent time with Maya.

* * *

2

THE HUNCH

IN December, just a few days before Diya's call, I found myself plagued by an unsettling sensation. An inexplicable unease seemed to wash over me, leaving me with a sense of foreboding. There were no visible signs of trouble, but an intangible intuition was nagging at my consciousness. Thoughts of Maya consumed my mind, accompanied by a growing worry that she might be unwell. It was a strange and elusive sensation, like a whisper of concern hinting that something bad loomed in the horizon. No matter where I went, her presence lingered in my thoughts, haunting me relentlessly. I tried to shake off the feeling, but it clung to me stubbornly, casting a shadow over my days.

My hunch had become a silent guide, engulfing my mind with thoughts of her, prompting me to consider calling her. Many times, I had reached over the phone but stopped myself. I hid my emotions

well and did not want others to know how deeply I missed her. It was beginning to get too much to take, so one day I made the call. Alas! It went to her voicemail. Before I could leave a message, she texted me asking, *"Talking with mamu. Everything ok?"*
"Yeah," I replied.
"No really. Tell me," she wrote back.
"Really, it's nothing. I just wanted to check on you," I reconfirmed.
"Sure?" she questioned again.
"Yes, yes," I reassured her.
She sent a smiling emoji and that was it. She did not call back. Later, when discussing the time frame of the incidents, it was right about this time that she had considered getting her check-ups done.

* * *

The day I met her while taking her to the hospital, I could notice the change in her voice. It was distinctly nasal. I had even asked her to blow her nose and had asked whether she had caught a cold.
"This is how it is. My nose is not stuffy. Nothing comes out," she'd respond in dismay.

* * *

Before calling Maya, I recall reaching out to Jenny to inquire about her. In a moment of uncertainty, I swiftly deleted the message before Jenny could read it. She was someone with whom I had shared my vulnerabilities, a person I trusted amidst the guarded façade I put up with others. Sensing that I had deleted a message, Jenny promptly called me back and inquired, *"What is it that you had to tell me but changed your mind after sending?"*

I had never opened up to anyone to the extent of laying bare my emotions. Unsatisfied with being brushed off, Jenny called me later, and I confided in her that I was missing Maya, and that her thoughts were haunting me constantly. I was seeking reassurance about Maya's well-being.

"Aww," she responded. At that moment, I began regretting sharing my feelings, thinking I should have kept them to myself. Despite my reservations, Jenny showed empathy. However, she hadn't spoken to Maya recently and couldn't provide the information I sought.

Later, Jenny texted me, sharing that she had just spoken to Maya, who sounded healthy and in good spirits. While this news brought a wave of relief, the uneasiness lingering within me refused to dissipate. In the days that followed, I made efforts to distract myself and avoid dwelling on thoughts of her. Yet, every activity we once relished together now felt tinged with a sense of emptiness. Maya's absence served as a stark reminder that moving on was far from effortless. The absence of communication from her, coupled with the dearth of information, only served to compound my worries further.

Occasionally, I would come across Facebook posts from Maya's colleagues, tagging her in photos where she would be smiling, raising a glass for a toast, or her friends tagging her while making *momo*[4] in her apartment and enjoying time with friends. Seeing this

---

4   Steamed dumplings.

was consoling, as it gave the impression that she was surrounded by friends and possibly moving on.

* * *

Maya and I shared a considerable circle of mutual friends. This group included individuals who invited us to birthdays, weddings, kids' parties, and various other occasions. Our connections with these friends were strong, with everyone being close to both Maya and me. While some may have been closer to her, they knew me equally well, and we always spent time together.

Things were undeniably different now – our separation had not only altered our own dynamics but also affected our relationships with our mutual friends. They found themselves in a quandary when it came to event invitations, grappling with the awkwardness of potentially having both of us present. In an effort to navigate this delicate situation, they often faced the dilemma of whom to include. Recognizing the inherent discomfort of being together in social settings, one of us would inevitably step back.

Whenever I received invitations, I would cautiously inquire, *"Did you also invite her?"* It was a subtle attempt to sidestep the complexities of our changed relationship. Our friends would reassure me, explaining that Maya had other commitments for the day and wouldn't be able to attend, but they hadn't overlooked extending the invitation to her. Sometimes, they'd joke, *"We spent time with her yesterday, today it's your turn."* However, even with these lighthearted exchanges, the topic of our relationship remained largely unspoken between us and wasn't openly discussed. Consequently, I remained unaware of how Maya truly fared amidst our separation.

Maya wasn't particularly active on social media platforms. Messages sent to her on Facebook Messenger could easily go unnoticed for weeks on end. Despite her reluctance, I was the one who had initially signed her up for a Facebook account. The few tagged posts of Maya portrayed happiness, but only she knew deep down the true story behind that façade. Social media, in our view, often presented a distorted reality, emphasizing a curated version of one's life. But the pictures gave me a sense that she was not alone, and her friends were a constant presence. Jenny became my sole source for updates on Maya, though I knew even Jenny would filter information so as not to hurt my feelings if she thought it may.

Maya and I both disapproved of people oversharing their personal lives on Facebook. She rarely scrolled through her feed, and days could pass before she logged into her account. We found it perplexing when people posted about a gift they were about to give, urging others to keep it a secret. *"Isn't this dumb?"* we would ask each other, shaking our heads in agreement. At that time, we were grateful that Facebook hadn't consumed our lives. Guilty to admit, I now had a change of perspective. In hindsight, I wished Maya had been more active on social media, as I was yearning for glimpses of her life through regular posts.

* * *

THERE SHE GOES

IT had been approximately two years since our separation. On that day, I experienced a profound sense of loss, as if a part of me had been taken away. The notion of losing a part of oneself is often expressed as a cliché in movies, soap operas, and the like. However, when it became my reality, I truly understood the depth of its meaning.

Few days or months before leaving, Maya hadn't been herself for a while. One day, while my mom and I were in the family room watching TV, Maya entered with a serious expression. I recognized that look, and it was evident that whatever she was about to say wouldn't be pleasant. Standing in the middle of the room, she took a deep breath, as if swallowing years of discontent, and declared, *"I've decided to leave!"*

The moment she uttered those words, a seismic wave of disbelief and heartache swept through me, leaving me in a state of emotional disarray. The world seemed to momentarily halt as the weight of her announcement sank in. The once familiar and comforting foundation of our shared life crumbled, replaced by a hollow ache that echoed through the very core of my being. I never understood what a heart break was until then. I just couldn't believe it. We were having our dark days, but I had never imagined that this day would come. It was difficult for her too, but she had gathered enough courage to make the announcement.

She was serious and she didn't plan on retreating. I couldn't bring myself to talk yet. My mom, with a heavy heart asked her where she'd go, and Maya explained her intentions. I finally found my voice to tell her that she should stay, and I would leave. She was not letting this happen. She shrugged me off saying she was already moving her stuff to a friend's place in Stamford, and she would leave the following week.

"Until death do us part!" This solemn vow was etched in our hearts and minds. Little did I know at the time that it would be the very thing that'd separate us. I had taken our relationship for granted, assuming that we would navigate life together until the end. The bond we shared was strong, founded on openness, and comfort in each other's presence. Yet, a lingering sense of incompleteness persisted. Deep down, I acknowledged this void but chose to deny its significance, hoping that time would mend any discrepancies. Having known her for so long, the idea of a world without her seemed unfathomable, but she had sensed the disparities long before I did. Even with our deep friendship, she recognized that the love between us didn't align romantically or as life partners. This realization,

known to her even before our marriage, had lingered, and now, we both confronted the undeniable truth.

This day had been inevitable, and as they say, everything happens for a reason; this too had its own significance – reasons that transformed me as a person and altered my perspective on life and people. It instilled strength in me; it was as if I had constructed a shield around myself to ward off further pain. Trivial matters held little importance. Pain and sorrow, one goes through is defined by one's ability to cope with it. It is how each handles the situation, gives an opportunity to open doors for new learnings. Every individual being is different and has their own threshold for grief. This was mine!

In the wake of her departure, I found myself wrestling with the rawness of heartbreak, attempting to make sense of a reality that felt surreal and at times, unforgiving. The process of coming to terms with the separation became an emotional odyssey, marked by moments of profound sadness, introspection, and the gradual, often painful journey towards acceptance. I found myself sobbing at times; it took me many months of learning to deal with this emptiness. After much reading and meditation, I came to understand that this was our first step towards happiness. I was pleased that Maya had made this decision. Personally, I knew I wouldn't have had the strength to do the same; walking away would have been beyond me.

* * *

I vividly recall a moment when she expressed her anger, confessing that she felt miserable with me. It struck me deeply, for she was someone I cherished more than anything in the world. The notion of her feeling miserable in my presence was unfathomable and agonizing. I couldn't bear the thought of her suffocating in our relationship. If her happiness lay in leaving me, then so be it. As cliché as it may sound, I genuinely wanted her to find joy and contentment, even if it meant letting her go. Perhaps I had failed to provide the happiness she deserved, and if parting ways meant she could find true bliss, then I was willing to accept it.

Later, when we reflected on this moment and revisited the conversation we had, during a time when we were on better terms, she confessed that she hadn't meant it. She had said it in the heat of the moment, fueled by anger and disappointment. It was all inconsequential now. Much was said at the time, feelings were hurt, emotions ran high and all that was done could never be undone.

We had now parted ways. My wife had reached a point where she was giving up on me. The commitment to stand by each other through thick and thin was now tested. Even with the difficulties, I knew she cared. Even as she struggled not to display it openly during this tough time, her concern for me was evident. She held a deep affection for my family and genuinely cared for them. Admittedly, there were moments when she was frustrated towards my family. She felt they relied on me excessively, and that I prioritized them more than necessary. She believed my mom's attention towards my younger brothers overshadowed the challenges I faced in constantly coming to their aid. Despite Maya's repeated efforts, she couldn't cultivate love for me. In that regard, she too had failed our marriage I suppose.

* * *

There are always two sides to a story. She may have been in the right, but I was not always in the wrong. In a dual narrative, each holds their own truth, colored by personal experiences, emotions, and interpretations. The complexities of human relationships become apparent as each storyteller unveils a version of events that feels authentic from their vantage point. The truth, in this context, becomes the objective reality and a mosaic of individual perceptions, retelling someone else's shared history with one's perception.

Talking about it now would only reopen the wounds that took us so long to suppress. I admired the fact that Maya had gathered up the courage to walk away from me. I wish every woman or a man who felt miserable in a relationship could just walk away, no matter how hard it is. I feel the end of something always leads to a new beginning – a fresh start. If something is meant to be, it always works out, and if it wasn't, it never will.

Opinions may vary, but personally, I don't believe in subscribing to seek external help to better my relationship. I find it perplexing to invite a third party to instruct me on how to love someone I already know so intimately. If a relationship requires extensive effort to be sustained, I firmly believe it's not meant to be. Even if it yields temporary success, it often involves one person compromising their own happiness to spare the other from pain. To me it's a recipe for a miserable existence. Can you not tell when the spark has faded away?

Some claim that after marriage, the spark and attraction tend to fade. Obviously, one can't expect the honeymoon phase to last forever, but it shouldn't deteriorate to a point where mutual disdain takes over. Every word spoken becomes offensive, every action perceived with negativity, and the once-warm touch turns cold, causing all that was good to wither away with time. Sadly, many relationships prevail in the most toxic environments, but ours wasn't one.

I know I loved her, but I am uncertain whether hers ever existed. We were now leading separate lives. She left the very first house we bought together. The first step towards our American dream. Now she rented a place in Stamford and lived alone. I would have left the house for her, and I would have gone. Yet, she never took this offer when I suggested, and deep down I knew she would have never taken it.

At the time she left, I drowned myself in alcohol, running away from everything that seemed to go wrong. I was being sued at work for reasons beyond my control. The trust that I placed in some investors had backfired; they were only interested in financial gains, and when I couldn't deliver, they turned it into a legal matter. It was a situation I'd never faced before, and I didn't know how to deal with it or who to talk to. Maya wasn't communicating with me properly. Whenever I tried to discuss it, it backfired. She would say, *"I told you not to get involved."* Though we spoke, the interest seemed to have faded away.

* * *

Saying I started drinking after Maya left, would be inaccurate. We both drank occasionally. I had a higher tolerance. Once a friend, Avi had visited Maya's family in Nepal. After witnessing the amount of alcohol Avi could consume, they had made a comment about it. In his defense, Avi replied, *"This is nothing. You should see the amount your son-in-law drinks."*

I always say, choose your words wisely. Even though Avi had said it in passing, Maya's family took it way too seriously. They must have discussed this with Maya, and because of that, alcohol became restricted. The person who was okay until yesterday about me drinking was suddenly checking my moves. Unable to drink at home, I took the opportunity when we went out to friends' places or when I went for work meetings. The tension at work also led to increased drinking. She disapproved of the field I had chosen for work. However, I wanted to flip properties and invest in them. The work involved various stresses, and she didn't want to see me go through it. I don't blame her. Who would want the police showing up late at night to arrest their husband? *(I won't go in details, but I later filed a motion against the cops and won the case for wrongful allegation.)*

When one thing went wrong, everything seemed to go wrong. Just like that, one sip of whiskey led to another until I found myself drowning my sorrows. I became dependent on it. Before I knew it, I was drinking excessively. Maya was concerned. She got me help and wanted me to go to rehab, and I hated it. I was angry and felt I didn't need to be there. Nobody does. I couldn't relate to anyone there; I was not one of them. Nobody was. I stayed for ten days and returned. I stopped drinking and I felt good. But my problems weren't gone, and I relapsed.

I could see the distance between Maya and me growing. Everyone had turned against me. During the toughest time in my life, I had no one. Every conversation turned into an argument. I believed I was right. I couldn't recognize myself as the intoxicated person who slurred his words. I didn't realize that days would pass without me showering. I despised light, being in groups, everything. I wished for eternal darkness as I felt like no one understood my pain.

There were nights I would see Maya staying up in bed, visibly sad. She would gaze blankly at the walls or engage in typing on her laptop. Later, I discovered that those late-night sessions often resulted in lengthy emails to me, where she laid blame on me for her sadness. The content would be too painful, and sometimes I couldn't bring myself to go through the entire message, choosing to ignore it instead. I was in denial that my actions were causing her pain.

In response to her concerns, she even bought breathalyzers, a decision her family had disapproved of. I'm not proud to confess, but I knew how to manipulate the results by carefully calculating my alcohol intake. By the time she returned home, my blood alcohol level would register at 0%, should she decide to check. She did check every day when in doubt, until eventually she gave up doing so.

One day, my family staged an intervention. Maya, having taken a day off from work, joined forces with my mom and brother to initiate a conversation with me. I resisted sitting down with them, anticipating the topic of discussion. Confrontations and surprises were aspects I detested. They brought to my attention that my alcohol consumption had become excessive. Anger flared up within me; I raised my voice, even telling Maya that if she had an issue, she should leave me. I had taken her presence for granted, confident that she wouldn't leave me. Little did I know, I would learn that the hard way.

* * *

Maya was gone. Someone so close, someone whose breath I could feel every night by my side had drifted so far away.... and I knew then, she would never come back. I don't remember what I did after she left. I don't remember how I spent the days. I may have blacked out. I was in shock. Maya walking away from the relationship had not hit me yet, but when it did, it hit very hard.

I was a wreck - nothing seemed to interest me anymore. I didn't want to wake up and get out of bed. I didn't want to meet anyone. There were a few friends I was talking to who lifted my spirits, but they were not around me and I couldn't reach for a hug or a consoling word when I wanted one. There were no shoulders to lean on. Everyone who I thought were friends seemed to have turned out to be fair-weather friends. When I was at the low point of my life, there were no one. Or perhaps there were, but I just failed to notice any.

I missed Maya. I missed her more than ever. How I wish I had handled things differently. Looking back, everything I did seemed justified, but now in hindsight, I realize it could have used a little refinement. I was blind to the value of what I had.

Friends didn't bother dropping in much. Conversations were often casual, with some teasing me about how I felt with Maya not being around. Unfortunately, not everyone was sensitive to my feelings. In response, true to my nature, I didn't bother to sugarcoat my responses and I definitely didn't hold back on the sarcasm.

One among all, Jenny always checked on me. Maya seemed to have confided in her a lot. Maya had also asked her to convince me to go to rehab and paid for a session lasting thirty-five days. This happened after she ended our relationship. What does this reveal? Certainly, Maya wasn't heartless; she cared deeply for me and couldn't bear to see me throw my life away.

It took a lot of meticulous planning for Jenny to convince me. She did not want to come off in a wrong way. Of course, I refused when she brought up the idea of me going to rehab. It was when she told me it was Maya's idea that I calmed down and listened. I had hurt her enough, and I didn't want to do it anymore. She was gone but she cared and this time I was going to make it right. I agreed and left for thirty-five days. This was the last time I was going, and I was taking it seriously, and seriously I did. It's been more than five years since I had my last glass of alcohol and haven't had any cravings for it. I plan on remaining sober for the rest of my life! I'm proud of having done it without going for any AA meetings or by following a mentor. I picked up that glass and I knew it was only me who would be able to put it down and never pick up again. I resorted to meditation, took up yoga, and began long distance running. I would do anything to keep myself busy and distracted; self-care became priority.

* * *

There was one incident where I nearly relapsed. I had gone to India and Nepal for my twenty-five-year high school reunion. I think we all know how reunions go – it's synonymous for indulgence with childhood friends. I hadn't seen my batchmates for decades. 'Party hard' was the mantra, and it took insurmountable willpower to keep away from all that alcohol. A reunion without alcohol, simply unthinkable!

A little back story before we left for India: The guys had convened in Nepal and visited me in my apartment. There was much excitement, and everyone shared updates about their lives. They made themselves a drink and offered to pour me a glass of whiskey. I politely declined, but after they left, a strong temptation took over and I fixed myself a glass. I went to the kitchen and took a big sip. In my moment of weakness, an inner voice stopped me from gulping it down. I was literally about to undo my six months of sobriety. I fought the urge and spat it out. My face broke into a smile, and I knew at that moment that I had laid my demons to rest! I resolved never to do it again. Had it not been for this moment, I may not have been able to enjoy my reunion as much as I did. I finally had the will power to choose my health over all things. I managed to have one of the best times of my life. I was free from the clutches of alcohol, and the clarity was beyond comforting.

* * *

Time passed quickly, and to keep myself occupied, I decided to pursue a 'proper' job as Maya had always wanted. I applied for over twenty jobs daily, often finding myself interviewed by individuals who had just graduated high school. Many offers I received were commission-based, and my MBA degree seemed irrelevant without experience. Eventually, I landed a job as an inspection officer for insurance companies. This role involved snooping around houses and taking pictures as per the company's specifications. I faced challenges, even having the police called on me for trespassing, but I managed to explain my valid reasons. Even though I wasn't fond of the job, I did my best and earned a promotion within a month. Fortunately, due to COVID-19, I didn't stay in this position for too long.

Circumstances led me through tough situations. I had always been self-employed, opening my first sandwich restaurant right out of college at the age of twenty-three. My MBA in Finance came to little use as I lacked work experience. I had worked in the restaurant chain as a student and promised myself to buy one after graduation. With barely a thousand dollars in my bank account, I borrowed, and managed to secure a down payment to purchase a restaurant in Branford from a Chinese couple. There were always naysayers but with grit and determination, I overcame the hurdles and became a franchisee. A ten-year stint at my sandwich store without a single day off except for the four days off to Norway with Maya for her training. I remained focused on my goal.

Being a franchisee was tough, as the company prioritized its gain over the success of franchisees. Opening stores within a mile of each other for greater visibility was a common strategy, causing financial strain on franchisees. When opposed, they offered the option to purchase the new site, which was not always feasible. Although I faced losses, I ultimately decided to move on. Despite having a university diploma and the intellectual capacity, I found that my lack of a resume showcasing experience hindered my chances of getting hired in different roles.

One of the most satisfying aspects of being a restaurant owner was providing jobs to those who valued the opportunity. By the time I parted ways with the business, I had managed and co-owned a total of seven stores, employing over forty students who were able to get through college because I gave them a job. I am still friends with many of them, and I couldn't be happier with the impact I had on their lives.

* * *

DIYA'S ARRIVAL

DIYA had informed me that she and her husband, Biru, would fly in on the first available flight. She sought my opinion on her decision to come to the USA. I expressed that I didn't think it was necessary until we knew the diagnosis. I assured her that I would take care of Maya in the meantime. If she felt it would bring her peace of mind, the decision was hers to make. Diya decided to come, and they would arrive two days after Maya's first appointment. Given the COVID-19 season, they would need to undergo quarantine upon their arrival.

It was a freezing January day, with most of the earth's surface covered with snow. The streets remained slushy, and the addition of salt had tainted the once pure snowflakes, rendering them dirty and unwelcoming. Skid marks from tires formed asymmetric patterns of haphazard lines. The wind was still frigid, sending unexpected, frightful shivers down one's spine. Biru and Diya were coming from Dubai, where the temperature was likely still in the 90s, while New York awaited them with a bone-chilling stingy 18 degrees Fahrenheit.

I arrived early and brought two extra jackets of mine. Knowing them, I anticipated they wouldn't be properly dressed for the harsh weather. They landed in JFK airport in New York and after about an hour in line at the passport control, they emerged. The first thing I noticed was that Biru was wearing a fashionable but thin leather jacket, and Diya had on a fine fall coat, seemingly unaware of the chilling weather awaiting them.

After exchanging uncomfortable hugs and greetings, I offered them the coverings I had brought. Both initially declined the offer. I didn't insist, and as we were heading out, someone opened the entrance door of Terminal 4, letting in the chilliest gust of ice-cold wind they probably hadn't experienced in a long time. Instantly, both asked for the jackets. I smiled and handed them over, whispering, *"Told ya!"*

On our way back, we caught up on the good old days. It seemed like their attitude towards me hadn't changed, and they spoke to me with the same respect and comfort as before. I felt at ease and realized I was overthinking. I had imagined the meetup would be awkward, considering things were not the same, and I hadn't seen or spoken to them for a long time.

* * *

The last time I had met them was in the fall of 2019, shortly after Maya and I separated. During my visit to Nepal for my high school reunion, I decided to see Maya's family. Although I hadn't planned to meet Biru and Diya, I made sure to bring them gifts, as we always did. Diya even invited me out to eat, and we went for lunch once, along with her brother. I hadn't informed them about my visit beforehand. When Diya found out, she had sent me several welcoming messages, urging me to meet them. At the time, it felt very odd.

Diya and I always got along, or so I thought. I cherished her like a sister. Although I saw her as a bit of a pampered kid, I appreciated her for who she was, especially because she was Maya's younger sister. Maya held Diya in high regard, and her constant praises of Diya only strengthened my fondness for her. While we did have our arguments, I never took them too seriously, viewing them more as a friendly banter between two siblings.

When Maya and I faced challenges in our relationship, I reached out to Diya numerous times seeking comfort, but I found none. In hindsight, I should have realized that expecting Maya's family to understand my perspective was unrealistic. How could I ask them to understand me when their own daughter was struggling? Family loyalty runs deep, and no amount of explanation would change their support for Maya, regardless of any faults on her part. This likely explains why Diya never reached out to check on me. We eventually discussed this during her visit, where I voiced my feelings and she acknowledged her oversight, apologizing and saying, *"I should have known better and checked on you. I'm sorry."*

* * *

As we drove back from JFK, engaged in light conversation, one sister called the other, igniting a continuous flow of dialogue between them that lasted until we reached Stamford. It was a familiar scene for me. Even when Maya and I lived together, Diya and Maya would frequently call each other, immersing themselves in lengthy phone conversations. Their topics ranged from emotional discussions to giving advice, from nagging to storytelling. Diya often had a lot of gossips to share, recounting stories about her brother-in-law's affair and his wife's reaction during the scandal; her self-consciousness leading to cosmetic surgery decisions to remove her moles, and her journey in weight management, often punctuated with bursts of laughter. Diya also talked about the discrimination she faced from her mother-in-law compared to the other daughter-in-law. I typically respected their privacy, although some of the gossips were too intriguing to ignore.

I grew up with boys. Two younger brothers. We have a good bond but never talked for such long periods. Our conversations would last not more than two minutes.

"How are you doing?"
"I'm good."
"You?"
"I'm good too."
"Eh ok…. ummm"
"Did mama tell you about (so and so)??"
"Yeah."
"Alright then, will catch up soon."
"Ok take care!"

My mom would keep us all updated, so there was no need to call each other for updates. I suppose it's different among sisters. They would discuss how their mom could be so annoying, or how their dad was so stubborn and refused to wear his reading glasses, or how Kiran was rude to their parents, or how Diya had spied on her sister-in-law, or even how their distant aunt had forgotten to wish their mom a happy birthday, and so on. But it was enjoyable listening to their sisterly gossips.

* * *

As I drove them home to Trumbull, I knew how much they would cherish seeing each other. To surprise them, I took a detour to Stamford. I cautioned them that there would be no hugging or close contact, and we must maintain a six-foot distance. We all agreed to this and stuck to it. Initially, the plan was just to catch a glimpse of each other, but they insisted on going for lunch, with Maya sitting further away and wearing her mask. I agreed. Later, they suggested going to a coffee shop while maintaining the same precautions. It was evident that they were savoring every moment and trying to prolong their time together. Once again, I agreed. Thus, they enjoyed a good three to four hours of catching up, and I'm certain Maya was happy, as were we.

Biru and Diya were quarantining in my house, which was a risky decision considering the COVID-19 pandemic. We were all paranoid about the virus, given the news of increasing deaths and its easy transmission. Them being in my house meant that I could be exposed to the virus if they had been exposed, putting both me and my mom at risk, but my mom didn't mind, understanding that it was either me or my mom risking it or Maya.

The next day, I invited Maya to come over. She hadn't visited our home since she left. I knew she would want to see her sister. When she asked if it was a good idea, I reassured her that as long as we all wore masks, it should be fine. Maya arrived a little later, likely feeling nostalgic being in the house after more than a year. After all, we had built many memories there. While she visited, she stayed seated next to the fireplace, and we all maintained distance from each other.

For a moment it felt like the old days. All of us were together. Maya had Sanu, our Shih Tzu, in her lap. Maya was crazy about Sanu, and she often played and talked to her as we would do with kids. Just like separated parents took turns with the kids, she did have turns with the dogs. I wouldn't mind if she decided to keep them even though I loved them equally. But Maya being alone and being gone for longer periods of time for work did not seem feasible for the dogs.

After three days of self-quarantine, I took them over to Stamford. The atmosphere was filled with hugging, laughter, jokes, and their constant sisterly gossip, enveloping everyone in bouts of laughter. We attended various appointments together, but I couldn't shake off the feeling of being left out. Despite being her husband, I sensed that they perceived me as flawed in some ways. While we cared for each other, I wondered if I still had a voice in the decisions regarding her treatment. Would my suggestions be entertained? Many questions lingered, and I remained mostly silent, not contributing much except for driving them around. I would be included in their activities if I was already there with them, but otherwise, the three of them would venture out together.

* * *

THE DIAGNOSIS

THE call came. It was *rhabdomyosarcoma*, a cancer more commonly seen in children but exceptionally rare in adults. This aggressive form of soft tissue sarcoma could manifest tumors in various parts of the body. The news devastated all of us.

As I was preparing to head to Maya's place, she called to break the news herself. It was horrifying to hear, but she remained remarkably calm, and so did I. Keeping the conversation brief, I assured her I was on my way. Cancer was a word I never associated with Maya, and its presence sent my mind racing and my heart pounding. Yet, deep down, I held onto the belief that despite the challenges ahead, Maya would emerge victorious, and I would be there to adorn her with the laurels of triumph. Though I envisioned success, I couldn't foresee just how grueling the journey to recovery would prove to be.

I arrived at the apartment before them, so I waited in the parking lot. When they arrived, I got out of my car, and someone had already opened the back door to the apartment building. It was dark. I saw someone approaching, so I thought it was Maya. We hugged, staying embraced for about a minute without saying a word. After we let go, I turned around to realize that it was Maya holding the door. I had mistakenly hugged Diya, not Maya. They both have a similar stature, and to add to that, Diya was wearing Maya's winter jacket that I had gifted her on her birthday a few years ago. Reluctantly, we all smiled. Chaya, Maya's friend, had driven down from Providence upon hearing the news. She said she felt the need to be there for Maya.

When we went up, there was an eerie silence. We didn't know how to react or what to talk about. It was tough to act normal. Diya went to her room and wouldn't come out for quite some time. I went in to check, only to find her weeping. I sat with her and offered some words of consolation while I was trying to hold myself together too. I told her we needed to be strong no matter how broken we were. It would be tough for Maya to see her sister and close ones sad, and we did not want her thinking that we had lost hope. We looked at each other and promised to do so, and halfheartedly smiled and hugged each other.

I'm not sure if it was my words or something came into Diya, as if an awakening, but she was different from that moment onwards. She had mustered up the courage to act normal. Chaya had ordered dinner and we gathered up around the dining table to munch on the greasy Chinese food, which tasted fabulously delicious. Maya even cracked a joke saying Jamie had called and told her, *"Maya, no matter what, I will be with you until the end."* We knew what she meant, but it just sounded wrong.

Maya went on to say, *"I was like hmmm.... what end? You mean death? Am I going to die?"* and burst out in laughter. I'm sure we all pretended that it sounded funny and let out a fake laughter.

* * *

THE BEAUTIFUL CALL

I always thought cancer happened to other people. It was tough to fathom the fact that it had come so close to home, knocking on our very front door. My maternal grandmother had succumbed to breast cancer and had passed away at the early age of fifties. I knew it was tough for my family, but I was a kid then. All I could remember is visiting her in the hospital every evening with homemade food and spending several nights at the hospital to accompany her. When the news of her demise came, I was in boarding school, and I don't remember crying or being sad. Perhaps, because I was still in seventh grade and did not realize the depth and pain of death and moreover, I was not so close to her and knew deep inside I would not miss her much.

It was different now. Every suffering of Maya hurt me. To imagine the emotional turmoil that she was going through hurt me more.

Maya, once vibrant and full of life, had transformed into a somber individual. Though she didn't shed many tears, her heart seemed to weep a river of sorrow, and I could sense the profound hurt she sheltered within.

One day she had an early morning appointment with a doctor in Memorial Sloan Kettering Hospital (MSK) New York and several other appointments would follow that day. Biru was leaving the same day back to Nepal leaving Diya behind to be with her sister. The night before the appointment, the girls decided to spend the night in a hotel in Manhattan so it would be easy for them the next day. We had driven down to the city and checked into the hotel. While in the room, Maya was expecting a call from one of the oncologists from Yale New Haven Hospital who had initially examined her and recommended her to MSK Hospital in New York.

It was a video call, and when the call came, Maya answered. Biru, Diya, and I stood behind the phone facing Maya while she talked. I don't remember much of what the doctor said but a sentence he said still lingers in my head as if he was saying it now.

"Maya, we looked at your case. Looking at you now over the phone, I can see that you are healthy and doing well. I wish I could say this to all my cancer patients but to you I can confidently tell you that we can cure you!"

I choked. I could feel my heart bursting with joy and a sudden burst of tears were about to explode. I didn't need to hear anything else. I slowly walked to the bathroom so as not to give away my emotions and burst out in silent cry of joy. Tears flowed and I didn't stop it but continuously flushed the toilet or kept the tap running so I wouldn't be caught in the act. After a few minutes I walked out making sure my eyes didn't look puffed up or engorged. When I got out, Maya was just bidding the doctor her goodbyes and exchanging thank yous. Once she was done, we hugged each other and stood there happy. Biru, hungry as always, had ordered *Chicken over rice* which we quietly ate perhaps contemplating in our own ways and thanking our higher powers for looking out for Maya.

I was also glad that no one noticed that I had wailed in the bathroom. I was wrong. I found this out a few days later. Maya had gone out for lunch with a few of her friends. When the girls were out dining, one of them had asked if Maya had ever witnessed me cry during this entire ordeal. Maya had replied, *"I think he did that night when the doctors told me I would be cured. He slyly went to the bathroom, and I think he was in there crying!"* I was caught. I thought I was a step ahead, but I was wrong.

When Maya expressed her observation of that night, I denied it. Maybe she believed me, but I would be caught red handed many times as she would go through the treatment. Now it was tough going through the journey without shedding a drop of tear.

* * *

Being sent to a boarding school from the first grade onwards meant growing up surrounded by boys in a hostel environment where crying was deemed a sign of weakness. The notion that *"boys didn't cry"* was ingrained in my mind from a young age. I was taught to be resilient and to never show vulnerability. In our school, boasting a large circle of friends, I can't recall any instances of seeing each other cry. The fear of being perceived as weak or effeminate by our female counterparts was a constant concern. *"What would the girls think of us if we cried? They would see us as a bunch of sissies,"* was a prevailing sentiment among us.

We didn't want the bullies to get the best of us. We wanted to appear strong and were ready to get into fights no matter if the aggressor was years older than us. We had to keep our dignity. After all we were the *"Incredibles,"* a name my friends and I called ourselves when we were in sixth grade! We were naughty and missed being suspended or expelled in more than one occasion for vandalism and other petty naughtiness. We were not even teenagers then. What were we thinking?

As the oldest in my family and among all my cousins, I bore the responsibility of looking after my younger cousins while their parents were at work. At the age of twelve, I found myself changing diapers, feeding them, and tucking them into bed - all four of them, to be precise. Despite feeling overwhelmed at times, I felt compelled to suppress my emotions. Whenever I cried, I was reminded, *"Hey, you're a grown-up now. It's not becoming of you to cry like a baby. What will others think?"*

* * *

THE TREATMENT

ONCE Maya was diagnosed, the doctors wasted no time in initiating her chemotherapy. Recognizing the aggressive nature of rhabdomyosarcoma, they were eager to begin treatment without delay. The first chemo session was scheduled for February 18th, 2021. A snowstorm was expected that day and although I had offered to take Maya and Diya, they politely declined and had already arranged for Sanjay, a mutual friend, to drive them. Despite my insistence, they remained firm in their decision, citing concerns about inconveniencing me. It wasn't about the trouble for me, but rather a sense of discomfort and unease on their part, perhaps stemming from a reluctance to rely on someone they had distanced themselves from or fear of judgment from others.

While Maya underwent her chemo, Sanjay and Diya passed the time at Amy's apartment, a friend of Maya's. I was unaware of the details of chemotherapy procedures and only had limited knowledge from the research I had done. I didn't anticipate that Maya's treatment would take the entire day. Due to the snowstorm, Sanjay and Diya found themselves stranded at Amy's place for the duration of the day, waiting for Maya's session to conclude.

Maya had to undergo fifteen more rounds of high-dosage chemo, which the nurses described as nearly four times stronger than the chemo typically administered for breast cancer. The pressing question remained: who would accompany her to her next appointment? If I wasn't going, would friends be able to spare the entire day to accompany her and wait through the sessions? While Diya assured me that Maya had many friends willing to volunteer, I couldn't shake the feeling of being sidelined once again. Concerned, I waited anxiously all day for updates, breathing a sigh of relief only when they returned safely late at night. When I spoke to Diya that night, she reassured me that Maya was resting and recovering, albeit exhausted

Later, friends confided in me that they were relieved to see me step in. They too, had wondered who would accompany Maya to her sessions, given their own busy schedules. Coordinating time was difficult for them. They knew I would drop everything to be there for Maya. Some even joked that I was like the knight in shining armor coming to her rescue, except, I didn't have a horse nor armor!

The next day when I went to her place, Maya was up, cheerful and doing household chores. All the readings I had done about chemotherapy seemed to paint a different picture. I hoped it would remain this way throughout. The true horror of the treatment unfolded three to four days later. Maya was nauseous, vomiting, dizzy, and experiencing a strange metallic taste in her mouth. She found it difficult to eat or sleep, and the medications provided little relief. She constantly squinted in pain, and we could only sit by her side, feeling utterly helpless.

From the moment she stepped into the treatment facility, the sterile environment and the scent of medical supplies became familiar to her. The routine of chemo sessions became a central part of her life, evoking a mix of anticipation and anxiety each time. The powerful drugs coursing through her veins targeted not only the cancer cells but also took a toll on her healthy ones. Fatigue became a constant companion, making even the simplest tasks feel like a daunting challenge. Nausea, at times overwhelming, tested her resilience, and the unpredictable changes in her appetite made mealtime a delicate balance.

Words of comfort would do less heed, so it made sense to keep quiet. We could just show empathy, but it was Maya who was the one dealing with the poison in her body and trying to cope with the changes her body was trying to adapt. The uneasiness bothered her. She couldn't describe it as she had never gone through such a feeling. It was heart wrenching to see her this way, and this was only the first. We had fifteen more sessions to go, a whole year of torture. If everything went well, as per our calculations her chemo sessions would be over December 31st of 2021.

* * *

I've known Maya to be a brave girl, able to endure physical pain without being delicate, unlike many other girls I knew. I recall a time when she was uprooting poison ivy with her bare hands, only to end up hospitalized the next day with her entire face and body swollen with hives. Not having recognized the plant and its aftermath, she never complained, and I had to rush her to the emergency room, even though she initially refused to go.

There was another instance when she accidentally collided with a pillar in our basement. I heard a loud 'thud' that felt so intense, I could almost feel the pain myself. She sat down abruptly, pressing her hand to her forehead. As I hurried over to assist, I noticed a swelling the size of a ping pong ball forming on her forehead. Despite the pain, she managed a smile and looked up at me, asking, *"Shit! This will never go away, right?"* Her innocence and candidness caught me off guard, and I couldn't help but burst into laughter.

The physical pain Maya endured in the past, such as from poison ivy or hitting her head, was something she could handle and control. However, chemotherapy introduced a completely different challenge. It affected her appetite severely; she couldn't eat and even the mere mention or smell of food made her nauseous, leading to frequent vomiting. Not being able to enjoy the foods she loved saddened her deeply. She described her experience as being in a state of 'mental darkness,' highlighting the emotional and psychological toll of the treatment.

* * *

Hair loss, a visible marker of her battle, brought a profound shift in her appearance. She would gaze into the mirror and quip, *"I look like an alien."* Witnessing her reflection change served as a constant reminder of the sacrifices she was making in her journey towards healing. With her once long, straight hair now disappearing, it was a stark reminder of the effects of chemotherapy. I did thorough research to find ways to prevent it, but there were no solutions.

Her chemo sessions were scheduled every three weeks on a Friday. In the two weeks following each session, she gradually regained some stability, allowing her to resume daily activities and enjoy the taste of food once again. As the third week approached, she faced the prospect of repeating the entire ordeal, a thought she dreaded immensely.

A few days after her first session, Maya started to observe more hair falling out, a little more than the previous day. To address this, she opted to cut her hair short, a decision that surprisingly complemented her appearance. As the hair continued to fall out unevenly, she made the bold choice to shave it all off. The following day, she requested that I bring the hair clippers to complete the shave.

By the time I arrived with the clippers the following day, Maya's hair already appeared uneven. Diya had arranged a chair in the living room for Maya to sit, and I began the task of shaving her head. It was a difficult moment for me. I struggled to identify my emotions, but I felt a profound sense of sadness enveloping me. I glanced at Diya, who seemed to be avoiding eye contact as she busied herself with cleaning up the fallen hair and attending to other tasks, perhaps preparing dinner. Despite her efforts to stay strong, her nervous tone of voice betrayed her deep sadness.

As the razor buzzed in my hand, drowning out all other sounds, I remained silent. Biru chimed in with suggestions on how and where to use the clipper first. Biru suggested we both should shave our heads too to show support. I kept quiet, but I couldn't help but wonder if he ever had any worthwhile ideas. I felt that watching Maya bald was already a scene we did not want to face, and now the prospect of all three of us being bald in the same room felt like an unwelcome addition to an already difficult situation. Fortunately, Diya said, *"No babe, you don't suit with bald head, you look like Jughead!"* Her comment brought a smile to all of our faces, and the matter was dropped.

Yet, Maya found strength in her own vulnerability, embracing headscarves and hats with grace, and discovered resilience in the face of transformation. She actually carried the bald head fine. We said she looked like Sinead O'Conner. After the haircut and a quick shower, Diya and Maya sat trying on some earring to go with the new look.

* * *

THE SUPERWOMAN

EIGHT hours of chemotherapy can exhaust your vital organs completely. There are numerous factors that need to be closely monitored. At times, Maya's platelet count would drop dangerously low, and most often her White Blood Cells (WBC) stubbornly remained below normal levels throughout the treatment. Initially, her platelet consistently fell below critical levels, necessitating emergency trips to the hospital during odd hours for blood transfusions and hydration.

Given that individuals undergoing chemotherapy often face difficulties in eating and drinking, ensuring adequate hydration becomes essential. Maya began to struggle even with taking a sip of water. Recognizing the risk of dehydration, her doctors advised intravenous (IV) hydration to ensure she received the required fluids. This involved administering fluids directly into her bloodstream through an IV line, bypassing the need for oral intake.

During the initial stages, when Maya's platelet levels were low, as soon as the nurse suggested a transfusion, we rushed to the hospital. As this became a regular occurrence, Maya became reluctant despite my pleas. She would say, *"Ah, one day won't make a difference. It'll be back up tomorrow."* True to her words, it often would be, and her platelet levels would recover without immediate transfusion.

* * *

One day after her blood work, at 7:15 pm, the nurse called with urgency and instructed Maya to go to Urgent Care immediately since MSK, where she had received her transfusion, was closed for the day. The phone call was on speaker, and I could sense the nurse's concern. Maya's platelet count was at 16 x 1000 microliter (mcL), significantly below the normal range for a healthy adult, which typically falls between 150 x 1000 to 450 x 1000 mcL of blood. A low platelet count poses a serious risk, as it impairs the body's ability to form clots, making the individual vulnerable to life-threatening internal bleeding. Additionally, a compromised immune system due to low platelet and WBC increases susceptibility to infections. While cancer may take time to progress, an infection could swiftly become fatal. This was a matter we couldn't afford to overlook, highlighting the critical nature of her condition.

Maya was in the midst of cleaning the kitchen and did not want to go that evening but instead go the next day. I agreed to do so only if she sat quietly and watched TV. Reluctantly, she agreed. The next day, we left for the city early for her appointment. After her blood work, to my dismay, the platelet count had risen above 20 x 1000 mcL. While the nurse explained that the safe threshold for platelet count was between 50-100 x 1000 mcL, Maya's current count was not life-threatening and did not warrant a transfusion. I felt dismayed because I knew Maya would likely use this incident as a justification to delay future appointments, reminding me of this day when I was unnecessarily concerned. While she occasionally deviated from instructions, a gentle nudge would always guide her back to the right path, demonstrating her commitment to her health and treatment.

* * *

I could not blame her for what she went through. To add to the side effects of chemo, there were side effects of medications as well. *Gabapentin, MiraLAX, Senna, Nexium, Claritin D, Oxycodone, Lorazepam, Mirtazapine* to name a few. Each would interfere in her way of thinking, causing cognitive hindrance and affecting her decision-making ability. Sometimes her dosage of medications would be more than a meal she could intake. Nausea was nothing uncommon. Sudden cramps, constipation, hot flashes, and constant blockage of the nasal passage would wear her down many times. Quite often, after getting done with Positron Emission Tomography (PET) scan, she would come out complaining about the metallic taste in her mouth. Perhaps during this entire time, she did not have any sense of taste. Chemo had either killed all her taste buds or rendered them dormant.

Nausea was a nuisance, a state Maya loathed undergoing. We exhausted every measure available to alleviate it. Sometimes the medication proved effective, while other times it fell short. Upon researching, we discovered anti-nausea wrist bands and oils to apply behind the ears, touted to reduce nausea. We tried both methods, but to little avail. We even explored acupuncture as a remedy for post-chemotherapy nausea. Maya made several visits to an acupuncturist but eventually ceased going. Despite our efforts, she had to rely on medication and hope for relief.

Maya had an immense love for food. It was a joy to witness someone relish your cooking, and she was a prime example. *"Yum!"* was a common word that escaped her lips as soon as the food was served. Her face would light up, her eyes widening in anticipation before she indulged in the meal. She often added a sprinkle of salt or other garnishes to enhance the taste, striving for perfection. Maya didn't hesitate to go for second helpings if the food pleased her palate. Feeling full was inconsequential; she would softly murmur, *"Oh my God, it was so good,"* admitting to her greediness with no regrets.

The inability to fully savor the taste saddened her deeply. Moreover, she couldn't enjoy the aroma of the food. Nevertheless, Maya made an effort to appreciate the visual appeal of the dishes, even though the absence of taste and smell hindered her enjoyment. Occasionally, frustration would overwhelm her, but she swiftly composed herself before anyone could detect her distress. Eating after chemo sessions proved especially challenging. She consumed food out of necessity, but anything she ingested triggered nausea. Contemplating food during those moments was arduous, as it exacerbated her discomfort.

Maya's mother and sister were particularly attentive to ensuring Maya ate well. Food was a frequent topic of discussion, with her mom expressing concerns and taking proactive measures. She often fretted about preparing lunch even before we finished breakfast. Her vigilant gaze continually assessed our plates, encouraging us to take additional servings, a gesture driven by love but occasionally felt like a subtle form of coercion.

Maya's chemo sessions were typically scheduled early in the morning. Her mom would wake up early to prepare her breakfast and pack her lunch. On chemo days, Maya often experienced "anticipated nausea," where the sight of food, despite hunger, triggered the urge to throw-up. I could see her struggling to swallow her food and, at times, had the courage to tell her mom that she couldn't finish it. There were instances when she would throw-up soon after leaving the apartment. Even days after chemo, anything associated with the treatment made her nauseous, leading to the disposal of many water bottles and lunch boxes used during the sessions. Most of the time, she couldn't finish the lunch her mom prepared. Occasionally, she would ask me to order food via Uber Eats without her mom's and Diya's knowledge, finding solace in such moments.

When I picked her up after her sessions, she would plead with me to eat the food her mom had prepared, not wanting it to go to waste. Her conscience wouldn't allow her to discard it, saying, *"It would hurt her feelings."* I'm not a big eater, but I obliged when Maya asked me, whether I liked it or not. We did this discreetly in the garage before heading up to the apartment. Sometimes, regret would set in as I found myself stuck with leftovers. Upon our arrival, we would act as if nothing had happened. Maya's mom would greet us while checking Maya's lunch box to see whether she had finished it or not. *"Welcome! You guys are back. Are you hungry?"*

"Yes, very," I would say feebly, while Maya would look at me sympathetically. Maya's mom, seeing the empty lunch box, would happily come up to me and whisper, *"She ate! She ate everything!"*

It wasn't that Maya wasn't eating anything at all. As anticipated, Maya had lost her appetite and the desire for food. However, it was even more vital to sustain her immunity. I would confirm with the doctors and nurses if it was okay for her not to eat much for a day or two during chemo. They would agree as long as she wasn't going for days without food, which she never did. It was tough during the chemo days but bearable. The difficulty intensified the next day. Amidst the many battles she was fighting, this was one of them. Maya would sit and make it look easy, eating. When her mom would ask her to go for a second helping, I would intervene, preventing her from forcing Maya to eat.

Seeing the difficulty Maya was having with food, Diya decided to hire a nutritionist. Where did she find one? In India! This nutritionist would send a list of food to be fed to Maya which Maya disliked. She would advise Maya to change her diet completely, urging her to eat, *idli dosa and sambar-* all South Indian food that we never prepared in our kitchen or were accustomed to. I would feel annoyed when she suggested Maya stop eating what we were eating. I would question her, *"Are you telling us that the food that we've been eating since we were kids, is unhealthy?"* She would deflect the question without providing a direct answer.

Once when Maya was hospitalized with severe throat ache, the doctors in Stamford hospital encouraged Maya to consume protein-rich liquid diets like *'Ensure.'* They provided guidance on certain foods Maya could eat to regain her strength. When I updated the nutritionist about this, she dismissed the hospital's dietary recommendations, stating that Maya had no choice but to eat what they provided while in the hospital. She further advised Maya to discontinue following the diet suggested by the hospital nutritionist once discharged. It was only a matter of time before Maya asked her to be fired.

It amused me that Diya trusted the medical professionals from everywhere around the world except in the United States. She sought out a nutritionist from India, a therapist from Nepal, and initially suggested homeopathy in Mexico. She even sent all the reports to doctors in India and Nepal to get their second opinion. I would intervene, saying that the doctors here were following proper procedures and to trust them, but she wouldn't. Biru would say, *"Doctors here are never right."*

They would say this aloud, including her father, in front of Maya. I thought it was very insensitive on their part. Here, Maya was content with the unwavering care of her healthcare team, from the oncologist to the compassionate nurses. They had helped her develop a sense of trust amid all her vulnerabilities. Maya's resilience had shone through as she faced the unknown, drawing strength from the hope that each treatment brought her closer to remission.

On the other hand, we had a family who had no faith in the treatment right from the beginning. Maya would tell me, *"I don't care what they feel; I like the way my treatment is going."*

* * *

Many times, people would just show up or call wanting to visit Maya. It would be odd to refuse, so we timed it in a way that it would fall on the third week after her chemo. It was during this period that Maya would be regaining her strength, and even though the WBC count remained low, it wasn't concerning. She enjoyed the company of her friends. They would show up, and if Maya was up for it, they would sit down for long hours chatting and laughing. Sometimes they would have karaoke nights where everyone sang their worst. It would be a torture to hear some sing, but Maya enjoyed it, and the singing would go on past bedtime. Depending on how she was feeling, the girls would organize a few girls' night outs within the vicinity so if Maya was tired, it would be easy for her to come back. When Maya felt weak, few girls would come over and spend quiet evenings with her. They would either spend time watching movies or come over to cook for her.

Sometimes Maya's well-being was unpredictable. We would have guests come over, and suddenly she would feel weak. She would lie on the couch amidst all the friends, listening to their conversation with her eyes closed. We would think she was asleep, but she would surprise us by laughing along and offering her input if she had the strength to do so. No amount of praise is enough for the courage she mustered up so her loved ones wouldn't be hurt while she herself was hurting deep within. Despite her own struggles, she would organize camping trips, beach getaways, picnics, and trips to the city for her family. She would express feeling bad about her parents sitting in the apartment all day while they could be among friends back in Nepal. I would constantly remind her that her parents would rather be with her here and now than anywhere else.

"*I know but I feel bad,*" she would say.

That summer, the doctors had asked her to skip a week of chemo so she would prepare for surgery. She was excited and started planning a trip away. She had been wanting to do a family trip, and this was her moment.

I was home working. She called and I answered. "*Listen,*" she said, "*We are going to Lake George. Biru, Diya, and I along with the kids are leaving tonight and since dad and mom don't want to go tonight, you come with them the next day!*"

"*Huh? Are you telling me or asking?*" I responded, feeling a bit taken aback by her assertiveness.

"*Heh Heh, I'm telling you!*" she replied with a hint of amusement in her tone.

I remember it was a Wednesday when she planned this trip. She hadn't bothered to ask if I was busy or if I had other plans. "*You are so unpredictable,*" I would say, agreeing with her.

* * *

Maya would organize a *mehndi* night (a tradition before the wedding) for my brother and his bride-to-be. She wanted to perform and also encouraged everyone to come up with a dance. "*It can be solo or a group dance,"* she instructed. She had asked me to practice with her and suggested that the two of us would be on stage together. I didn't have to think much before disagreeing. I wasn't going up on stage to make a fool of myself dancing to a Bollywood song. She was excited about this event and got everyone else excited too. She planned the decorations and assigned tasks to everyone. Everyone cooperated, and the event came out to be a big success. The owner of the restaurant, where we had the party, was surprised to see his place so beautifully decorated and joked that he would hire Maya for all event planning.

She was looking forward to doing a solo dance after she couldn't convince me to dance alongside her. Unfortunately, she got hospitalized but was discharged just a few days before the event. She wasn't giving up. She would watch the dance moves on her iPad while in the hospital bed and practiced them visually for less than a week but managed to woo the crowd with her elegant moves.

All the girls had also practiced a group dance, and they performed equally well. Now it was the boys' turn. However, no one was willing to dance, and Maya was a bit disappointed. I had to step up. No, I wasn't going to dance alone; I was going to drag everyone onto the dance floor. Just before the party, I convinced all the boys that we should practice a move, which we did an hour before the event outside the restaurant. We gave it our best shot and the guests loved it because it was atrocious! But at least everyone had fun.

* * *

Emotionally, Maya navigated a rollercoaster of feelings. Fear and uncertainty loomed large, but she met them with a quiet courage. The support of family and friends became her anchor, providing not just assistance with practical matters but also the emotional sustenance needed to endure the challenges. She found solace in connecting with a few friends and coworkers who shared similar experiences, forming bonds in them where stories were exchanged, and empathy flowed freely. Maya was determined to fight this disease and overcome the adversities that cancer had brought into her life.

***

MAYA'S FAMILY

WHEN the diagnosis occurred, Maya and her sister decided not to tell their parents. I insisted that they had the right to know and if they did not have the courage to tell them, I would. They refused. Instead, they thought they would let them know when the time was right. *"When's the right time?"* I pressed, but I received no answer.

The parents were beginning to suspect that it was a serious situation, and they called me almost every night seeking updates. Each time, I found myself fabricating excuses for why both sisters weren't responding to their calls. I would suggest they might be tired from numerous appointments or simply state, *"I don't know. They must be out."*

One day, Maya's mother called me, stating, *"I know it's cancer!"* I was taken aback, yet relieved that they had finally informed her parents. I remained cautious, suspecting it might have been her mother's attempt to prompt me to disclose information. To tread carefully and verify her suspicions, I inquired about what led her to believe so. She mentioned she had been researching symptoms on YouTube, and all signs pointed to cancer. Encouraging her to maintain a positive outlook and refrain from drawing premature conclusions, I urged her to stay optimistic.

She would lament, *"I know you guys are lying to us and not telling us the whole truth."* I was stuck in a dilemma. I didn't want to lie to them, and at the same time, Maya had instructed me not to tell them anything. When Maya finally told them a few days later, I called her parents and apologized for keeping it from them.

* * *

Unlike the norm, where parents would instinctively rush to be by their child's side in times of illness, convincing Maya's parents, especially her father, was an emotionally daunting task. While the homes of others echoed with the comforting presence of concerned parents, ready to lend support, in stark contrast, convincing Maya's parents required immense persuasion and convincing. Many times, before their arrival, Maya's dad and I had numerous conversations. Each time we spoke, I'd hang up the phone convinced he was coming, only to find myself going through the persuasion process all over again the next time. I had to detail Maya's daily struggles and stress the urgency of familial support during such a critical time. Convincing him was a slow process, but eventually, it paid off. I had to stress to him that cancer was a serious matter, and tomorrow was uncertain, so they needed to come as soon as possible. After much persuasion, they finally settled on the date of May 6th, 2021.

When I mentioned to Maya, *"I think your dad will be coming too,"* she didn't believe me. Later, when I confirmed, she was in disbelief. She said, *"Good job! Only you are able to have him listen."* She knew that if anyone could convince him, it would be me. She mentioned that he liked me like a son and so would not let me down. When the day came, I went to pick them up from the airport and brought them to Maya's apartment.

* * *

Maya had suggested that I stay with her parents while they quarantined in her apartment. It was a well-thought-out plan. Maya, along with Diya and Jamie, would go to Trumbull to stay with my mom. This arrangement seemed fair, considering the potential infection risk during the flight. It seemed more plausible that they went to Trumbull instead of staying with the parents.

By the time we arrived home, it was late, and I could sense their anticipation to see their daughter. Waiting three days felt like an eternity. The next day, I took them to see their daughters, ensuring we had masks and maintained our distance. I recall her mom crying throughout the journey, and I hoped she would hold her composure when we arrived.

The meeting at Trumbull was pleasant, filled with smiles and laughter. I set up a bonfire in a chiminea, and everyone gathered around. Maya's parents and I sat on one side of the fire while others faced us. We were just quarantining but they treated us as if we carried the virus! The distance was maintained, and when night fell and the bugs started becoming a nuisance, we decided to leave. The father and mother were grateful to have spent time with their daughters instead of waiting until the quarantine was over. On our way back, Maya's mother broke down again, making the drive very uncomfortable. Maya's dad and I stayed quiet, reaching home without uttering a single word.

* * *

A month had passed since they arrived. Maya's dad and I would go out for walks in the evenings to get him accustomed to the roads in Stamford and to make him familiar with the directions. One day during an evening stroll, he coyly expressed his desire to go back to Nepal. He was missing his friends and did not like it here in America. I gave him a stern look, and asked, *"Are you serious? You forgot what we talked about?"*

This wasn't all I said, but the convincing lasted the entire half-hour walk we took along the sides of Long Ridge Road, where Maya's office was located. When we were just getting back, I reached out to shake his hand and asked him to promise me that he would stay until the chemo was over and never talk about going back. He shook on it. It was a very reluctant shake, but he had committed to it. This time I knew he would abide by his promise. Many times, he may have cursed me out for my knack of persuasion, but I was not giving up for the sake of Maya. I often wondered if everyone else's parents needed so much coaxing and pleading to be by their children's side during such times of adversity. There is no doubt that they loved

Maya, but it seemed like they cared about their own convenience more. So, I think!

He lived up to his promise and never talked about wanting to go back. This time, he knew there was no escaping it and decided to stay until the chemotherapy was over.

Maya's dad being around was like having a pillar of strength, both for Maya and me. He always supported me in the things I did. We spoke to each other as friends. I even played the role of a masseuse and a barber for him. He had a specific way he liked his hair to be cut. Once it grew to the point of touching his earlobes, he would become irritated. Spending twenty dollars on a haircut seemed ridiculously expensive to him, nearly thirty times more than the usual haircuts he got back home. Thus, I became his on-call barber. It wasn't a tough job as I was used to cutting my own hair as I too had taken up on that skill after having had many unhappy barber visits and not having the cut, I wanted.

Maya had never imagined her parents would stay for so long – entire nine months. She didn't doubt her mom's commitment to staying. It was her dad who was tough to convince, and if he decided to leave, her mom would never let him be by himself and would leave with him—nothing else mattered! Fearing the possibility of them leaving, to keep them busy Maya would assign them with different tasks. Her dad took charge of cleaning the apartment and doing the dishes. He made fantastic tea, so every evening when I arrived, he would get up to get started, and we would sit down to catch up about the day.

Her mom was supposed to cook. Despite having a bad back and often seeming in pain, Maya sometimes called her lazy. To defend her point, Maya would say that while shopping, her mom wouldn't notice the time go by, without once complaining about her pain. However, at home, she became immobile.

For the first few months, I was always cooking dinner for them and would leave as soon as it was ready so I could be back home to have dinner with my mom. Some may have said something to Maya's mom in my absence; a few days later she started cooking every night. When I asked what had happened, she would respond by saying she did not want to trouble me much.

One day, Maya's dad attempted to lift the twenty-gallon Poland Spring water container and place it in the dispenser, injuring his back in the process. I was frustrated, wondering why he had to do it when I specifically asked Biru to handle it. I hadn't done it myself as it still had water in it when I was leaving. Unfortunately, Biru had forgotten in his haste to go for his date night.

I could see that her dad's vitality had been drained out of him. He seemed to have transformed into a very weak, elderly man after this incident. He asked for a massage, and I obliged. He remarked that the women in the house did not apply enough pressure compared to a man doing it. After a few days of massage, he appeared to be better. His face regained some of its brightness.

They were becoming more comfortable with me as time passed by. When Maya's mom would see me massaging her husband, she would grumpily complain from the sidelines, saying, *"Nobody massages me. It seems nobody likes me."* I could sense that she wanted one too, and those words were her way of hinting at it. I would knead her shoulders, but she would ask for a full-body massage. I wasn't comfortable with the idea of rubbing my mother-in-law all over her body. It made me feel awkward and uneasy. My hands would freeze at the thought. To make things even more uncomfortable, she would say, *"don't be shy."* Maya would notice my discomfort and intervene. Later, I would tell Maya that as much as I respected her mom, I felt very uncomfortable massaging her, especially when she asked for massages on her lower body, including her buttocks.

* * *

I started dedicating more time to being with them. When Maya wasn't feeling well, I made a point to arrive early. While Maya rested in the other room, I would sit with her parents, engaging in conversation. Maya had now moved to a bigger apartment after confirming her parents' arrival, and there was plenty of room for everyone. I took on the responsibility of cooking dinner most evenings and also took care of cleaning the apartment.

One day, after steam cleaning and vacuuming the apartment, I gathered the trash and headed to the basement. As I was exiting the elevator, with the vacuum and two trash bags in hand, a friendly older lady greeted me, *"Working late today?"* I simply nodded and smiled in response. Later, as I disposed of the trash and returned to my car, I couldn't help but reflect on the encounter, realizing that someone had mistaken me for a janitor.

I didn't mind it. I wanted to do so for Maya, so if anyone mistook me for a janitor, it would be my own doing. Biru wouldn't lift a finger. He never cleaned up or cooked, except sometimes to make his kids cereal. He would sit at the dining table in front of his laptop, surfing the web for Tissot or Rolexes. Diya had told her parents not to order Biru to do stuff around the house. I didn't digest this well and asked her, *"Why not?"* She said he was not used to working around the house or being ordered to do things. Walking away, I smirked and said, *"As if I am."* Diya must have had a clever comeback, but I didn't wait to hear it.

Despite my pleas for them to stay, Maya's parents left in March of 2022. I emphasized the positive impact they had made and how Maya cherished their presence, hoping they would extend their stay. They remained unsympathetic to my requests and were steadfast in their decision not to stay any longer. The initial plan was for them to leave about a week after the last day of chemo. But due to hospitalizations, we were behind a few weeks, and the oncologist had decided to give Maya maintenance chemo, to avoid the risk of the cancer coming back.

The family opposed this decision, dismissing the 10% reduction in the likelihood of relapse as insufficient to justify the ordeal that Maya may have to go through again. Even if this gave Maya a chance to live by 1%, I would have wanted her to take it. Thankfully Maya was up for it. I don't understand to this day how one could so casually leave when your own daughter was struggling day and night. How could you be thinking of partying while leaving behind Maya? My desperate plea for emotional and collective support and strength that only a united family could provide, fell on deaf ears.

Maintenance chemo wasn't as challenging as Maya's regular dosage of chemo. She didn't experience nausea or pain, and her hair started growing back. Her energy seemed to return, and she slowly regained strength. This improvement led Maya's parents to believe she was healed, and they thought they didn't need to stay as long as I was there. *"You are doing everything anyway,"* they would say. I will never comprehend how they could leave her alone, regardless of my presence. That will always be a source of wonder for me.

* * *

One day, when the girls had gone out shopping, I found myself alone with Maya's dad, who seemed eager to have a conversation. As I sat beside him, uncertain of what to expect, he began discussing Maya's property back home in Chitwan. It was a sizable piece of land that they had owned for a long time in a rapidly developing area. I couldn't discern the reason for this conversation, and it left me feeling puzzled.

They had taken us there a few years ago to have it transferred into Maya's name. The intention was for Maya to have some property in Nepal; otherwise, all the parents' property would be inherited by the son. Some believed it was also to prevent Kiran's wife at the time, Kinara, from making a claim on it. They didn't seem to have a favorable opinion of her. Ironically, it was Kinara's father (Kiran's father-in-law) who had facilitated the transfer. It turned out to be an unwise move, as he had seen the property in the city where he didn't own anything. Now, the land that should rightfully belong to their daughters after the husband's parents, was slipping away. To keep the story short, after their divorce, Kiran and his family fought hard to ensure Kinara wouldn't get the land or anything in the divorce settlement, and she had to settle for a much smaller resolution.

Now, Maya's dad wanted me to take over and do something with it. When we had first gone there, I had expressed an interest in building a resort. After all, that place was booming, and many businesses and hotels have flocked to that region now. I listened to him carefully, but unsure as to why he was talking about it with me, I asked him. He said that I had shown interest in it once, so I should do something with it instead of leaving it barren.

I smiled and told him that it was a different scenario then and now it was different. We were husband and wife then, and now we were separated. He said he thought we would get back together and further told me that he was happy to see us spending so much time together. He said that Maya looked forward to me coming over and it made her happy. In short, he said both his wife, and he were happy to have me as a son-in-law and thought that Maya and I should get back together.

I smiled and I told him that this was not what Maya and I wanted. We were meant to be friends, and we should remain that way. I requested him not to even entertain this thought with Maya as I did not want her to be pressured and give in to her family's demands, just like she always gave in to her sister's. She had the tendency to do so. I would see a teary-eyed man just staring at me and wondering how I had become so heartless.

* * *

During Maya and my challenging times, I would often confide in her father about my feelings. He had suggested that we take a break and live separately for a few months until things settled down. I had expressed my concern, telling him that if we did so, our relationship would never be the same. However, he had assured me that things would improve.

* * *

"Remember?" I asked him, reminding him of that day. He looked at me, and finally, a tear made its way down his cheek. He wiped it off discreetly and muttered a few words. He said it would make everyone happy if we were to get back. I told him that Maya wouldn't be happy, and I wouldn't want to spend my life with someone who was unhappy with me. I had told him time and again that if Maya found someone she loved, I would be very happy knowing happiness awaited her. That was all I needed to see, and I meant it and mean it to this day. But I also told him, *"Let's wait and see what the future has in store for us."*

I assured him that my daily visits to take care of Maya were not motivated by hopes of getting back together with her. It was purely because of the love I had for her, and never once did I expect anything in return. I even told them that if they were embarrassed about the world knowing I was helping out, no one needed to know.

He sat there speechless, and I stood staring at him. Suddenly, we heard the door open, and I was grateful that this uncomfortable silence was broken. The girls were back from their short walk from Burlington.

* * *

Maya's mom would often express that I was Godsent, and she would wonder what Maya would have done if I had harbored animosity and hatred like many other jilted husbands. She disliked being reminded that we were not together, even going as far as concealing it from her family members. Once, when Maya was in Nepal attending the *Bratabandha* ceremony of Diya's kid, a religious ceremony marking the transition to manhood for boys aged 8-12, she sent me a picture of Maya dressed up in a traditional married woman's attire, complete with her *Mangal sutra* and *Tilahari*. She followed the picture with a smiling emoji. I understood her intention as she was not the kind to send pictures or even reply to messages. I dumbly replied, *"She looks nice!"*

When Maya's mom's friends called her and questioned why they were in an apartment instead of the house, she would fabricate a response: *"Because it's closer to the hospital so we decided to take it, but my son-in-law is here with us."* Even with my repeated reminders that the truth would eventually come out and not reflect well, she would simply ignore me.

When I recounted such instances with some close friends, they would suggest that Maya's family was exploiting me. *"They would never do that,"* I'd retort. And even if they did, it wouldn't change my actions; I would have helped regardless. Similar to Diya, Maya's mother could be deceitful. She had a knack for taking advantage of people's kindness. They were adept at assessing their relationships and knowing who to keep close and whom not to. This was an evident fact, as Maya herself didn't hold back from sharing these traits among her friends.

* * *

Maya had expressed a desire for a wig, so one day she, her mother, and Jamie went wig shopping. When they returned in the evening and Maya wasn't around, her mother kept mentioning a particular wig that Maya had liked. I wanted to buy it for her. Before I could mention my intention, her mother asked me to sit next to her. I initially declined, saying I was comfortable standing. She became annoyed and insisted I sit. I found it unsettling when she suddenly became overly nice and asked me to sit next to her—it always made me wary as I didn't know what to expect.

When I finally sat down next to her, she mentioned that she had discussed the wig Maya liked with Diya, who was in Nepal at the time. They had decided to purchase it for Maya. I was pleased to hear this. However, she then told me that it was Diya's idea for the three of us—Maya's mom, Diya, and myself—to share the cost. I agreed willingly and handed my credit card to Jamie to place the order. While they did transfer the money, I couldn't help but wonder if they truly felt the need to split the cost with me. After all, I had intended to purchase the wig regardless and had bought one for Maya a few months earlier as well. It struck me as ironic that Diya, who often boasted about her wealth, was now suggesting that I split the cost of the wig for her sister.

I didn't dwell on it much. The wig arrived a few days later, and Maya was delighted. Her mom presented it to her, saying, *"Here's your gift we got you. Diya and I had discussed it."* I'm unsure if she ever mentioned to Maya that I was also a contributor. I didn't bring it up with Maya either.

Typically, it was Maya's mom who would request favors from me. Maya's dad seldom asked me to do anything around the house, maybe because he didn't do much himself. They would sit and confide in me about the family's deepest secrets, leaving me puzzled as to why they were sharing such information with me. Sometimes it was enjoyable, but at other times, I wished they hadn't told me these things.

Maya's mom also disclosed that Diya had suggested it was because of me that Maya had gotten cancer. She even shared this with my mom. It was an incredibly insensitive and thoughtless remark. My mom was deeply hurt and confronted her about why she would say such a thing. *"She believes Maya worries about him too much and is always stressed. Stress causes cancer,"* Maya's mom explained. I couldn't believe that even after making such an accusation, Diya could still confront me without any hesitation. It took my mom a long time to overcome this. I urged her not to give too much importance to ignorant and shallow people.

Maya's mom also confided in me that since Diya was a child, she always sought out wealthy individuals to date, and from her perspective, getting involved with Biru was the best thing that could happen to her. *"He was a good catch,"* she would say. She shared an incident from Diya's school days when she found a neatly folded paper with some cash inside. It contained a detailed calculation of expenses and how much to spend on various items. According to her mother, this was from someone whom Diya was 'using.' *"Poor guy, he thought he had a chance with Diya,"* she would remark.

The individual had left her significant sums of money, far more than any middle-class parents would typically give their teenage daughter as an allowance. This person had left Diya with that money when he had to travel somewhere. When he was present, he had always picked her up from school and given her money. Now that he was away for some time, he didn't want her to be without any. He too had to keep her hooked with the pampering.

When I inquired about what happened to that guy, her mom said she left him as soon as she started dating someone else. She further went on to say that he was very hurt and even had come to ask for her hand in marriage when Diya was of the right age.

"What did Diya say?" I asked.

"Who's going to marry that ugly guy?" was her reply.

According to her mom, *"She had used him and dumped him when she didn't need him. She did so with so many other boyfriends she had. She's a cunning fox. A brown cat!"* Her mom said, smiling, as if taking pride in her daughter's conquests. Referring to her boyfriends, sometimes even Maya would joke saying, *"I don't know for how long she's going to have this fish in the hook."*

* * *

Kathmandu is a small city, and everybody seems to know everybody. Coincidentally when they found out that Diya was my ex-sister-in-law, few of her ex-boyfriends that I happened to meet, vouched for her mother's claims. They would say they were used, but they had used her in their own way too, and they were lucky they realized it sooner rather than later. They were just happy they weren't married to her.

As per her exes, Diya, a woman with a strategic approach to her romantic entanglements, chose each relationship for her personal gain. Her motivations were transparent, as she sought financial security and a lavish lifestyle ever since she was a kid. Unapologetically pragmatic, she seemed to navigate the world of dating with a calculated finesse, choosing partners based on their wealth and influence rather than emotional compatibility. While her companions indulged her with opulent gifts and extravagant experiences, Diya skillfully maintained a façade of genuine affection. Many times, she used her charm and allure to secure the material comforts she desired, navigating the dating landscape on her own terms. While this portrayal may seem harsh, it reflects the nostalgic lamentation of disgruntled exes.

Diya seemed content with Biru, who appeared eager to fulfill her every desire. It appeared as though she had him on a leash, as he sought his wife's permission for everything. One beautiful aspect of their relationship was their two lovely children, whom I deeply cared for. Maya's dad, however, held a different impression of his son-in-law.

When Biru would come to visit his in-laws (in Nepal) in his superbikes, he would say, *"Showoffs! This is pure showoff, flaunting what they could afford. In a city where there are no roads, they want to own superbikes."* He would roll his eyes while I laughed in awe. Amidst such a spicy conversation and upon sensing his bitterness, I would dig deeper and ask him, "*If it wasn't ancestral wealth, would he……?*" Before I could finish my query, he would respond, *"No never! To make it, one needs brains. He doesn't have one. He would have never made it. The man has no manners and disrespects his employees! What he does for us is a sham and does it only because of Diya."*

I wasn't aware of Maya's dad's feelings towards his son-in-law, who appeared to be an ideal match in many respects. He was wealthy, regarded as good-looking by some, and displayed an unwavering devotion to their daughter, epitomizing uxoriousness. However, Maya's dad was dissatisfied with how they raised their kids. He was old school, and there were aspects he couldn't accept. He strongly disapproved of how his grandkids were being brought up, fearing they would become weaklings. He was very unhappy with their parenting skills, and unsurprisingly, the kids were highly susceptible to infections and illnesses, much like their father.

"This is the reason you shouldn't be too dainty," Maya's dad would say. *"You have to play in the dirt just like any other kids, be rough and be a normal kid. Breathe the same air we breathe and eat the same food that we eat."*

Once, in Nepal when I was at Maya's house, Biru and Diya had come to visit. Their son was about three years old. I started to play with him, and at one moment, the kid came and hugged me. On seeing this, Biru walked up to the son and said, *"What did I tell you about hugging people? You are not to hug anyone except papa and mama!"*

During Maya's treatment, the kids had grown comfortable with me. I often played with them, telling jokes that sent them into fits of childish laughter. The son even declared to his grandparents that I was his favorite person in America! I taught him fist bumps and pound hugs, which he found cool. We usually did this when Biru wasn't around. One day, Biru saw us doing it and asked, *"What are you guys doing?"* Though the kid enjoyed it, Biru told me, *"Be gentle, Hanchu da! He's just a kid, and I don't want you to hurt him."* Sadly, his son never engaged in it with me again.

Maya's dad had witnessed this, but these were parents benefiting from the youngest daughter's favors through her husband's wealth. What could they do when they couldn't speak up? Stay quiet, and they would be happy.

* * *

On one of Maya's dad's birthdays, the three siblings decided to buy him an SUV. They would divide the cost between themselves and finance the rest. Diya came up with the idea and proposed that instead of financing through a bank, Biru would just pay for it and this way they would avoid high interest cost. This was a great deal we thought. Only to find out later that Biru too was charging them interest, a percentage point less, I believe, as per Maya. Maya had lamented, *"I can't believe these guys are charging me interest."*

I guess when you have money, you become greedier. Maya's dad once shared with me that Biru was planning to buy a land to build their family home. He had asked Kiran to do the running around, Kiran would find properties, but Biru had other plans. One day, without anyone's knowledge, Biru had already purchased the land he liked. Maya's dad was not happy to see his son cut off from the commission. As the sellers paid commission, Biru would have nothing to lose should he have involved Kiran, after all he had done a lot of running. Kiran was well deserving of the commission, and it would have been a huge paycheck. Later they found out the reason why Kiran was not included. It's because Biru had pocketed the commission, and his family did not know.

* * *

Kiran was different; he didn't engage much with Biru but frequently found himself in arguments with his sister, Diya, especially when he thought she wasn't being rational. When disagreements arose, Diya's response was consistent. She would call Maya in the United States and vent, expressing frustration about how unreasonable her 'good-for-nothing' brother was and how he failed to understand her. She would remind Maya of being selfish for leaving her alone. As Maya listened, she would look at me with a sad expression, unsure of how to react, while her sister cried on the other end of the call, thousands of miles away.

Biru and I had a scuffle, which I wrote about in detail in chapters to follow. After the incident, the family decided to keep it a secret, instructing me not to tell anyone, but I had insisted that I would tell Kiran. They agreed. Kiran is talkative, but when I told him, he had listened to me for about twenty minutes without interrupting. When I was done, to my surprise, Kiran responded differently, *"Bro, I listened to you for twenty minutes without saying anything; now I want you to listen."* Expecting admonishment, I was taken aback by his words.

"Bro, they're there for a short while just visiting and you are going through it. I have to deal with them every day, how the fuck do you think I handle it? You should have beat the shit out of him," he concluded, leaving me stunned by his unexpected reaction.

I was surprised to receive such a response from him. I hadn't realized there was so much resentment within him. Kiran had previously mentioned his frustration, expressing that he was tired of being treated as a subordinate. Despite running a showroom himself, he had to work under Biru. Kiran's wife, Mala, consistently suggested starting their own business to avoid dealing with Biru's management. According to Kiran, Biru wasn't a good boss. In case of discrepancies at work, instead of addressing Kiran directly, Biru would communicate them to Kiran's parents. Unable to comprehend the situation, the parents would worry, adding to Kiran's frustration.

Kiran further shared that every Saturday when Biru came to their place, he would claim to have a meeting most of the time and retreat to a room. When lunch would be ready, his mom would ask Kiran to go call Biru. He would go reluctantly and find him playing video games on his phone. Despite calling out to him, Biru wouldn't answer. Even when informed that lunch was ready and everyone was waiting, Biru would respond with just a nod without sharing a glance.

Kiran could not wait for the day when he was no longer subordinate to Biru. If Biru ignored him the first time when called for lunch, Kiran's tone in the second reminder would be, *"You Motherfucker! Are you deaf? Come and eat your fucking lunch bitch!"* This got me laughing. Kiran would then say, *"I'm serious bro, I am tired of putting up with his shit. You should have beat the shit out of him when he taunted you. You don't even work under him! And Diya has become just like him. She speaks his language and sometimes I wonder if she's still my sister."*

This was a kind of relationship I had with Kiran. I wouldn't hesitate to share things with him, and he would have his own way to reveal his animosity towards his sibling. He was my brother-in-law by relation, but we were good friends, or so I thought!

* * *

THE SURGERY

MAYA'S surgery was scheduled for August 15th, 2021. The medical team had meticulously coordinated Maya's treatment plan, scheduling the surgery a few months after commencing chemotherapy. The decision to delay surgery initially was driven by the significant risk it posed to Maya's life due to the tumor's extensive growth, nearly reaching her brain. Positioned between her eyes, nasal cavity, and the brain, the tumor's substantial size necessitated a strategic approach. Therefore, the plan involved administering chemotherapy to reduce the tumor's size, enabling a subsequent surgical intervention to remove as much cancerous tissue as possible.

I recall the occasion when I accompanied Maya and Diya to the doctor for a scheduled appointment to discuss the upcoming surgery. Biru joined us for the visit, and as the two sisters went in to meet with the doctor, Biru and I waited in the car. The wait extended to about two hours, during which Diya provided periodic updates to Biru, who then conveyed the information to me about the doctor's discussion.

After this lengthy wait, Diya called Biru. His expression turned somber, marked by a furrowed brow, and as he spoke on the phone, I could sense a heaviness in his words. Concerned, I asked, *"What's the matter? Is everything okay?"*

He looked up to me with a blank stare, fidgety and restless, constantly settling his thinning hair. I asked again, *"Biru, what's the matter?"*

"According to the doctor, they have to remove her eye," he replied, his words shocking me.

"What? Are you sure? Why?" I pressed for more information.

"Oh, I don't know, you ask them," he replied constantly shifting in his seat and still playing with his already messy hair.

I didn't know what to make of it. I knew Biru was a bad conveyer of messages, so I had my fingers crossed, but I was pretty sure he had misunderstood the information. While we waited, I constantly looked out to the hospital main entrance to see if they were coming out. When they finally did after the much dreaded and uncertain wait, I saw the two sisters walking out, smiling, and chatting. Once in a while Diya could be seen looking up to the sky with her mouth gaping and bursting out in laughter. There was no way they would be so casual after being delivered such bad news.

When they settled into the car, Maya apologized for the extended wait. I reassured her, urging her not to worry, and immediately inquired about the doctor's consultation.

"She discussed the surgery date and the post-operative protocols," Maya replied.

"What about the removal of the eye?" I asked.

"Oh, the doctor explained that in the past, that was the only method used for surgery. There was no alternative at that time," Maya explained.

Maya further explained and expressed gratitude for modern medicine. Now, the operation would be purely 'minimally invasive surgery.' This approach involved using small incisions and specialized instruments to perform surgical procedures, minimizing trauma to the body, and resulting in quicker recovery times for patients. The operation had its own share of risks, but the doctors were confident that it would be successful.

I sighed a breath of relief and cursed Biru in my head. How could he not understand someone explaining something so serious? Would he not care to ask to make sure if what he had heard was correct? But it didn't matter to me. What he had said did not mean anything except it had tensed me out for a bit. It was all good, I thought, and drove them home.

After getting to Maya's apartment, we relayed the message to her parents. They expressed their concerns and asked questions accordingly but stayed strong, or perhaps pretended to be so, not to let their guards down in front of Maya.

* * *

We were to be at MSK at 7 am on the day of the surgery. The night before, we had a family dinner at Maya's apartment. The three of them were packing to take along the next day. I still needed to go home and pack. The doctors had estimated that Maya would need at least four days of recovery before being discharged. Biru, Diya, and I had decided to stay at a hotel nearby. Our plan was to leave at 5 am to ensure we arrived on time for the surgery.

After dinner, I headed back home with my mom. On our way back, my mom suggested that I stay the night at Maya's to avoid being late. While it sounded reasonable and convenient, I listened to her but had no intention of spending the night at Maya's place.

It had barely been ten minutes since we left when Biru called and informed me about the change of plan. They had decided that we leave the same night, and he suggested that I come back. I agreed and told him I would do so after dropping mom off and after picking up my belongings.

By the time I returned and picked them up, it was already midnight. We got to the Bentley Hotel on York Avenue at 1:20 am. After checking in, the two sisters shared a room, while I had to share a room with Biru. We had time to catch about three hours of sleep.

The next morning, we walked to the hospital, which was also located in the same street a few blocks away. It would take us ten mins to get there by foot. We were asked to wait in a room where others were already waiting impatiently. Everyone looked nervous in those early hours. I noticed a few people sobbing. I would slyly glance at Maya. She looked equally nervous but did not want it noticed. While seated, I would notice her restlessly shaking her legs, which made her body tremble. She would blankly look around and stare at her restless fingers that fidgeted among themselves over her shaky lap.

I asked her, *"Maiya, are you ok? Everything will be done before you know it."* (I called Maya, Maiya out of love. It was a name I chose to call her when she decided to call me Baba.)

"Yes, everything is fine, everything is fine. It will be okay. It will be okay." She repeated everything twice, trying to reassure herself while simultaneously revealing the nervousness and fear she was trying so hard to hide.

* * *

Only one person would be allowed to stay or wait for her during the surgery. I would have loved to, but Diya had taken for granted that she would be the one staying, and I was in no position to argue otherwise. So, after hugging them goodbyes and passing on my good wishes, Biru and I headed back to the hotel, reminding Diya to keep us updated about the progress. After being reassured, we headed back. Biru had requested a different room for the coming days. They had theirs, and I had mine, and I was thankful that I didn't have to share a room.

Diya was not sending me updates, so I had to rely on hearing from Biru once he was updated by his wife. There were not many updates to take heed of except that the surgery was going well. It was taking longer than expected, but there was nothing to be alarmed about.

Later around 3 pm, Biru came to my room to have a chat. It was then Diya had called to say that the surgery was successful, and they were moving Maya to a room to recover. When I asked Biru as to what Diya had said, he had his own way of expressing it. He said, *"The doctors are saying the surgery was successful. I'm sure this means she'll live. Right?"* It was a very obtuse way of conveying a message. How insensitive it was to even think that Maya may not make it out of the operating room. He had managed to imprint the harsh reality of the unexpectable. He also told me that Diya had sent him a picture of Maya and asked if I wanted to see it.

No matter how the picture was taken, I knew it would be hard for me to see her in the state she was. I instructed Biru not to show it to me directly but to send it via text so I could view it later. Despite my request, he insensitively proceeded to show it to me anyway. I wanted to punch him in the face but instead asked him to leave me alone, holding back my emotions. As soon as he left the room puzzled, I fell to the floor and cried my heart out.

It was so painful to see the picture of Maya. She looked like a corpse with her mouth gaped open, with tubes inserted through her nose. I had never seen her in that state, nor did I ever want to. Though she was unconscious when the picture was taken, she looked as if she was in deep pain. I had witnessed many painful expressions of Maya during this cancer ordeal, but this picture looked the most painful and very hurtful of all, perhaps because it was my first time seeing her this way.

After gaining my composure, I needed some fresh air. I walked out of the hotel room and made my way to the Riverside drive. Finding a secluded bench, I sat and broke down again. I couldn't control it. The image of Maya kept lingering in my head and could not help but feel bad for what she was going through. I felt utterly helpless, as this situation was completely out of our hands to change. I don't remember how long I sat there, or how many people walked or jogged by me, or if anyone noticed my state.

Time passed, and night fell. I hadn't answered any calls; every call that came in was to inquire about Maya. I was in no condition to talk. I wished I had been the one waiting in the hospital instead of her sister. How much I needed to hold her and tell her no matter what, I wouldn't leave her side and would never give up on her. But such consolation wouldn't heal her; if it could, she would be healed by now. I wouldn't even be allowed to see her that day, so I headed back to the hotel.

Visiting hours extended only until 8 pm, so when Diya returned, I went up to their room to get more updated details from her. Along with other stories she even shared that due to the anesthesia, Maya was a bit delusional and did some funny things that cracked us up. After exchanging a few more incidents, Diya asked me about planning for the next day. I suggested that since she had been there all day, she should take some rest, and I would go in during the first hour the next day. She could join at any time, and I would leave accordingly.

I sensed that, despite my eagerness to stay close to Maya, Diya harbored reservations about leaving her sister's side. She offered reasons, expressing concerns that the nurses required frequent reminders to attend to Maya's needs. Diya characterized me as 'soft-spoken and polite,' implying that I might struggle to assertively handle interactions with the nurses. It left me contemplating whether her words suggested a lack of confidence in my ability to navigate healthcare professionals and officials in the United States, despite me having been here for twenty-four years, while she deemed herself more adept, coming from Nepal.

Before I could say anything, Biru interrupted and suggested, *"Why don't we have breakfast together at 9 am tomorrow and then decide."* I agreed and headed to my room. I went to sleep late, but was awake promptly at 6 am, showered, and got ready to go.

I waited patiently for their call, checking the time as it passed: 7 am, 8 am, and then 9 am, with still no response. By 9:15 am, I decided to text Diya, asking, *"Are you guys still sleeping?"* There was no immediate reply. Eventually, around 9:47 am, she called me.

"Hi Hanchu da, Good morning!" she greeted.

"Good morning," I responded. Hearing some background noise, I inquired, *"Where are you?"*

"We just had breakfast and now we're in front of the hospital, ready to go in," she replied.

I was taken aback. *"I thought I was going in first. This is what we discussed, and you didn't even call me for breakfast?"*

"We didn't want to disturb you," she replied.

Feeling upset, I said, *"Whatever, if you didn't want me going you should have told me earlier. I've been waiting all morning, and you know how much I want to see Maya. Never mind, Diya, whatever..."*

She sensed the tone of my voice and said, *"Why do you always think I'm pushing you away, we are family."*

Feeling frustrated, I retorted, *"It doesn't seem like it, and it doesn't matter anymore. Tell me, what am I to make of what you just did? Is it not clear that you didn't want me to see her and that you wanted to get there before me? You didn't even want me to go for breakfast with you even though your husband had clearly suggested that we should."*

She said she didn't remember Biru insisting we go for breakfast together, and neither had he mentioned anything that morning. I pondered, what should I make of this? It wasn't just my imagination, and if Diya truly forgot, why didn't Biru remind her? We were in New York together for a reason; wouldn't it be courteous to have breakfast together?

Feeling upset and conflicted, I hung up without further discussion. I didn't know what to do. I decided to return home to Connecticut for the day and come back later. A few minutes later, Diya called me again and asked me to come, but I refused and told her I was already far away. I was still at the hotel when she called, but I decided I would lie about my whereabouts.

I saw Biru at the reception while I was checking out of the hotel. He had just finished a call with his wife. Sensing the tension between us, he politely informed me that Diya wanted me to come and stay with Maya because she wasn't feeling well. Biru mentioned that Diya might not be able to spend the entire day at the hospital. I asked as to what was wrong with Diya. Biru told me, *"She says it's cough."*

"Was she coughing this morning?" I asked.

"No, she seemed perfectly fine." Biru confirmed.

With that information, I decided, *"Oh well then, she can stay. I'm heading to Connecticut, need anything from home?"*

Biru quickly responded, *"I'll come with you."*

"*Oh no,*" I thought. I wanted that alone time, and now I had to engage in conversation with him myself. Hoping he'd reconsider, I asked him, "*Won't Diya need you?*"

He shook his head, "*No, she's in the hospital anyway, and she has enough help there, so I'm coming.*"

We set out for Connecticut, and after dropping him off in Stamford, I headed home to Trumbull. It had barely been ten minutes since I arrived home and caught up with my mom when Biru called, "*Are you on your way here?*" I regretted bringing him with me. Now I had to rush back again because his wife was craving for something from the local store. After quickly packing a few of my own things, I went to pick up Biru and headed back to the hotel.

Later that night, Biru and Diya came to my room. I greeted Diya normally, and she apologized for the misunderstanding. I said it was okay. She told me to go there the next morning, and I was happy to agree, even though I asked, "*Are you sure?*"

I was excited for the next day. I wanted to take flowers. I made sure to call the hospital to check if I would be allowed to do so. They said yes! I wasn't familiar with the area, so I looked up Google maps for some flower shops in that vicinity. I had walked that street many times but hadn't seen any. I located one in the First Avenue and planned my route there for the next morning. I decided I would leave about forty-five minutes early even though it was barely ten minutes' walk to the hospital. I'd rather be early than late, I thought.

That night I probably fell asleep at 1 am but was wide awake by 5 am the next day. I showered, browsed the web, and checked my emails multiple times while still pacing back and forth in that small hotel room. I left early, as planned. I located the flower shop on First Avenue and having bought a bouquet, I headed to the hospital. I felt like a nervous schoolboy trying to impress his first love.

'*Uh oh,*' I thought to myself. This has happened before. In New York, when I get into a store and get out, I lose the sense of direction unless I have told and reminded myself which direction to walk when I get out. Like the kids blindfolded while trying to hit the piñata and having been rotated and losing the sense of direction, I was walking in a totally different course and found myself in front of my hotel. So much for getting early, I thought, and started walking back. I arrived at the hospital five minutes after ten. I went to Maya's room and was delighted to see her.

* * *

Maya was asleep but woke up when she saw me. She had a big smile on and didn't seem like she was in pain. In a way, I was glad to see her this way. If I would have been there yesterday, she probably still would have been in pain. I gave her the flowers, which she held while lying down, with the ever so generous smile she never held back. I clicked a few pictures to send to her mom but noticing that Maya's eyes and face were still a bit swollen, I made her wear my sunglasses and pose with a victory sign. Obediently, she followed my instruction as I told her that I would send that picture to both our moms so they wouldn't worry.

The previous night, Maya's mom had called me in tears, expressing her pain and suspicions. She felt that Maya was in distress as Diya hadn't sent her any pictures or allowed her to talk to her. The picture I sent made her laugh, and she thanked me numerous times for making her feel better. She did ask why Maya was wearing sunglasses, and I told her the truth. I said, *"Aunty, it's difficult for me to see Maya with swollen eyes. I wouldn't want you to see her that way and draw conclusions. I want you to know she's much better, and the swelling is receding,"* and assured her that I would send more pictures. This picture was enough to ease a mother's heart.

Maya and I spent the morning chatting, but only when I sensed that Maya was up for it. She had a tube through her nose, but it didn't hinder her from talking. She ate and smiled, reassuring me that she was in less pain compared to the day before. Nurses regularly came in to check on her and monitor her vitals. The room was small, resembling a box of machinery with wires and tubes, but the large windows brought in plenty of light, which Maya appreciated. Even though the room overlooked another building, the room's brightness made it welcoming. The nurses were friendly and attentive to Maya's needs, which contradicted what Diya had mentioned about needing to have them on a leash.

One nurse even went out of her way to find a vase and beautifully arrange the flowers from the bouquet, placing them on the windowsill. The reflected light on the dew-covered flowers made them even more enchanting under the bright afternoon sunlight streaming through the hospital window.

Diya later came around 3 pm to relieve me. I left them, content and delighted to have spent some time with Maya. As a treat to myself, I indulged in a *Chicken over Rice* bowl from the Halal Brothers food truck in the same block. These trucks were a common sight on New York City streets, offering incredibly delicious meals at an affordable price. The sumptuous dish, featuring your choice of meat with rice, a few vegetables, and the spicy secret sauce, made Halal Brothers a sensation in New York Street food.

I returned to my hotel room, turned on the TV, and eagerly devoured the delicious meal in my ravenous hunger. Satiated, I began returning all the missed calls from the well-wishers of Maya. While I spoke to people, I couldn't help but wonder about their true intentions. Were they genuinely concerned about Maya's well-being, or were they simply calling out of courtesy? Some I knew sincerely cared, while others seemed to have never shown interest before. It was disheartening to realize that those I expected to reach out first never bothered. It made me question the nature of our relationships and whether the connections were as meaningful as I had believed.

As time passed and I sought communication and support, I came to realize that only a handful of people truly embodied the phrase, *"Friends in need are friends indeed!"* Many who were present during good times, events hosted at my house, parties, and when they needed my help seemed to have disappeared. It felt as though they had gone into hibernation, leaving me to navigate this challenging period alone.

And then there were a few people I labeled '*second loud noise.*' These were the *friends* who reached out, expressing profound concern, and detailing how deeply troubled they were upon learning about Maya's condition. They claimed restless nights, incessantly haunted by thoughts of Maya. I couldn't help but wonder, if these '*friends*' struggled to sleep, how did Maya's parents manage? How did my family, Diya, and I find solace at night? This remains a lingering question to me.

* * *

The next day when I visited Maya she seemed to be in pain. They had a tube inserted in the lower portion of her back into her spine to drain out the spinal fluid, a common occurrence after undergoing surgery of such magnitude. The excess fluid would automatically be excreted into a small pouch hanging by her bed. Now that the tube was removed, it was common for Maya to feel a slight headache due to the pressure. She was also beginning to have a small discharge from her nose. If there was throbbing or severe pain, or if there were profuse discharges, it would be a matter of concern. They kept her in observation, constantly checking on her. She was in immense pain but not to the severity that would concern the doctors. After a day or two, the pain subsided, much to everyone's relief. Maya looked normal again, able to talk and watch standup comedy on her iPad, which kept her spirits high.

Three to four days of hospital stay turned out to be a week. Accordingly, we had to extend our stay in the hotel, which they always said was overbooked but never failed to find a room when we needed one. On the seventh day, knowing she wouldn't be discharged, I suggested that Biru and Diya go around the city while I stayed with Maya all day. I told them it would give them time for each other and would also be a break from hospital runs. They happily agreed and decided to take a trip to Roosevelt Island and various other places, sending me pictures of their trip. I would show them to Maya, and she would smile. Maya was glad that they were having fun and occasionally thanked me for letting them take time off.

We were informed that there was a probability that Maya would be discharged the next day around noon. Of all the days, Biru and Diya decided to go to Stamford that night to spend some time with the kids. They were taking my car, which I agreed to, but asked them to be back early so they would be on time for discharge.

The next morning, the discharge happened before noon. Biru and Diya, tardy as always, were still about an hour away. The hospital would not wait, as they had to make room for the next patient. We were escorted downstairs by the nurse, leading Maya in a wheelchair. I told Maya we would take the Uber to the hotel and rest up until they came.

I called an Uber, which arrived instantly. The driver turned out to be a fellow Nepalese who engaged in unwelcomed chitchat. Thankfully, the hotel was a short drive away. I held Maya in my arms and led her through the elevator into my room. She felt nauseous and queasy but jumped straight to bed and pulled the blanket over herself. I had set the air-conditioning too cold for her liking. Since I had a suite, I reminded her that I would be in the other room if she needed me. She nodded and said she would take a nap. After adjusting the temperature a few degrees higher, I left.

In about five minutes she called out, *"Hanchu!"* I rushed into the bedroom, worried but unable to make out the reason for her call. I saw her peering out of the blanket and asked, *"What's wrong?"*

"Can you bring me miso soup?" she requested.

"Is that why you yelled out for me?" I asked, slightly relieved.

"Yes, I want miso soup," she replied.

I smiled and nodded, amused by her request, and headed out to get her the *miso* soup. It was typical of her to have such cravings during odd hours. I reminisced about the good old days when, while watching TV in the quiet hours of the night, she would sit up with her eyes sparkling and ask, *"You know what I feel like having?"*

I would think to myself, *"Uh oh."* She was probably craving for *Chinese food, Idli dosa, chickpea salad, wai wai, jhaal mudi....* Everything that would be difficult to get at those odd hours of the night.

When I came back with the *miso* soup, Diya and Biru were already in the room, ordering lunch, taking the liberty of ordering me something as well. I didn't care, and they knew I wasn't fussy about food, unlike Biru, who wanted a Wendy's burger in a Nepalese restaurant!

It was heartening to see Maya regain some energy after enjoying the soup. She sat up on the bed while we had our lunch, even taking small piece of fries from Diya's plate. Since Biru and Diya had checked out the night before, they didn't need to pack anything. After retrieving my car from the underground parking conveniently located in the hotel basement, we set for home, ready to be welcomed by her excited parents, especially her mother, who sometimes got more excited than anyone else in the family.

As soon as we arrived home, Maya exchanged a few words with her parents before expressing her desire to rest. She headed straight to her room and lay down, covering herself with the thick quilt as if it were one of those cold winter nights. Knowing Maya always felt cold, I observed her mother's insistence on using a lighter blanket, but I respected Maya's preference and let them be. I then joined her dad in the living room, where we shared a few words.

***

RADIATION

AFTER overcoming each obstacle, new ones seemed to appear, presenting challenges we hadn't anticipated. Maya was becoming accustomed to the chemotherapy and understood what to expect after each treatment. While she was healing from the surgery, she still experienced discomfort in her nasal breathing. To prevent dryness, she had to apply ointments and perform nasal irrigation daily. Unfortunately, she had lost her sense of smell, and there was uncertainty about whether it would ever return. The doctors assured us that this was a minor concern compared to the larger battle against cancer and advised us to focus on her overall healing. They emphasized that once the cancer was eradicated, we could address these "petty" concerns.

Losing the sense of smell, a vital sensory ability, was an unwelcome deprivation. Given Maya's circumstances, she had more pressing concerns to address. *"Yeah, we'll take care of it later,"* she would say with a smile, prioritizing her immediate health needs over minor inconveniences.

The doctors provided us with the radiation schedule: thirty sessions, scheduled for five days a week over the course of six weeks. We reassured ourselves that it would pass quickly. At this point, Maya showed no reactions to the new schedule. If she noticed any changes in the upcoming appointments on the portal or if a new schedule was assigned, she would casually remind me without delving into her feelings. What could she say? There seemed to be nothing to express; she kept everything inside and maintained a smile on her face whenever possible. This became our daily routine, and we understood that we still had a few more months to endure before it would all be over.

A week before the radiation treatment began, we had to visit the Proton Center in Harlem for a robotic simulation to create a 3D imprint of Maya's face and part of her torso. As usual, I drove her to the city, accompanied by Diya, who stayed with her while I waited outside in the parking lot.

The wait felt endless. While Diya was inside, she called me, and I anticipated an update. Instead, she asked me to get her some food as she was hungry. I considered fetching something from nearby stores but suggested Uber Eats instead. Unfortunately, she couldn't use it due to the lengthy delivery wait. Despite her hints about her hunger, I remained firm in my decision not to leave the parking spot. In earlier times, I would have gone out of my way to get her something, but these days I started to get a feeling as though she had begun to take my assistance for granted. I reminded myself that I wasn't inclined to run errands for Diya.

When they came out, I could sense the tension. Maya remained quiet and did not say anything. I figured that she was in no good mood. She was seated in the passenger seat as always and Diya at the back. I had asked her how it had gone. Before she replied, I started driving, not expecting any answer. A few minutes later, she started describing the process and burst out crying. I was glad she cried as it was the first time I ever saw her cry during the entire ordeal since diagnosis.

She described how they had to perform the simulation, encircling her into an enclosed object to get her exact measurements of the face and the torso. During the process, she had to bite on something that was inserted in her mouth while being engulfed in the "mask." Claustrophobic as she was at times, this was a very suffocating experience for her. She felt she could not breathe and likened it to feeling like "*Jason; With the goaltender mask.*"

"*Why do I have to go through this, why? What did I do wrong that I am being punished this way? I'd rather die. Why not just kill me or make me die instead of making me go through this,*" she vented heartbreakingly.

Her words cut through the silence, expressing the depths of her anguish and despair. Diya and I sat in solemn silence, understanding the weight of her pain and the burden of her suffering. There were no words of comfort that could adequately address the depth of her despair in that moment. All we could offer was our silent presence, bearing witness to her anguish and sharing in her grief.

Our eyes had teared up, still unable to find any words of consolation. I continued to focus on the road while Diya remained silent, our hearts heavy with sorrow. Even if we had something to say, we knew it wouldn't be enough. It's easy to offer condolences and say words like, *"I know what you feel,"* but they often fall short. No one can truly understand what others are going through except to imagine. Our imaginations too, may not fully capture the reality of what others are experiencing. Maya was going through a lot, and it was high time she vented out, and we let her.

A few minutes later, Maya wiped her tears and said, *"I'm sorry, I had to let it out."* Diya and I both agreed and responded, *"We're glad you did. We hope you feel better."*

"Yeah, much better. Now I want coffee and a Subway sandwich," Maya replied.

I took the nearest exit in Westchester and found a Subway restaurant. Since I wasn't hungry, the two of them went to get a sandwich. I knew their mom had already prepared dinner but didn't bother to remind them and let them have their time together. While they ordered, I waited in the car. They came out smiling and talking to each other. Maya had gotten me a cup of coffee, and once they were settled in the car, we set off.

When we got home, her dad was seated in his *throne,* a swing chair that Maya loved. I would be the first one he would hook his gaze on every time we got back from appointments and wait for a sign whether everything went well or not. He would understand through my expressions, and many times we communicated through sign language. When he looked at me, I indicated that I would tell him momentarily. He nodded and after briefly visually scanning his daughters, continued writing in the journal he had taken up during his visit to the United States.

Later, I explained to him that it was a bad day and how she had reacted. He stared at me blankly with immense sadness. He wasn't very good at showing his feelings, but I knew he was hurting to see his daughter suffer so much and go through so much pain. The times when I had good news for him, he would say, *"Good, that's very good news!"* and get up on his feet and ask everyone if they wanted tea, heading to the kitchen. That day he stayed put.

* * *

As the days for radiation approached, we began discussing our options—whether to rent an apartment in New York close to the hospital or to commute. Maya believed it wouldn't be necessary to get an apartment there since the radiation procedure would take, at most, an hour. If we scheduled it for the early hours of the day, the commute would only be about forty-five minutes, avoiding traffic. I agreed, as did her dad. We even considered the possibility of renting a place if Maya found the commute challenging. However, Biru and Diya were insistent that we stay in New York. They loved the city and believed it would be convenient for taking the kids around.

I spoke to Maya and suggested that instead of involving them in the search and expenses, we should secure one ourselves. Maya was hesitant at first, but after I left, she took it upon herself to explore Airbnb and book a place. Unfortunately, the host seemed new to Airbnb, as he never bothered to check his listing or respond to Maya's messages, and the reservation expired without any response.

Upon seeing the initiative taken by Maya and me, Diya and Biru, driven by a desire for independence and perhaps seeking credit for their decision, embarked on a mission to find a place without consulting any of us. They even refused help when my brother, well-versed in the intricacies of the real estate market in New York, offered to assist with the search. The revelation about securing accommodation for Maya's radiation treatment came just a day before it commenced.

While we were relieved to learn about the arrangements, it turned out that they had booked four separate rentals. The challenge arose as the check-out from one rental couldn't be synchronized with the check-in of another. Consequently, we found ourselves having to pack up our belongings, return to Connecticut, and then make another trip to check into the new rental whenever our move-in date was scheduled. The logistical arrangements made by the couple seemed perplexing yet once more.

As a consequence of their foray into unchartered territory, the chosen apartments did not align conveniently with Maya's radiation schedule too. The lack of foresight and consideration for Maya's need became apparent when the second apartment had to be swiftly abandoned, prompting a hasty move to Stamford in just about a week. The abrupt relocations added an extra layer of stress and inconvenience, highlighting their inconsideration for not being team players. Seeing my dissatisfaction with the decision, Maya told me that they had tried their best, and since nothing else was available, this was the best they could come up with.

"*Whatever,*" I thought, and decided to go with the flow, waiting for further instructions.

I drove them to Harlem the night before the radiation session on a Sunday. Maya had undergone chemotherapy the previous Friday. After they settled into a nice, lavish condo rented for a week, I headed to the hotel room I had booked for myself. I didn't want to stay in the same apartment with Maya's family. When they found out I was staying in a hotel, Maya's dad insisted that I move in with them, but I remained firm in my decision.

The day of chemo usually wore Maya down, and now she had to undergo radiation simultaneously. I expected the worst but hoped for the best. I couldn't get the picture of her breaking down during the visit for simulation off my head. She would now go through the same process, and the outcome did have side effects. We had read and also heard from people who had undergone radiation that the side effects could sometimes be worse than the chemo.

The drive from the hotel to her place was just about fifteen minutes without traffic and having to drive to her place at 6 am wasn't bad. I always arrived about five to ten minutes early and waited outside. Once she came, it was a two-minute drive to the Proton center. The procedure itself took only about forty-five minutes, and then after dropping them off, I would head back to my hotel and either work or just relax for the day. Sometimes, a friend or two would stop by and take me out for dinner. They would say that I needed to be taken care of too, and I appreciate these people in my life.

Needless to say, the first day was tough. She couldn't go through the process and had to leave. She experienced anxiety and panic, still needing time to digest the fact that she always had to wear the mask during radiation. The mere thought of wearing it filled her with fear. There was no escaping it and she knew it. So, the next day she gathered up all her courage and underwent the treatment. It wasn't easy, she would explain, agonizing over the thought of it. The doctors then prescribed her anti-nausea medication, which helped her throughout the thirty days of her radiation.

* * *

The first unit Biru and Diya had rented was spacious, with huge rooms and attached bathrooms. It also had large windows allowing plenty of sunlight to enter, which Maya would have loved if she had been in the right state of mind to take delight in it.

Sometimes after radiation, I would relieve the family, who would go for a walk while I stayed back with Maya. She would be sleeping most of the time, and once in a while, when she felt a little energetic, she would come out and spend time in the living room with me. She would rest her head on my lap while I massaged it, and I would play reruns of *Law and Order*, hoping she would take notice and indulge watching. Minutes later, she would get dizzy and sick and would head back to her room to try to fall asleep. When the family returned, I would whisper goodbye to her and bid farewell to the family, who would insist that I stay for dinner, for which I always had an excuse not to.

* * *

Harlem had its own way of showing its charm. One day, I was by Maya's bedside while her dad and Diya were in the living room. Suddenly, I heard Diya scream. I rushed out, instructing Maya to stay back. When I reached them, they were both standing and staring out the window. I hurriedly asked them what happened and intended to go out to check. Diya replied, *"A man just jumped over this window and climbed up."*

"What?" I exclaimed in amazement. The unit had twelve-foot-high ceilings and it seemed impossible. Ignoring their warnings not to go outside, I opened the door, asking them to remain inside. When I went out, I saw other neighbors staring up in the direction the *"person"* had gone. Upon further inquiry, we found out that the person renting the third floor was mentally unstable and had indeed climbed up the walls. Someone had called the police, and he was later taken into custody. Diya was in shock, and I don't recall exactly where Biru and the kids were at that time. I was glad they didn't see it, as I'm sure the kids would have been more frightened by the scene, which seemed like a piece taken out from a psychotic horror movie!

This place was situated near 121st Street in Harlem, an area with a notorious reputation. In the past, 126th Street had been known as one of the most violent streets in Harlem; we were just a few blocks away. For individuals relocating from Nepal or even the suburbs of Connecticut, this environment was difficult to comprehend. It was evident that the recent incident had left the others feeling shaken. Fortunately, they mentioned they would be checking out on Friday, moving to a different apartment just a few blocks away the following Monday.

When Diya and Biru returned to Maya's apartment in Stamford, for the weekend, it seemed like they breathed a sigh of relief. They no longer had to hesitate before taking walks with their children, regardless of the time of day or night. Harlem presented a starkly different scenario, and we still had four more weeks to endure. Deep down, I wished they had listened to our suggestion to commute from Stamford. Maya's dad and I silently discussed our mutual feelings, expressing them only when the couple weren't around to avoid causing any hurt.

The next apartment was a few blocks away and not as spacious and bright, with no sunlight to embrace you. It wasn't a basement, but it felt like one with dingy windows, and rooms big enough just to fit a queen-size bed. As Diya's son would describe it, *"Hanubaba" (as he addressed me), "it's like a pigeon cage,"* and would burst out in laughter with his sister in their own sweet, innocent way.

At the time they checked into the second unit, I had decided to check out of the hotel and instead commute from Trumbull. Maya was against it as she thought it didn't make sense for me to drive all the way there at 3 am to take her to the Proton center, which was just about two minutes' drive. I refused and was unwavering in my decision to be there, as it meant a great deal to me. I couldn't rely on Biru to drive her there, as sometimes he would be caught up in meetings and I doubted he could give a hundred percent. Moreover, Maya wasn't very comfortable with him accompanying her. I never understood how he always had meetings conveniently when the entire Nepalese population would be sleeping due to the time difference.

One day, when Biru, Diya, and the kids had gone out for a walk, a stranger had approached them and murmured something. He was perhaps homeless and was begging for money, but he appeared scary enough for them to reconsider their stay in Harlem and decide to move back to Connecticut. They even thought they saw him carrying a gun. As a result, they canceled the reservations for the next few apartments, and the landlords were kind enough to refund the security deposit, despite it being against Airbnb's policy to cancel past a certain allotted time.

It was a relief. We no longer needed to pack up everything every week and live like nomads. Maya was fine with the new arrangement. So, starting from the following week, I left Trumbull around 4 am and arrived in Stamford around 4:30 am. Sometimes, if I arrived early, I went upstairs to the apartment, wake them up, and left by 5 am. Diya often accompanied us, sitting quietly in the back, but she stopped coming along after a week. It seemed that the early wake-up calls were taking a toll on her.

During our trips, Maya would sometimes catch up on sleep, while other times she would engage in conversation, with soft blues or jazz playing in the background. I preferred the soothing tones of blues or jazz in the early morning. Maya would usually be okay with it, but occasionally she would demand, play *"Metallica"* or *"We Will Rock You"* by *"Queen."* You never knew what mood she would be in.

* * *

During Maya's third week of radiation, on a Sunday, I was preparing to visit her place. My mom expressed her desire to accompany me. Typically, I aimed to arrive around 4 or 5 pm. However, that day, as I had a hunch before, I once again felt a queasy sensation, sensing that Maya might need me. Biru and Diya had already returned to Nepal. I informed my mom that we should head there earlier than usual and suggested leaving around 2 pm.

It was Asma's birthday that day, and she lived just two minutes away from Maya. Mom wanted to take a bouquet for her and drop it off before we headed to Maya's place. To avoid making an additional stop after leaving home, I went to get the flowers in the morning. Later, when we reached Stamford, we found ourselves at a stoplight, waiting to make a right turn, when suddenly I made a left towards Maya's apartment instead. I assured my mom that we could drop the flowers off later when we returned. I just had this strong feeling that I needed to be at Maya's place as soon as possible.

My mom was surprised and said, *"It's just two minutes."* I had already taken a left and was just a minute away from Maya.

When we got to the apartment, there was an eerie silence except for snores coming from Maya's dad's room. Maya was lying on her usual couch in the living room but did not respond when I said, *"Good afternoon, Maiya."* Her mom had just come out of the bathroom and was walking towards Maya with a wet towel but did not turn to acknowledge us.

I called out to her, *"Aunty!"* but she didn't turn around. Instead, she reached up to her eyes. I noticed she was wiping away tears, and upon seeing this, I hurried over to Maya to check on her. As I approached her, her mom exclaimed, *"No matter how much I tell her, she doesn't close her eyes,"* and she threw a towel over Maya's face in a mixture of panic and frustration, unsure of what else to do.

I looked at Maya and noticed her eyes were fluttering. I asked her calmly, *"Is that right, Maiya, you can't close your eyes?"* She nodded. I asked her to try closing her eyes again. She would try but was not able to. She seemed unconscious but was responsive. In a matter of minutes, her eyes opened but I could not see the retina. She was looking up exposing only the sclera. It scared me but I remained calm. I called out to my mom and pointed out to a small bottle of spray and asked her to pass it to me.

I sprayed the entire content of the bottle into her nostrils. I saw life coming back to her. Her breathing slowed, and she sighed a breath of relief. Her eyes were no longer fluttering and gently opened. She looked at me and smiled.

"Feeling better?" I asked. She nodded in response and looked at the dogs, who were trying to get on the couch, signaling with their soft yelp. She gently lifted them and put them by her side, starting to pat them. After a few minutes, I asked her to lay on her side, and as soon as she did, she threw up.

* * *

Just the day earlier I had gone to CVS to pick up Maya's prescriptions, as I usually did when it was ready. There was an extra item, *Narcan*, the spray I used on Maya earlier. It was to be used when someone overdosed with opioids. When I came home and noticed it, I had asked Maya, *"Why do they keep sending this to you? Were we supposed to get this?"* She didn't know.

We had received a set of *Narcan* prescribed a few months ago as well. At that time, I thought it was mistakenly prescribed and hadn't paid much attention to it. However, the previous night, with some extra time on my hands, I felt compelled to read every line in the instruction that accompanied it. Typically, I didn't bother with reading medication instructions, but something prompted me to do so this time, and I'm glad I did. Consequently, I knew exactly when and how to use it. Reflecting on this, I realized what might have happened if I hadn't read it and had discarded it like we did the first time.

Seeing someone overdose on opioids was an experience I had never encountered before. Maya had been instructed to increase her dosage of medication when she experienced intense pain in her throat, the area targeted by radiation. The pain was so severe that she couldn't swallow anything, and even attempting to do so caused her entire body to convulse in agony. The prescribed regimen included nearly 2000 mg of gabapentin and several dosages of oxycodone throughout the day whenever the pain flared up. Perhaps it was because I was familiar with the medications she was taking that I instinctively reached for the *Narcan*.

* * *

Later she lay down after throwing up, still with the dogs resting by her side. Her eyes were closed, but she was squinting in pain. I sat next to her, gently patting her head, and sensing the warmth that suggested she might be coming down with a fever, I suggested that we might need to go to the hospital. She turned towards me, her eyes still closed, and asked, *"You think?"* I replied, *"Yeah I do."* She agreed, and I immediately called the paramedics.

The paramedics arrived within three minutes and quickly assessed Maya's condition. Her body temperature was 102.4 degrees Fahrenheit. While attending to her, they noticed the used *Narcan* spray on the table and asked, *"Who used that? Was it used on her?"*

I stepped forward and admitted that I had used it. The paramedic nodded and remarked, *"Good call. Never know what would have happened otherwise."* They then inquired how I knew when to use it. I responded proudly, *"Instinct!"* They nodded in agreement and complimented me, saying, *"Your instinct may have just saved a life!"*

I took a deep breath and felt gratitude wash over me. What had prompted me to read the instructions last night? Why had I rushed to the apartment earlier than usual? What if I had gone to Asma's before visiting Maya? I was just thankful that I had been there.

Maya's dad woke up only when the paramedics arrived, having missed out on all the commotion.

* * *

The paramedics carefully lifted Maya and laid her on the stretcher, then swiftly transported her to Stamford Hospital, just a six-minute drive away. Due to COVID-19 restrictions, only the paramedics were allowed in the van. They provided me with instructions on where to find Maya in the hospital once we arrived.

Accompanied by Maya's mom, I drove to the hospital and went straight to the emergency room. The nurses had already initiated an IV, and Maya's white blood cell count was dangerously low at 0.01 percent. She urgently needed a transfusion and had to be admitted as soon as a room became available. In the meantime, she would remain under observation in the emergency ward.

After dropping off Maya's mom at home, I asked Sanjay, Asma's husband, to escort my mom back home. Returning to the hospital, I remained with Maya. Eventually, her room was prepared, and she was transferred upstairs at 4:45 am. Due to hospital visiting hours ending at 8 pm, I wasn't allowed to accompany her to her room despite my request.

I spent the entire night awake, returning the next morning to check on Maya. Thankfully, she was showing significant improvement. As we discussed the events of the previous night, she mentioned that she had thought she was fine and couldn't recall much else that had happened. I embraced her and urged her to inform me whenever she felt weak in the future. She agreed and drifted back to sleep.

As I settled in with my laptop to work, the weight of the situation weighed heavily on my mind. It was the first time Maya had been admitted to the hospital, forcing her to miss not only her scheduled chemo session for that Friday but also several crucial radiation treatments. Her condition simply wasn't stable enough to undergo the treatments, leaving us all deeply concerned about the impact on her ongoing medical care.

* * *

12

THE MISUNDERSTANDINGS

AMIDST the overwhelming emotions, misunderstandings began to surface. While everyone shared the common desire for Maya's recovery, each person had their own approach to caring for her. Following the doctor's instructions, I insisted that Maya refrain from driving for five to seven days after chemotherapy. Diya held a different view, believing it was acceptable for Maya to drive while they went shopping.

One evening Maya, her dad, and I decided to take a short stroll around the building with the dogs. After barely ten minutes, Maya began feeling dizzy and nauseous, prompting us to return to the apartment. While waiting for the elevator, Maya almost unconsciously began to drift backwards. Fortunately, the wall was close enough to prevent her from falling. Concerned, I held her and asked if she was okay. With a blank expression, she replied, *"I thought I was going to faint."*

When I arrived at Maya's apartment the next evening, I immediately noticed that her car was absent from its usual spot in the garage adjacent to mine. When I entered the apartment, I didn't find Maya or Diya. I asked Maya's dad about her whereabouts, and he informed me that she had gone to the mall with Diya, a ten-minute walk from her apartment. Maya often walked there.

I expressed my surprise to her dad, questioning why she had chosen to drive to the mall, especially considering its close proximity. It seemed unnecessary, unless Diya had plans for heavy shopping that required the car. He met my gaze with a helpless expression, acknowledging my discontent. However, he also indicated that they likely wouldn't have listened even if he had tried to dissuade them.

When I called Maya, she instantly sensed my reason for calling. In a somewhat cagey manner, even before I could express my concern, she reassured me, *"We're not too far and will be back before you know it, oki?"*

"I hope so Maiya. Please be careful." I replied and hung up.

Maya's friend Chaya, along with her husband AJ and their kids, were visiting from Providence that day. They arrived before Maya and Diya returned from the mall. While waiting for them, we spent some time chatting, and Maya's dad kindly prepared tea for us. Just as the tea was ready, Maya and Diya arrived. Maya entered with a guilty smile, signaling to me not to be upset, and quickly made her way to the restroom. Though I didn't say anything, I simply nodded and averted my gaze, silently expressing my disapproval of her actions.

* * *

Maya and I had a similar conversation before, back when Biru and Diya first visited after Maya's diagnosis. On that occasion, the four of us had gone for a walk. Once we returned to the apartment, as I was preparing to leave, Biru and Diya requested a ride to Target. Maya opted to join me in dropping them off. As we made our way there, Maya asked if I could stay with her until Biru and Diya returned. She expressed her concern that they might ask her to pick them up, but she wasn't feeling up to driving. When I questioned why they weren't considering her fatigue, Maya simply replied, *"When they shop, they forget everything."* As expected, they called shortly after to be picked up. I allowed Maya to rest while I went instead, as they had accumulated a considerable number of boxes and required transportation, despite the apartment being only a seven minute walk away.

It seemed like Biru and Diya tend to forget about Maya's condition when they get caught up in their activities. Maya, even when feeling tired or unwell, often ended up accommodating their needs, even if it meant inconveniencing herself. In the past, Maya had expressed her concerns about driving when she wasn't feeling up to it, but her sister's forgetfulness or disregard for her well-being led to situations where she had to step in or make sacrifices.

It's understandable that Maya might have felt torn between wanting to spend time with her sister and needing to prioritize her health. However, it was crucial for Diya to be more considerate and mindful of Maya's situation, especially during times when she was undergoing medical treatment or feeling fatigued.

With my repeated attempts, I often intervened, aiming to foster an open and honest conversation with Maya and her sister regarding the importance of setting boundaries. I emphasized the necessity of ensuring that Maya's needs were acknowledged and respected, especially during social outings or activities. Regrettably, my efforts proved futile.

* * *

Diya's selfishness became evident in her selective adherence to the doctor's instructions regarding Maya's rest. When it suited her own agenda or convenience, she conveniently overlooked the doctor's advice, allowing Maya to continue without adequate rest. When it didn't serve her purpose, Diya adopted an unusually strict approach, denying Maya even a single break.

This behavior often displayed a self-centered attitude where Diya prioritized her own interest over Maya's well-being. The inconsistencies in following medical recommendations highlighted a lack of genuine concern for Maya's health and showed Diya's readiness to compromise on crucial aspects when it suited her personal goals. I could sense such selfish conduct and feared its potentially detrimental effects on Maya's health and recovery. I constantly emphasized the need for a more supportive and consistent approach from those involved in her care. As you continue reading, you will notice other instances where such behavior was prevalent on more than one occasion.

* * *

Later, when Maya's dad and I were in the kitchen, Diya walked in. I expressed my concern, telling her she shouldn't have allowed Maya to drive, especially since it hadn't been five days since her chemo. In response, she rolled her eyes and exclaimed, *"Why? You guys want her to live life like a handicapped person?"*

"Diya, all I'm saying is to let her drive only when she's feeling better," I replied to her insensitive comment.

She retorted, *"She is better, and she wanted to drive."*

"Well then, you should have stopped her because just yesterday she nearly passed out. What if that happened when she was driving? In a matter of seconds, she could get into an accident," I replied firmly.

"Oh God, you guys!" she exclaimed before walking away.

Chaya entered the kitchen and inquired, *"What are you guys arguing about?"*

When I told her the reason, she responded, *"Why don't you let Maya make her own decisions? It's her life."*

* * *

'Make her own Decisions?' Allowing Maya to make her own decisions, particularly when it comes to aspects like eating, taking medications, engaging in physical activity, and following medical advice, poses significant risks. Her choices may include refusing to eat, neglecting medications, avoiding walks, lifting heavy objects despite doctor's warnings, and neglecting rest, among others. Allowing Maya to

make these decisions could have serious consequences for her health and well-being.

I recall a friend sharing a regretful experience where he allowed his father to make his own decision regarding cancer treatment. His father opted for homeopathy instead of traditional chemotherapy and radiation. Unfortunately, this decision resulted in his father's passing within a month. This serves as an emotional reminder of the potential consequences of allowing loved ones to make decisions that may not be in their best interest, particularly when it comes to matters of health and medical treatment.

That was the breaking point for me. I found myself unable to speak another word to them. A heavy sense of agitation consumed me, causing my hands to tremble. I couldn't discern whether it was anger or hurt at being told by an outsider to stay away from the family circle. Hastily, I fled the kitchen and sought solace in the living room, where Maya's dad, AJ, my mom, and Maya's mom were seated. Sensing that I was on edge, Diya emerged from the kitchen and approached me, saying, *"Listen, Hanchu da."*

"Diya, please leave me alone." I replied firmly.

* * *

Experiencing a situation where you're subtly hinted not to interfere while you're deeply invested in caring for someone like Maya evoked a mix of emotions within me. The frustration and upset were intense, especially when the person offering the advice, in this case, Chaya, seemed to have limited knowledge about Maya's specific needs. It was disheartening to be told to let Maya make her own decisions by someone who was never around or who sporadically visited and perhaps did not comprehend the intricacies of the situation.

The sense of being misunderstood or undervalued in my caregiving intensified my emotional toll. Balancing the desire to support Maya in the best way possible with the external pressure to step back created a profound internal conflict within me. The strain stemmed from the genuine concern and commitment I had towards Maya's well-being. Chaya may have said it with good intentions, but such comments made it challenging for me to navigate the dynamics of well-intentioned but potentially misguided advice from uninformed visitors.

* * *

All eyes were on me now, and the tension in the room was profound. Chaya's attempt to calm me down only fueled my frustration further. My trembling hands made it impossible to hold the teacup steady enough to take a sip. In a sudden surge of agitation, I abandoned the tea, hastily put on my shoes, and announced my departure to everyone present. Assuring my mom that I would return to pick her up later, I hurried out of the room.

As I made my way to the kitchen, Diya called out my name, attempting to intervene. Ignoring her pleas, I poured the untouched tea down the sink and stormed out of the apartment. Without waiting for the elevator, I sprinted down the stairs, the rush of adrenaline urging me forward. Once in my car, I sped away, the turmoil within me matched only by the chaos on the road.

Still trembling and feeling the rush of blood to my head, I cranked up the air conditioning, drowning out my thoughts with the blaring sounds of *"Peace Sells"* by Megadeth. With each mile, the pain and heat in my head intensified, but I pushed on, desperate to escape the suffocating emotions that threatened to consume me.

My phone started ringing off the hook. The calls were from AJ, Maya's dad, my mom, Maya, and Diya. I didn't answer, but after constant calls, I replied to Maya's dad's call and told him, *"I'm sorry for leaving this way, Uncle, but please don't ask me to come today, I just won't."* He understood and told me he would see me the next day.

The following day, I chose not to return despite their calls. Instead, I concocted an excuse to make the drive all the way to Boston to pick up something for Maya. On Sunday, however, I had no choice but to rejoin the group as we were all invited to a friend's place for dinner, and I was responsible for driving everyone there. By then, I had managed to regain my composure, and it seemed like everyone had forgiven my outburst.

Reflecting on the situation, I realized that harboring anger only leads to personal loss. It was a bitter realization, especially considering that AJ and I had planned a long hike together, coinciding with his visit, which happened to fall around his birthday. I had been eagerly looking forward to it, but my anger had caused me to miss out. AJ is one of the few close friends with whom I can speak openly and without fear of judgment. I apologized to him over the phone, as they had already departed Sunday morning. That was the only day I didn't visit Maya during her entire treatment.

The message from *Sadhguru* echoed persistently in my mind. His words about how allowing anger to take hold gives power to the other person, ultimately leading to our own suffering, resonated deeply with me. I wholeheartedly agreed with this sentiment, recognizing the destructive nature of anger. Yet, despite my agreement, I couldn't help but acknowledge the challenge of consistently embodying such wisdom. Becoming a saint seemed like a far-off aspiration, but I remained committed to continual self-improvement, taking small steps towards growth and reflection.

While I acknowledged the importance of recognizing when I had erred and being willing to apologize or make amends, I didn't feel the need to apologize in this particular situation. My stance was not out of stubbornness but rather a conviction that my actions, while fueled by frustration, were justified given the circumstances.

Another reason I got so riled up was upon being asked, *"Do you want her to live like a handicapped person all her life?"* The suggestion that I wanted Maya to live like one, was not only hurtful but also completely unfounded. It disregarded the daily struggles Maya and I faced and the efforts we made to navigate her illness with dignity and resilience. It was frustrating to hear such a statement, especially from someone who may not fully comprehend the depth of our experiences. In that moment, I felt the urge to retaliate with equally cutting remarks, to expose the flaws in Diya's perspective. However, I refrained from succumbing to that temptation, recognizing that retaliation would only escalate tensions and sow further discord within our already strained relationships.

* * *

Diya had a specific way of organizing the pantry, and she often took the time to rearrange it to her liking. On one particular day, we were in a rush to get to Maya's Computed Tomography (CT) scan appointment. Maya, who was restricted to only a few nuts and seeds, quietly mentioned she was hungry as we were leaving the apartment. Despite her insistence that I shouldn't worry, I hurried back upstairs to grab something for her.

Navigating Maya's pantry, which was arranged according to her preferences, proved to be a challenge. Maya had instructed me on the location of the nuts, but the pantry was in disarray, with items arranged differently than usual. In my haste, I shuffled through a few things around until I found what I needed and rushed back downstairs to fetch Maya for her scan, intending to organize the pantry later.

After several hours at the hospital and returning home fatigued, I forgot about the pantry rearrangement. Maya, changing into her pajamas despite the daylight outside, joined us for our usual conversation with her parents. Suddenly, Diya erupted in frustration, exclaiming, *"Oh my God! Di and mamu, how many times do I have to tell you to not mess up the things that I arrange? How many times?"*

I sensed that her outburst was indirectly aimed at me as well, even though she couldn't bring herself to say it outright. *"Diya, stop yelling at her. You know very well who did it and you can tell me directly."*

She replied, *"It wasn't directed to you, and I didn't know it was you"* and stormed into her room.

I disliked it immensely when Diya raised her voice at Maya, as shouting seemed to be her default method of communication within the family. Maya needed compassion and support during this delicate time. It pained me to witness her mom scolding her for not eating more than what she was capable of, and it frustrated me when her sister insisted she should exercise, beyond Maya's physical limitations. Even though Maya was frail during this period, Diya expected her to participate in a rigorous *"Yoga bootcamp."* Maya struggled silently, never revealing the extent of her discomfort to her sister. Instead, I would often find myself comforting her later, massaging her tired muscles after enduring the strenuous regimen Diya imposed on her.

Such conflicts continued to arise, fueled by the strain of witnessing our loved one's suffering, which clouded our judgement and reasoning. Consequently, I found myself becoming increasingly irritated by Diya's actions, and she seemed to interpret everything I did as a signal that I disliked her.

* * *

One night, during my mom's visit at Maya's apartment, dinner time arrived, and no preparations had been made. Taking on my usual role, I volunteered to cook for the family, as everyone else appeared preoccupied with their own activities. I assured them that I would prepare a simple meal for dinner.

Opting for *Aloo Dum* (potato curry) paired with Malaysian *roti* (bread), which only required heating in the pan, I headed into the kitchen to get started. After heating the pan, I started peeling the potatoes. However, amidst my preparations, I overlooked the fact that the pan had overheated. When I placed the *roti* in the pan, it ended up burning slightly.

Diya, who happened to be in the kitchen at the time, exclaimed, *"Oh Hanchu da, you burnt the roti!"*

I reassured her saying, *"It's ok Diya, this one is slightly burnt but I got it."*

But Diya persisted, insisting, *"Oh, you don't know how to make roti, come I'll show you."*

Feeling confident in my cooking skills, I replied, *"I do know how to make roti, Diya. I got this covered. You go ahead and do your stuff."*

However, Diya persisted despite my refusal. *"No come, let me show you."* she insisted.

I replied, *"If you think you know how to make roti so well that you can teach me, then you make it. Two people don't need to be doing it and I'd rather do something else,"* and I walked out of the kitchen.

"You don't have to be mad just because I said I'll teach you," Diya responded.

"I'm not mad, if you think you can make it better than me then do so," I retorted.

Diya swiftly took over the cooking, making sure to make her dissatisfaction known by clanging utensils and angrily tossing them into the dishwasher. No one confronted her, as she was the youngest darling of the household who always seemed to get her way. It seemed she had difficulty getting along with me because I refused to comply with her demands if I believed they were incorrect.

Feeling disheartened, I opted not to eat dinner that night. Once my mom had finished her meal, we bid everyone goodnight and left. Diya and Biru were in their room, so I simply said goodnight through the closed door and departed without waiting for a response.

The next morning, Maya had an early appointment, and as usual, I arrived a little early and went up to the apartment. Following my routine, I greeted everyone with a cheerful *"good morning"* as I always did.

"Good morning Diya, good morning Uncle, good morning kids," I greeted as I walked to check on Maya. It struck me that Diya hadn't responded to my greeting, which was unusual. I went back to the room where she was and asked, *"Seriously Diya? Now you don't want to talk to me?"* She didn't say a word and walked right past me as if I didn't exist. I thought to myself, *"Well if this is what she wants, then so be it."*

From that day onwards, I didn't utter a single word to her. I avoided making eye contact and only responded if she asked me something in a very precise way. I simply didn't care anymore. I kept my distance and stayed out of her way. In the days that followed, she attempted to engage in conversations or act as if nothing had happened, but I remained silent. I refrained from teasing her about certain silly things as I usually did, and she took notice. It seemed she missed the attention from me, and perhaps resented the fact that everyone else seemed unfazed, at least at that moment. Days passed with this uncomfortable silence lingering between us. This incident occurred before we moved to Harlem for radiation treatment, and it was one of the reasons I didn't want to be under the same roof as them.

* * *

One morning in New York, during radiation, Maya wasn't feeling well, and every noise seemed to aggravate her condition. Amidst her discomfort, I heard boisterous laughter coming from the dining room—a voice unfamiliar to me. Concerned, I went to check and discovered that it was the condominium caretaker whom Diya had invited for breakfast out of kindness.

Initially, I felt inclined to ask him to lower his voice, considering Maya's sensitivity to noise. But I refrained from doing so, realizing that Diya's gesture was well-intentioned. Maya's mom continued to enter Maya's room, seemingly worsening the situation by expressing her annoyance at the noise and criticizing Diya for inviting strangers into the condominium, as if implying that I should take some action.

The individual's loud and obnoxious behavior became increasingly unbearable, especially considering Maya's discomfort. Each burst of laughter caused Maya to squint in discomfort, prompting me to intervene and ask him to lower his volume due to someone being ill in the other room. Although I intended it for Maya's well-being, the caretaker likely took offense and left after bidding Diya farewell.

Unfortunately, yet again, Diya perceived my actions in a negative light, failing to comprehend that my concern was solely for Maya's comfort. Later, she relayed to her father that I seemed to disapprove of everything she did. My intentions were rooted in compassion, but our communication seemed to falter.

* * *

Diya, since her childhood, exhibited a knack for avoiding responsibilities and chores, especially when it came to tasks around the house. However, this time while visiting Maya, it was different as she was trying hard. Unfamiliar with the kitchen atmosphere, she would call me several times via video calls asking how to chop turnips, or asking for help to identify spices, or asking recipe for certain dishes. In contrast to her sister Maya, who embraced simplicity, Diya often managed to escape the obligations of daily life. Whether it was evading household chores or finding a way out of responsibility, she had the talent of avoiding the less glamorous aspects of life.

Furthermore, she appeared to have a penchant for stretching the truth and emphasizing her perspective by assertively using her voice. Being the youngest in the family, this tendency was even more pronounced, as she realized that her youth afforded her a certain leniency. It wasn't uncommon for her to resort to a bit of fibbing or employ a raised voice to emphasize her point, ultimately enabling her to navigate situations in a manner that suited her preferences.

I wasn't sure whether she was upset that she wasn't getting the attention that she was used to or what it was. While she was used to getting things done around the family, I stood out differently. I would tell her to her face that the decision was wrong if it was. When I went to the kitchen to make dinner or any other meal, she would rush in. I would think she was doing it to give me a break. If I resisted, she would ask, *"Are you competing to show who's doing more?"* *"It's not a competition,"* I would add, telling her we all had one goal: to see Maya better. I didn't care if anyone knew what I was doing.

When friends told me that I was so noble for doing what I did, I replied, *"We never know what we can do until we must."* They would still argue otherwise, saying they would never be able to do as much or were confident that their significant other would never be able to do so given the same circumstances. But here on the other hand, when Diya was mad, she would create a commotion and tell her parents as to why no one saw how much she was doing for Maya. It wasn't teamwork for her, it was all her. There was no end to it.

In the midst of Maya's battle with the disease, I found myself in a situation that unintentionally stirred a sense of jealousy in Diya. My untiring support and dedication to Maya during this challenging time earned me the recognition and gratitude from Maya's parents. While there was no doubt about Diya being genuinely happy for Maya's well-being, the acknowledgement of my efforts highlighted a contrast with her own contributions. This possibly prompted her to reflect on her role in Maya's journey. Diya, aware of the importance of my role and support, may have grappled with mixed emotions, recognizing the depth of my involvement, and yearning for a similar acknowledgement of her own efforts. Such interplay of emotions created tension in our relationship, and the family took notice.

* * *

One evening, as I was preparing to visit Maya's place, she called me and informed me that Diya wanted to talk and urged me to listen to what she had to say. Despite Maya's insistence, I expressed that I wasn't emotionally prepared for such a conversation that day but reassured her that we would eventually talk. Maya persisted, but I remained firm in my decision.

Upon arriving at Maya's apartment, I coincidentally met Maya's mom in the elevator as she was heading out for a walk with Diya's daughter. She offered a reassuring wink and encouraged me to have a constructive conversation, emphasizing the importance of clearing up any misunderstandings without getting angry. With her words in mind, I proceeded to the apartment.

When I entered, I found Maya's dad, as usual, seated, and I greeted him. I could sense tension in the room. Surprisingly, Maya's dad wasn't in his usual position of authority, allowing me to comfortably take his seat without feeling the usual pressure. Later when I was checking my phone for messages, I was caught off guard by Diya.

"Hello Hanchuda," she greeted.

"Hello Diya," I responded.

"How are you? We need to talk," she said.

"I'm good Diya but please I am in no mood to talk," I replied.

"But I want to," she insisted.

"But I don't," I insisted back.

"You've been coming to this apartment, and we don't talk, Its odd. I need to know you will be there for me if I need you in future," she expressed.

"I think it's better that way. At least we don't get in each other's way, and we don't know what the future holds," I reasoned.

"So, you're telling me you won't be there for me?" she questioned.

"Perhaps but we don't know. Right now, I am here only for Maya not you," I asserted.

"No, but I feel odd that you are coming here every day," she continued.

"What are you trying to say? Are you telling me not to come?" I asked.

"Yes," she replied.

"Excuse me? Are you serious? How selfish can you be?" I retorted.

"Get out? Get out of here fucker!" she yelled.

And then it started. Here was someone I had known since childhood, someone I had always been fond of, kicking me out of her sister's apartment, knowing very well that I was there just to take care of Maya. While being utterly obnoxious, she persistently questioned whether *"I would be there for her when she needed me."* Not once she acknowledged that I was there for Maya. Now she was kicking me out because she wasn't getting me to do things her way. It was a very selfish move, but I should have known. Every move she made somehow had to benefit her in return.

I replied, *"Do you realize that I am still her husband? If I want, I could kick you out of here, so don't even get there."*

Words were exchanged, carefully chosen to inflict maximum hurt. I know I said harsh words, and she certainly didn't hold back either. We were family, and yet, it seemed like we were tearing each other apart.

Biru was in the shower during the entire commotion. When he heard the noise, he emerged with a towel wrapped around his waist.

Seeing him approach, I felt a sense of relief, assuming he would intervene and calm his wife down. As he drew closer, I noticed he was muttering something, which I assumed was an attempt to quiet her down. To my shock, he walked up to me with his fist clenched and threatened, *"I'm going to smack your face, you motherfucker."*

I was stunned by his threat. It only took a second to understand the gravity of the situation. Without hesitation, I responded, *"Hit me. Go ahead, hit me if you can. But mark my words, if you do, I'll break those hands and shove them in your mouth. Hit me you asshole!"*

I remained seated, defiant, with squared shoulders and a steady gaze, ready to face whatever came my way. Despite Biru's threatening posture, Maya and her dad tried to intervene to stop him from potentially striking me. He could have attacked as no one was holding him back. I continued to taunt him, unsure of what I would do if he actually followed through with his threat. Would I retaliate physically? No! I couldn't. Not in front of Maya's parents and certainly not when Maya herself was in such a fragile state. Besides, I had made a promise to Maya that I would never engage in physical confrontations after an incident in *Thamel* a few years prior. In that altercation, I had stood up against two individuals who were preventing me from buying food for street kids. They had assumed it was a pretense, but I had remained steadfast in my commitment to helping those in need without resorting to violence.

Of course, no fists were exchanged. Everything stopped when Maya cried, *"Stop! Stop!"* She broke down crying. The couple were going out for their date night, so Maya asked them to leave. Biru apologized to Maya and said, *"I'm so sorry di. We didn't mean to stress you out."*

"Get out," Maya yelled.

Biru and Diya went to their room. Later, Biru emerged, dressed in his signature attire of tight jeans and an overly snug shirt. He stated, *"I'm sorry but I cannot stand it if anyone disrespects my wife, not even my brother. I'm not scared of making enemies. I have a lot of them."*

I responded, *"What sort of a person are you? Jumping into a fight without understanding the situation? Reasoning holds no value to you? And having friends is something to be proud of, not enemies."*

"I don't care but next time this happens, I'll never do anything for you," he retorted.

"Fuck off! What have you ever done for me? I don't need you to do or have ever asked you to do anything for me so cut the crap."

This wasn't the first instance of Biru displaying such behavior; it appeared to be a recurring pattern in his interactions with others. From what I heard, he often reacted aggressively towards his employees, as well as his own family members, including his cousins, uncle, and other relatives. It seemed that he held his wife in high regard and was fiercely protective of her, refusing to tolerate any criticism or opposition directed towards her. This dynamic suggested a strong allegiance and devotion to his wife, leading him to vigorously defend her honor and reputation, regardless of the circumstances. Furthermore, Diya appeared to endorse his behavior, as she took no stance in discouraging him.

As they left, Maya's mother soon entered the room. She shared that she had encountered them downstairs, where Diya had tearfully recounted her version of the events to her.

Maya looked at me and expressed her frustrations, saying, "*Why couldn't you talk when she wanted to? All this could have been avoided.*" With a heavy heart, Maya retreated to her room, her tears flowing freely. I followed her, finding her in distress. I attempted to console her, explaining, "*Why is it that I am always at fault, in your eyes? It was your sister who stopped talking, not me. It was me who went to talk to her the next day, and she refused to engage. Moreover, I had expressed my reluctance, but you insisted. Besides, you've known me for so long now. Have you ever seen me remain composed when someone threatens my personal space or prepares to strike? Have you?*"

She gazed at me, absorbing the situation, and then enveloped me in a hug, offering her apologies for raising her voice. Maya acknowledged the truth in my words, recognizing that despite any past missteps I might have made, this time I was justified in speaking up. Even Maya's father expressed his displeasure with the way they had addressed me. In the Nepalese community, I held seniority over Biru and deserved respect, at least in Maya's father's eyes.

As I left that evening, I found myself devoid of emotion. Not angry, not happy – just numb and cold. Was this pain numbing me? I couldn't ignore the changes I observed within myself. That night, I confided in Maya, expressing my intention to reconcile with Diya solely for Maya's sake. However, I made it clear that I harbored no remorse for my actions.

The next day I wrote to Diya the exact words that I write below.

"Diya. Whatever happened yesterday should never have happened. Things were said that I know weren't meant. During this moment, we all need each other. After you left, I felt like shit to see Maya and uncle stressed. This is not something we both want. I'm not here to prove myself right or wrong. I've said time and again that I'm no saint. I wasn't ready to talk yet, and I was still digesting stuff. We both will never forget what happened yesterday, but we should put it aside as a bad hiccup and work together in getting Maya better…and believe it or not, for some weird reason I do care for you and your family very much! I apologized to Ryan too….so I think we let out frustrations more than needed…. I'm willing to move on and I hope you do too!"

(Ryan = Diya and Biru's son. He was in the other room during this ordeal and seemed shaken.)

In response she replied: "Dear Hanchu da… I agree with you, and I am going through the same thing. I appreciate your initiative and your efforts to resolve the situation. Biru respects you a lot and he felt bad as well. I know we are all doing it for my sister. I don't know why you have some misbelief about me, but I know I care for you, and I always wish you well. I am ready to move on… Let's treat each other respectfully and move forward in the best interest of my sister."

The next day when I arrived at Maya's place, I made my way to Diya's room and embraced her. Sensing the need for reconciliation, I suggested we take a walk together. Arm in arm, we returned to the living room where everyone was gathered. As Diya and I entered, her mother stood up and began applauding, a gesture of approval and relief mirrored by the smiles on everyone's faces.

As Diya and I stood together, Biru approached me, muttering something under his breath as he often did. I intervened, gently halting him, and indicating that we shouldn't revisit the issue. Instead, I offered him a hug, symbolizing a truce and a willingness to move forward together in harmony.

* * *

13

GIRLS NIGHT OUT

MAYA'S final dose of maintenance chemo was scheduled for Monday, with Diya's return flight set for the day before. Maya mentioned to me that the girls were planning a night out on Saturday to mark her *"last day of chemo."* I felt uneasy about celebrating prematurely, before achieving the intended goal, and voiced my concerns to Maya.

Understanding my perspective, Maya agreed and suggested checking with Diya to see if she would be comfortable with a smaller gathering of friends for dinner nearby instead. After consulting with her, Maya informed me that Diya had already made a reservation at a small bar in Jackson Heights, owned by her friend, and was excited about the plan.

Maya expressed her desire for her sister to be present for the celebration once her chemo was officially completed. Despite my reservations, I reluctantly consented, acknowledging Maya's decision. *"Well, it seems like you've already made up your mind, so might as well go along with it,"* I said with a hint of resignation. Maya smiled in response.

I felt a mix of emotions knowing that Maya would have a chance to enjoy herself, yet I couldn't shake off a sense of unease. Maya's immunity was still not being back to normalcy, the plan to go out meant being confined in a small, overcrowded bar—a scenario that raised concerns about her health and well-being. Some friends had already posted pictures on social media, prompting a few concerned calls from others about the seriousness of the situation for Maya's sake. I had no answer.

I understood Diya's desire to go out and celebrate, and Maya's inclination to comply with her sister's wishes, even if she knew it might not be the best decision for her health at the moment. It was a delicate balance between wanting Maya to experience joy and ensuring her safety and health remained a top priority.

* * *

As they made plans to take an Uber to the city, I felt it necessary to express my concerns to Maya. I gently reminded her that if she didn't feel well halfway through the celebration, it might not be ideal to bring the entire group back with her. I made up an excuse, mentioning that I had also made plans for dinner with a friend that day, and suggested we coordinate accordingly.

Maya responded with her characteristic skeptical look, followed by a blunt *"Bullshit!"* Even without her verbalizing it, I could read her skepticism loud and clear. She jokingly threatened to call my friend and confirm our supposed dinner plans. I simply shrugged and encouraged her to go ahead, knowing full well that she didn't have his number and likely wouldn't bother following through with the call.

On the day of the night out, I drove Maya and three other girls to New York City, while Diya opted to ride with others. When we arrived, the girls urged me to join them, but I politely declined, citing a fictitious dinner engagement. It was an excuse everyone saw through, but I stuck to it, nonetheless.

After dropping them off, I made my way to the parking lot in Jackson Heights. It was bustling with activity, and I had to circle the block twice before finding an entrance. The queue was causing a traffic jam, and when I finally entered, I encountered a Tesla blocking one side of the entrance.

I approached the attendant and remarked, *"Looks like you're busy. Do you need a hand?"* He gestured towards the Tesla and replied, *"I'd appreciate it if you could move that piece of shit out of the way."*

It appeared that someone had left the Tesla to be parked there, and the attendant was unfamiliar with how to operate it. I had never driven one myself, but I had been in a friend's Tesla before. Seeing the attendant's dilemma, I offered to give it a try.

The attendant handed me the key card, and I made a quick call to my friend who owned a Tesla. With his guidance over the phone, I managed to move the car to a suitable parking spot. It was a moment of relief for both the attendant and me, as we successfully resolved the situation without further hassle.

Recognizing me from my frequent visits to Jackson Heights, the attendant expressed his gratitude for helping with the car and inquired about how I managed to get it working. I shared the knowledge I had just acquired, and he seemed appreciative.

Planning to stay in the area for a while, I informed the attendant that I would remain in my car. He mentioned that they closed at midnight but assured me I could stay as long as needed. I had seven hours to kill, so I passed the time by making calls and catching up on some reading.

As midnight approached, Maya and the girls were still not finished. I left the parking lot and found a street parking spot about five minutes away from the bar. I stayed there for an additional two hours. Eventually, around 2 am, Maya texted me to see if I was still nearby, to which I replied that I was just finishing up. She informed me that they were done, and I headed over to meet them.

Another hour passed by in front of the bar, with some of the girls eager to try the Nepalese *"titaura shots."* Half of them ended up a bit tipsy, but they seemed to thoroughly enjoy themselves. After bidding their farewells, the girls finally piled into the car. Maya mentioned they would sing on the way back and began searching through her playlist.

As soon as I started driving, Maya dozed off, only to awaken once we arrived at her apartment. The girls kept me company, requesting to play songs that I had never heard of. When they played them, I found the music unpleasant—it was clear we had different tastes. While they were into mainstream pop, I leaned towards genres like progressive trance, techno, and Psytrance.

I found solace in the pulsating rhythms of Psytrance, where the hypnotic beats seamlessly mirrored the chaotic whirlwind of thoughts swirling in my mind. The intricate layers of electronic melodies and driving basslines provided a fitting soundtrack to the tumultuous emotions I was experiencing, allowing me to immerse myself fully in the music without the need to focus on lyrics. With each throbbing bass and intricate synth pattern, I felt a sense of release, as if the music was a conduit for channeling and expressing the inner turmoil I couldn't articulate with words.

*　*　*

Diya and Biru left for Nepal on Sunday. Maya was feeling a bit under the weather. I spent the entire day with her and left late at night after receiving assurance from her that she would be okay. The next morning, I arrived at her apartment around 6 am to check on her. Although she seemed better, she still appeared somewhat weak. After preparing breakfast for her, I returned home, urging her to call me if she needed anything.

Shortly after I arrived home, Maya called, expressing that she wasn't feeling well and suggesting we visit the hospital for a checkup. She insisted on taking an Uber, but I hurried back to her place. When I took her to the hospital, it became apparent that she needed to be hospitalized once again. Her blood count had dropped, and she was neutropenic once more.

When the doctor inquired as to what she had been up to, I hurriedly answered his questions. *"She had a girl's night out!"*

Maya looked at me and then glanced at the doctor and smiled guiltily. She knew I was right, once again, to stop her from going and she knew she hadn't listened. She had put her health on the line and had listened to her sister to go out dancing in a small, crowded bar celebrating her last day of chemo when she still had one session to go.

The doctor asked, *"Girl's night out? Where?"*

I replied, *"New York."*

"New York?" he exclaimed as he had specifically asked her to rest.

Maya and I later would talk to each other and conclude that if the doctor was a little more comfortable with us, he would have told her, *"Great job, you moron! You should have partied more!"*

* * *

14

THE CANCER RETURNS

TWO months had passed since Maya's last chemo session. During this time, she traveled to Houston to explore her new office and search for a house. While she was gone for ten days, I remained behind to pack up all her belongings. Everything was arranged to be shipped to my house during her time in Nepal and then sent to Houston.

The day after her return from Houston, Maya had a routine doctor's appointment scheduled in New York City. Since we also needed to pick up a few documents from the Nepalese embassy, we decided to plan it on the same day to save a trip. After dropping her off, I headed to the nearby embassy. While waiting there, Maya called and mentioned she wanted to share something but asked me not to worry. The tone of her voice didn't offer much reassurance. She explained that she had discovered a lump in her neck while in

Houston but chose not to tell me immediately to avoid causing concern. The doctors were planning to conduct a biopsy, and it would take some time to determine the situation. My heart sank, and a wave of fear and uncertainty washed over me.

Two days later, we received the report, and to our dismay, the cancer had returned. In just two short months. It felt like a cruel twist of fate, especially as Maya had been starting to find happiness again. Her hair was regrowing, and she had embraced her new look with grace. She was smiling more often, radiating warmth to everyone around her but that one call from the doctor shattered everything we had hoped for. The expression on her face as she shared the news with me is etched in my memory, haunting me as if it happened mere moments ago.

Our hearts broke as we grappled with the devastating reality. I felt utterly helpless watching her hopes crumble before my eyes. While I was in pain, Maya masked her own anguish with an unwavering façade of positivity. Yet, I could see through it. We held each other tightly, tears streaming down our faces. It was a moment of raw emotion, and I found myself breaking down in a way I hadn't in a long time. My façade of strength crumbled with just a single tear from her eye.

Witnessing her distress stirred a profound sense of empathy and sorrow within me. I longed to ease her pain, to shield her from the suffering she was enduring. If only I could bear this burden for her, if only I could take away her pain.

This was the morning of October 21st, 2022. The previous night, the results were out. I had stayed up anxiously, refreshing the portal repeatedly in hopes of finding some glimmer of positive news in the medical report. Despite my efforts to decipher the complex terminology, I couldn't find any solace. It was a moment of profound helplessness, a stark reminder of life's uncertainties. At 3 am, I heard Maya stir from her sleep to use the restroom. As she emerged, I noticed the slight discomfort etched on her face, a telltale sign of the pain she was enduring. She appeared fragile and vulnerable, and my heart ached for her.

Offering to massage her shoulders, I hoped to provide some small measure of comfort. For the next hour, as I gently kneaded her tense muscles, a flood of emotions overwhelmed me. Tears welled in my eyes; each drop a silent testament to the anguish I felt inside. Maya remained unaware, perhaps mistaking the moisture on her skin for the soothing oil I was using. I couldn't bring myself to share the burden of what I had discovered. Instead, I silently prayed that my fears were unfounded, clinging to the hope that the doctors would be able to provide clarity and guidance.

* * *

Every Morning, I always greeted her with a melodically funny, energetic "*Good morning*." Usually, she returned the greeting in the same tone. That day she did not. I got the feeling that she had talked to the doctor already. She was in the restroom. When she came out, she hurriedly walked towards me and said, *"So it's back,"* and she came and hugged me.

"I know, Maiya!" I replied meekly.

The look on her face, the smile just drooped, and the sadness was overwhelmingly noticeable. I am still not able to erase that look of sadness in her from my head. That was the moment, I felt weak. How painful it may have been for her to hear the news, just when happiness seemed around the corner. Her plans of hiking, taking up dance classes, quality time with her family, her sister's secret vacation trips just got dragged beneath her feet as a distant memory fading away.

We hugged and cried with not a word spoken. Our shoulders shaking in each other's arms. I could not choose any soothing words as there were none. We knew what this meant. But I held on to the glimmer of hope which I was not ready to give away. I don't believe in miracles, but I desperately needed to see one this time.

The second diagnosis hit both of us hard. I've never found myself feeling so helpless and never knew I had so many tears that I could let out. During the first treatment, we had a sense of certainty about the outcome. Chemotherapy, surgery, and radiation—followed by the expectation that the cancer would be eradicated. So was the expectation and so we had hoped the result to be. We feared the recurrence, but the doctors had said that it would give us two years to find out. Optimism presides over my thinking and hence, I thought that was how it would be. Plans had been made. After her relaxing time in Nepal with family and much-needed break, she would move to Houston to a more promising office hub that would provide her more opportunities to grow.

* * *

Life often unfolds in unexpected and sometimes cruel ways. The day we received the devastating news was also the day of my brother's wedding. With a heavy heart, I pondered whether we would be able to attend the evening ceremony in Brooklyn. I refrained from broaching the topic with Maya, knowing she needed time to process the shocking revelation.

Even with the immense emotional turmoil she was experiencing, I had no doubt that Maya would still want to attend the wedding. Her selfless nature and boundless love for her family and friends compelled her to prioritize their happiness above her own struggles. It was a testament to her strength and resilience, even in the face of adversity.

Later, I overheard her conversation with Jenny where she explained the diagnosis. There was a pinch of uncertainty and pain evident in her voice, but she casually told Jenny, *"It is what it is. We will dance it out tonight!"*

If she had expressed her wish not to go, I would have chosen to stay by her side. It was my brother's wedding, but attending without Maya would have felt like an empty moment. I believe my brother would have understood, and no one would have insisted that I leave her alone to attend. It is these kinds of cherished relationships, and my family's genuine love towards Maya that I appreciate every day.

Such irony! Someone was starting a new life as husband and wife while here things seemed to be falling apart. We could not see where we were going to end up. Positivity! Yes, I have it in abundance but somehow, somewhere it had struck me, and the horror of *"What if?"*

with a negative connotation seemed to be overwhelmingly taking over me, whilst at the same time drowning me in sorrow.

* * *

Maya looked beautiful in her dress she had so meticulously picked out. After nearly a year of chemo, she was finally beginning to gain her normal weight. Her cheeks were becoming plumper, and muscles were more visible. I often teased her that her breasts and butt were also getting sexier and that she could finally use a bra. She would smile and ask for reassurance as if she didn't know. *"Really?"* she would ask, *"hmmm"* she would say. She's always been a girl of few words when talked dirty upon.

Perhaps such qualities helped people around her cope with the pain during her treatment. She never failed to put up a smile for others or cook for them even though she was nauseous. I repeatedly told her that I should put her in a lease and keep her stationary. The doctors and nurses also called her the *"happiest patient."* Her blood count would be close to zero, but she never failed to answer the doctors with a smile when called upon. This girl needed to be happy. This girl wanted to live large.

At the wedding, she swallowed her pain, and so did I. Many did not notice, but how long could you keep that fake façade from the people who knew you close enough? Someone had noticed and asked. Maya shared it with that someone, and that someone broke down. Someone else noticed, and that someone broke down. Hence the vine had spread. By the end of the night, many were in tears. The wedding was not affected. After all, no one wanted to steal the moment from the bride and the groom who were so ecstatic and had planned the details of the event for the past year.

Maya herself danced the night out. Tears dropped from the corner of her eyes while she played out the dance moves that many think agile except herself. To top it off, the DJ had perfectly played the songs that we were accustomed to. Songs from the nineties that we could relate to, and so, Maya danced, trying to forget her woes and pain, at least for that moment. This is the Maya everyone knows. So why wouldn't anyone be saddened to see the pain she underwent? I watched from the corner of my eyes. Would I have been able to hide my feelings if I was in her shoes? How would have others coped?

* * *

The weekend following the wedding, Maya's friend Chaya and her family, along with Amy, provided some solace through their comforting presence. Maya bravely concealed her inner turmoil during their visit, but once they departed, the floodgates of emotion opened. Together, we shared tears and embraced, finding solace in each other's company.

Maya's demeanor shifted noticeably afterward. She withdrew into herself, often sleeping late into the day and remaining glued to the TV when awake. Instead of her usual lighthearted movie preferences, she gravitated towards darker, more intense films. Laughter seemed foreign to her, and even my attempts to cheer her up with silly antics were met with subdued responses.

Sometimes, I couldn't discern whether Maya was watching the TV or if it was watching her, as her gaze remained fixed, lost in thoughts too heavy to articulate. In those moments, I sat silently by her side, offering a comforting presence and a listening ear whenever she needed it. The depth of her sorrow was obvious, occasionally breaking through in unexpected bursts of laughter or tears.

On Monday, the atmosphere in the apartment was heavy with an uncomfortable silence that seemed to drown out even the background music and TV, despite their volume. The only living being unaffected by this somber mood was our Shih Tzu, Sanu, whose acute senses seemed attuned to our emotions. Sanu became Maya's steadfast companion during this trying time, providing her with a source of solace and comfort.

Maya's bond with Sanu was profound. Despite the heaviness in her heart, Maya poured all her love and affection into caring for Sanu. She slept with her, took her for walks, bathed her, and pampered her with treats and toys. Maya even bought a stroller for Sanu, anticipating moments when she might tire during their outings.

Remarkably, Sanu seemed to possess an intuitive understanding of our emotional state. She would take turns comforting Maya and me, curling up beside us and showering us with affectionate licks as if to convey her silent support and empathy. In the midst of our sorrow, Sanu's presence was a beacon of warmth and companionship, offering a glimmer of light in our darkest moments.

I constantly checked the portal to see if the documents had been uploaded for her scans. It wasn't. I may have checked the portal every minute. And finally, there it was after two days. Maya seemed to have checked it quite as often because when I saw it and was gushing out of the room to give her the news, she had called out to me too. She had got an email from the nurse saying the cancer had not spread and was limited in her neck. Well, this was very good news.

* * *

It's a strange twist of fate, isn't it? Just a few days ago, we were engulfed in tears upon learning of Maya's cancer diagnosis, and now we found ourselves embracing and shedding tears of relief because the cancer was localized to her neck. Yet, despite this glimmer of hope, I couldn't help but wish for the results we had received before—results that showed no cancer at all.

Why did it have to come back so quickly? Why now? These questions echoed endlessly in my mind, like a refrain without resolution. I find myself asking them over and over again, knowing deep down that answers may never come. But still, I can't help but wonder and hope for some semblance of understanding amidst this whirlwind of uncertainty.

Sam, Maya's lifelong friend and a physicist in another state, remained a constant source of support and guidance for me throughout this ordeal. When I shared the news of Maya's recurrence with her, Sam offered a stark reminder of the grim reality we were facing. She urged me to prepare myself for the worst, to accept the harsh truth of Maya's condition.

Her words hit me like a sledgehammer, shattering the fragile veil of hope I had been clinging to. For the first time, someone intimately familiar with the situation was hinting that Maya may be in the advanced stages of cancer. I couldn't bring myself to accept such a devastating prognosis. I refused to believe it.

I remember the moment vividly—I was parked outside Maya's apartment, sitting in my car, overwhelmed by a torrent of emotions. As I hung up the phone with Sam, I succumbed to the weight of my despair, tears streaming down my face as I rested against the tires of my car. It was a moment of great anguish, a battle between my desperate hope and the crushing reality unfolding before me. Deep down, I knew Sam's words carried weight; she was a doctor who had witnessed countless cases like Maya's. But still, I clung to hope, praying fervently that she was wrong, that Maya's fate would defy the odds.

* * *

Maya's experience with chemotherapy during her first treatment was incredibly taxing. The dosage she received was described by nurses as nearly five times more potent than typical breast cancer chemo. Given Maya's petite stature—weighing just 115 pounds—this intensive treatment regimen posed significant challenges, her body struggled to tolerate such high concentrations of chemo.

Over the course of sixteen sessions, administered every three weeks, Maya endured grueling treatments that took a toll on her physical and emotional well-being. In addition to chemo, she also underwent numerous maintenance chemo, surgery and radiation therapy, further taxing her already weakened body. The cumulative effects of these treatments pushed Maya to her limits, resulting in multiple visits to the emergency room as her body struggled to cope with the onslaught of medical interventions.

Recognizing the strain on Maya's body, her oncologist made the difficult decision to temporarily halt her chemo treatments to allow her blood counts to stabilize and her body to recover. This pause in treatment was crucial for Maya's health and allowed her a much-needed respite from the harsh effects of the treatment.

During a call with her doctor to discuss the plan moving forward, I asked, *"If a house on fire had to be put out and it could only be done so with ten days of nonstop flow of water, but if the firefighters took a pause for a day or two and then started to put out the fire again, the fire obviously would have gotten stronger, so the remaining days would not have been enough, right? Just like that, could it be that taking a break from chemo may have been the reason for this? You get my point?"*

But the doctor's answer to my question silenced me. She said, *"But don't you think it could be the chemo that has kept her alive for all this while?"* Her point hit home, but it wasn't easy for me to accept it. We had never discussed death, except for the insensitive remark from the jerk, Biru, during Maya's surgery. Now, the topic was coming up from those around us. My reluctance to hear or discuss it was clouding my judgement.

While discussing the plans moving forward, Maya asked the doctor, *"My sister wanted to know if I can get my chemo done in Nepal?"* I was horrified. Why would anyone in their right mind take someone from America to Nepal for treatment?

"You're seriously not contemplating this, are you?" I interrupted while she was still talking to the doctor.

"Diya wants me to, so I asked!" she replied.

I found myself grappling with numerous questions for the doctor. Why did hospitals not schedule radiation treatment during Thanksgiving and Christmas holidays? Did harmful bacteria and cancer cells take a break during those times, deciding not to infect? Did they observe ceasefires like in wars? It was perplexing. Illnesses and deaths don't pause for holidays; people still get sick and pass away. Couldn't there be alternate shifts working on those days? While everyone deserves a break, these decisions affect lives. It felt unfair when faced with such dire circumstances. Countless questions lingered unanswered, leaving me feeling helpless. All I knew was that my loved one was suffering, and nothing seemed right.

* * *

15

TRIP TO NEPAL

MAYA would have been done with the treatment August 15th, 2022. Everything seemed to be going as per plan. She was moving to Houston to a bigger office with more promising chances of personal growth. She worked for a European energy company. Maya loved her work. She loved everything she put her heart into. Of all those years of employment, I don't recall a moment she complained about her job.

I also don't remember Maya dragging her feet to work. She did call out occasionally and when she did make that call to her manager, she would say, *"Hi Mary Ann! Can I take the day off as I have a bad hangover?"* She also would share what drink she had had with her manager. When she was done with the call, I asked, *"Did you really have to tell her that you had a hangover and needed the day off?"* She would look at me and say, *"Why? What was I supposed to say? That's the truth, isn't it?"*

Even in playful attempts to pull pranks on friends, she'd refrain from being my accomplice, unable to partake in deception. I recall a time during our visit to my brother in Manhattan for the weekends when she borrowed my cousin's top. When she received a compliment while riding the subway, she promptly disclosed, *"It's not mine; it's hers,"* pointing to my cousin. I'd teasingly ask her, *"Did you truly believe the stranger cared about its ownership?"*

In response to Maya's candidness about her hangovers and calling out from work, I might appreciate her honesty while also gently suggesting that some details are best kept private, especially in a professional setting. I could acknowledge her commitment to truthfulness and integrity while emphasizing the importance of professionalism and discretion in certain situations.

Regarding the incident with the borrowed top and disclosure on the subway, I would playfully remind Maya that while her honesty is admirable, sometimes it's okay to accept compliments graciously without providing unnecessary details. I might tease her about her commitment to truthfulness, acknowledging it as a unique and endearing trait while also emphasizing the value of social norms and tact in certain situations. Ultimately, my response would aim to affirm Maya's integrity while gently encouraging her to navigate social interactions with a blend of honesty and discretion.

* * *

Before moving to Houston, she wanted to take some time off from work. Throughout her cancer treatment, even though she went through profound challenging experiences, marked by both physical and emotional trials, she never took off from work except for days she had chemo or appointments during odd hours. She finally had planned to take three months off; some friends coaxed her to ask for five months, and work was kind enough to grant it to her. She was happy and I was too. She deserved it. She'd never had such a long break.

Every year, when we went to visit family back in Nepal, the trip lasted for about a month. This would take away all her holidays, and then we would have to wait again for the following year. This time she had plenty of time. She planned to take classical dance lessons as she loved dancing. She danced well. Everyone thought so, except herself. She planned to go meditate, travel, and spend quality time with family. She planned to bask in the lazy Kathmandu sun and nap, savoring the warmth of the day. She wanted to relive all the nostalgic memories of being home as a child that she had so dearly missed.

Taking a five-month hiatus from work was a generous break. Her sister had organized surprise trips for Maya, intended to be kept under wraps. However, in our family, secrets tend to evaporate even in the coldest of environments, and nobody minds. Her dad shared the plans with me, and I, in turn, disclosed them to Maya. Their destination was the serene rural villages of Nepal, where the Himalayas adorned the backyard, seemingly close enough to reach out and touch them.

Maya had always been captivated by the allure of nature, especially when the mountains stood so near, as if awaiting her embrace. She loved city life, but at heart, she was a village girl, fond of gardening and reveling in the simple pleasures of playing with dirt. This vacation promised to let her relive those cherished moments, but as fate would have it, life had other plans in store for her.

The next few days were challenging. A ray of hope entered when her coworker Sharon, who was also undergoing treatment for sarcoma, advised Maya to seize the opportunity for a brief visit. Maya's doctor concurred with her decision. Consequently, she shortened the trip to approximately fourteen days, ensuring she could still go. While I was glad she had the chance, my concern lingered, wishing for the treatment to commence promptly to prevent the spread of cancer cells. Nevertheless, I trusted the doctor's judgement. During her absence, they needed to create a mask for her radiation treatment, a process that would take about a week. Maya also shared with me her desire to attend her nephew's ceremony, an event she had postponed for two years. She had said, *"That would make me very happy."*

In the pursuit of her recovery, happiness became not just a desire, but a necessity. As she navigated the challenges of illness, she came to understand the profound impact of mindset on one's healing journey. The power of positivity emerged as a guiding force, offering her the strength to fight, to persevere, and to embrace life with renewed vigor.

It became clear that a positive mindset was more than just a state of mind—it was a catalyst for resilience and hope. In the face of adversity, it provided a reason to keep pushing forward, to believe in the possibility of healing, and to find joy in the smallest moments.

Yet, she also recognized the inherent difficulty in maintaining such a mindset. While it was easy to advise others to stay positive, she understood firsthand the challenges of doing so in the midst of her own struggles. Despite the hurdles and setbacks, she remained steadfast in her determination to cultivate happiness, knowing that it was not just a choice, but a lifeline in her journey towards recovery.

So, changes to the air tickets were made. She was travelling with my mom. They got along well and had planned to spend two nights in Istanbul. Maya wanted to take mom for sightseeing and had other plans rolled up her sleeves. I could tell Maya would take pride in showing someone around in a foreign country, a satisfying feeling when you know a little more than the other person. She had already been to Turkey and had loved it. Maya loved visiting new places. She was excited, but now the plan had to be cut short.

* * *

While growing up, tourists always praised Nepal, marveling at its beauty. At that time, I couldn't comprehend what they found so enchanting; I only truly understood when I left Nepal for the United States and returned later. The landscape in Nepal revealed its majestic allure. While the United States also boasted its unique beauty, Nepal possessed an undeniable charm. It felt like time stood still, and the love for my birth country amplified every aspect of its appeal.

I recall a childhood game where we had to choose between health, wealth, and happiness. Wealth took precedence, followed by happiness, and health was often overlooked. It reflected the innocence of a childhood lived with the illusion of invincibility—strong, fearless, and unstoppable. Diseases were distant concepts, and even the mention of cancer now sends shivers down my spine, triggering vivid memories of Maya's pain and her courageous battle.

Our upbringing was in the Kathmandu Valley, nestled in its own densely populated and polluted charm. The bustling streets, murky rivers, countless motor vehicles, street dogs, and glimpses of cows leisurely sunbathing in the middle of roads—all these familiar sights never fail to bring a smile to my face. The city operated at its own pace, devoid of any urgency. The tardiness of the people used to bother me; a meeting scheduled for 9 am would never start on time, and the excuse? *"Nepal time!"* Maya and I often discussed this, and she eagerly anticipated experiencing it all over again.

* * *

Maya and my mom departed for Nepal on November 6th, 2022, with mom planning to stay about a month longer than Maya. After they purchased their tickets, I decided to join Maya on her return journey. I couldn't bear the thought of her traveling alone; she appeared fragile and stressed. I wanted to be there for her, providing support and companionship. In case anything happened, I wanted her to know she wasn't alone—I would be by her side. While the prospect of going to Nepal usually excited me, this time, my enthusiasm was nonexistent. Nonetheless, I welcomed the idea of a brief getaway and the chance to reunite with friends whom I considered my besties, offering a space where I could be my authentic self without fear of judgment.

My tickets were booked for November 9th, coincidentally my birthday, but the significance of the day didn't concern me. The previous year, I spent my birthday in Maya's hospital room, and this year, I would be soaring high in the air.

Maya had specific plans for her time in Nepal. She yearned to visit *Ghandruk*, a picturesque village cradled by snow-clad mountains and nestled gracefully amid the hills. Maya had been captivated by this place before; during her challenging treatments, she mentally transported herself to *Ghandruk*, finding solace and momentarily escaping her struggles. It was her way of healing and moving forward, and she felt compelled to return to this soothing haven as an expression of gratitude and hope.

Despite the brevity of her stay, just fourteen days, Maya was determined to make the most of it. A month would be insufficient, especially with the demands of ceremonies and endless family visits. When Maya expressed her desire to visit *Ghandruk* to her sister, the response was dismissive: *"It's such a tight schedule; we won't make it!"* Maya's unwavering reply was, *"I don't care; I have to go!"*

She did visit *Ghandruk*, playfully mentioning, *"I played my cancer card. If not now, then when?"*

I finally met Maya five days after my arrival. I wanted to give her space. I had a separate apartment to live in, courtesy of Arya and her family. But every time I went to Nepal, even though we always had this set up, I visited Maya's house and spent long hours with her family. This time it was different. We were visiting not for a vacation. We had this feeling deep within us, if not now, when? Will we ever get to do this? These words were not spoken but could be easily read in our eyes.

* * *

The lump in her neck had grown larger. As I touched it, fear gripped me, sending a sudden shiver that reverberated throughout my body. Whenever I encountered Maya, she was always donned in a hoodie. Being someone who tends to feel cold easily, she would wear sweaters even when the thermometer displayed 80 degrees Fahrenheit. This time, the hoodie served a different purpose—to conceal. I was aware of it but hesitated to voice my concern. I anxiously awaited the day of our return, eager to commence the radiation scheduled for November 21st.

The thought consumed me, gnawing at my peace of mind. I couldn't take the situation lightly. Had she not mentioned that this trip would bring her happiness, I wouldn't have supported her decision to travel. Travel could wait; her healing and recovery were paramount. She could explore the world once she was cured. Treatment needed to be our immediate focus. Undoubtedly, she harbored fears as well, but she adeptly concealed them. I could see through her and decipher her emotions like reading a book, recognizing when she was sad, excited, happy, or irritated, even when she refrained from expressing it on her face. Her subtle, inconspicuous gestures betrayed her, and she would be caught. She couldn't lie, so when

I noticed something and inquired, she would candidly reveal the truth.

Our return coincided with the World Cup Football event taking place in Doha. All flights were fully booked. We had initially traveled to Nepal on a one-way ticket, uncertain of our return date as the doctors hadn't finalized the radiation start date when we booked the tickets. They had informed us that radiation would commence either the week before Thanksgiving or the following week. Ironically, last year, she had completed her radiation a day before Thanksgiving, finally getting to enjoy that weekend after a prolonged period of treatment.

* * *

As my luck would have it, Diya had bought Maya's return ticket without Maya's knowledge, and it was business class. She didn't think of consulting me before doing so. She knew why I was there. Obviously, I wasn't expecting her to buy me a ticket, but at least she should have consulted so I would have had the time to make my own bookings and in the same flight. That was the whole purpose of being there.

The economy tickets at that time were twice the regular price, and the business class was four times the economy. I would have spent the money, but there were no seats available - neither in business nor economy on Qatar Airways. Finally, my agent got me a ticket via Cathay Pacific while Maya took Qatar. Mine was a longer flight but it was comfortable. She landed three hours before me in JFK and was received by my brother, and I would ask Sanjay to come pick me up. It was unfortunate that us traveling separately totally defeated the purpose of my visit.

We were back. Back to the truth, facing reality in the cold winter of Connecticut. The warm winter of Nepal at least helped us to escape the truth for some time. The congregation of Maya's family members and her mom's constant pampering, forcing her to eat despite her reluctance, had her gain a few pounds too. She looked healthy.

On my drive back to the apartment from the airport, the queer feeling of uncertainty never left my head. I could hear Sanjay conversing but may have annoyed him with my constant *"huh?"* as I couldn't focus or hear him talk. I was glad I was back, but I was also scared to see Maya put through pain once again. People said cancer is easy, it's the treatment that kills you. Now I knew what they meant. Maya knew that better than me. She was the one facing it and dealing with it. I was just a listening ear, and it hurt me equally when she said she was not able to enjoy the quality of life with the constant 'chemo fog' that hovered around her along with other side effects, leaving her nauseated, pukish, tired and constipated to add a few.

I had captured every moment of Maya's journey in pictures, hoping to go through it together and reminisce after she beat the disease. Now I could not even look at them. Looking at pictures hurt me, and now I had to see it as a reality all over again. I had to face the truth, and I had to be strong. I told this to myself every night and every day.

* * *

SELF BLAMES

IN times of adversity, it's common for individuals to perceive everything they do as wrong and to shoulder the blame. This universal human experience wasn't foreign to Maya, who found herself steering through emotional turmoil. Given her vulnerable state of sensitivity, I made a conscious effort to ensure that words and actions were carefully chosen to avoid any unintended harm. Mundane aspects of life that were once overlooked now held significant meaning, becoming oddly awkward.

While watching TV, if a mention of someone succumbing to cancer arose, I would discreetly observe Maya's reaction. Though I detected no visible response, I had no doubt that she reflected on her own situation with a tinge of sadness. Unfortunately, some people were less cautious and freely shared stories of individuals facing cancer or other illnesses, even death. I earnestly implore anyone with a loved one undergoing a similar experience to refrain from being the bearer of such distressing information. It's crucial to maintain a supportive and uplifting environment for those facing health challenges, shielding them from unnecessary emotional distress.

On one occasion, Maya set out with her cousin to return a few items at HomeGoods. However, she returned within minutes, visibly distressed, and called out to me, expressing her sadness of having crashed her car. Concerned, I inquired about her well-being, to which she replied affirmatively but tearfully lamented, *"Now I can't even drive anymore."* I embraced her, urging her to reconsider her perspective, and lightened the mood by playfully noting that even in her prime, she hadn't been immune to car mishaps. A smile graced her face.

While Maya may not be deemed a reckless driver, she had, unfortunately, acquired a slight reputation for being involved in accidents beyond her control—running a red light, navigating one-way streets, making inadvertent wrong turns, all situations beyond her anticipation and control!

The recent incident surely had stress written all over it. I had consistently advised Maya against driving if she didn't feel one hundred percent. Recognizing that driving could be stressful, especially for some individuals, I believed Maya fell into this category. In an effort to spare her from this stress, I willingly accompanied her everywhere. Despite my aversion to activities like shopping and mall visits, I found myself agreeing to join her, albeit with an earnest plea for her to minimize my trouble.

I considered window shopping a futile exercise, but this time, although I tagged along, I sought refuge in the car whenever possible. I occupied myself with music, made overdue calls to friends, or delved into a good book. My interest in social media, particularly Facebook, had waned, as it often portrayed others' lives in a rosier light than reality. The platform seemed to amplify the paradoxical human tendency to showcase one's achievements while secretly relishing the envy of others. Someone's joy could inadvertently become another's source of envy or misery, while another person's hardships might offer a contrasting perspective, proving that life wasn't as grim as it seemed.

After Maya's family left, I assumed responsibility for the entire household chores, a task she had somewhat humorously labeled as her "obsessive compulsive disorder (OCD)." While I disagreed with the label, acknowledging that Maya was only selectively OCD, I understood her preference for a clean home. Even with fluctuating blood levels during treatment, doctors permitted her to engage in minor chores, cautioning against exertion. There were good days and bad. During challenging moments, she would recline and communicate sparingly. On better days, restlessness took over, and she refused to stay idle. My persistent reminders to avoid overexertion often fell on deaf ears, as she pushed herself until fatigue. I constantly urged her not to deplete her energy to the point of feeling utterly useless. She acknowledged the wisdom of my advice but, true to her nature, resisted staying still and procrastinating.

One such day, when she was still under the spell of her treatment, I was preparing dinner. She came to me in the kitchen sobbing and muttering words that I had to have her repeat as the freshly frying potatoes and pressure cooker's whistles wasn't helping much to understand her softly spoken words.

She'd say, *"Hanchu, I am so sorry that you are having to do everything, and I can't even help you."*

I reminded her firmly while taking her in my arms and resting my chin on her head, *"Do you really think I mind doing stuff for you?"* She nodded, *"No."* *"So,"* I said, *"stop feeling bad because I am doing stuff around here. I would have done this regardless of what state you were in. Would I not? Have I not?"*

She agreed and I added, *"So please stop stressing yourself out. I am so glad to be doing this for you and grateful you are letting me do so. I'm not anyone else that you have to apologize and be formal with."*

"I know. Thank you, but I still feel bad that I cannot do things for you," Maya murmured, her voice heavy with emotion.

She grew increasingly vulnerable and sensitive with each passing day. I took over any heavy lifting or strenuous tasks, not because I doubted her capability, but to spare her unnecessary trouble. On good days, she couldn't sit still, always finding something to occupy her time. The nature of the day significantly influenced her mood, with gloomy, rainy, and snowy days draining her energy, while pleasant, sunny days worked miracles in uplifting her spirits. Humming old Bollywood songs and engaging in self-made musical improvisations were her outlets. She even conversed with the dogs and insects in the garden, displaying an endearing eccentricity.

* * *

During one episode of removing plant-eating insects and drowning them in soapy water, she would humorously beg for forgiveness. My mom and I shared amused glances at each other during these escapades, appreciating Maya's oblivious charm.

One memorable incident occurred when there was a ceremony held in our house. After the rituals, we were to make a wish. I made mine and she made hers. We didn't talk about it much. We had a huge yard and was plagued with groundhogs, and they would eat everything Maya planted. Surprisingly, we saw a sudden disappearance of these creatures over the next two years. Maya meekly admitted that she had wished for all the groundhogs to go away and surprisingly they did.

"Out of all the things that you could have asked for, you wished for that?" I asked grumpily. *"They're gone, aren't they? Aren't you happy?"* she would ask, smiling. Despite my grumbling about the triviality of her wish, Maya's playful satisfaction with the outcome was undeniable.

* * *

On another occasion, she expressed that people probably would avoid hanging out with her due to her perceived depressing demeanor. When her family were around, she felt sorry as she thought they were confined indoors because of her. I had to remind her constantly that there was no other place they would rather be than with her during such difficult times. I would also remind her that if she indeed appeared depressing, friends were not obligated to come see her. They were doing so because they cared. We didn't owe anyone any favors and neither did they. But she would throw all my reminders out the window and hide her pain and make efforts to take her parents out for sightseeing or to a winery. She did not mind visitors, but certain days would be tough to exchange conversations. With close friends, when they visited, she would lie down if she wanted to and just listen to their conversations, occasionally contributing with her smiles and few unintelligible murmurs.

I used to be hesitant when Diya visited with Biru and her kids. Diya's dedication to Maya's well-being was evident, but Maya often felt guilty of taking her sister away from her husband when he was around. Maya's concerns were valid, as Biru did have questionable priorities. Once I overheard their conversation briefly. Biru was suggesting a date night to Diya, during the time Maya wasn't too well. Diya said it wasn't possible as she needed to tend to her sister. Biru's response was, *"What about me? Don't I need your time?"* He's right but it was not the right time to be seeking his spouse's attention or intimacy. All of us ran around selflessly for Maya and here he was asking for a date night!

While he loved his wife, I believe, if Diya was not around, he would not be as supportive towards Diya's family. I had relayed this to Maya. She would shrug her shoulders and tell me that she found contentment as long as he loved her sister.

During a visit to Nepal, I witnessed an incident that left a lasting impression. While on our way to breakfast, Biru noticed that one of his dealerships had its shutters only partially open. In response, he called and receiving no answer, proceeded to call his general manager to get the manager fired. This extreme reaction shocked me, highlighting his lack of empathy and understanding. Another instance was when he boasted about his ability to run a marathon without any training, undermining my efforts in marathon training. His competitive nature extended to everything I did, believing he could outdo me in every aspect. Such instances, among others, painted a picture of a person who seemed to lack genuine regard for others.

* * *

17

EMOTIONS

ONE day, as I went to visit Maya at the hospital, I encountered Maya and Diya walking out of her room as I approached. Upon being spotted, I spontaneously broke into a Bollywood song and mimicked *Shah Rukh Khan's* signature style, opening my arms wide and attempting to replicate a dramatic expression as if someone had just sucked the air out of me. I even dropped down on my knees in the process.

She smiled and mumbled, *"What are you doing?"* I got up and hugged her, asking, *"How are you Maiya?"* She replied, *"Not too good."* Feeling foolish for my antics, I apologized. She smiled and whispered, *"At least, I smiled even though you looked stupid."* It was totally out of my character for me to perform such acts, but I thought it would cheer her up.

I walked along with them, completing a whole round on the 6th floor. The three of us barely talked, and I could see Maya processing her thoughts. As we approached her room, she asked us to go in as she wanted to be left alone to walk by herself. I hesitated but went into the room, only to jolt out and ask her if I could walk with her. She agreed, albeit mentioning she wasn't in the mood to talk. I took a step or two alongside her but eventually let her be and returned to the room.

After a few minutes, Maya returned. Biru and Diya had left to get some food from the cafeteria, leaving Maya and me alone. We didn't exchange a word. Maya sat on her hospital bed and began to weep. I kept my mask on and didn't lift my gaze from my phone. I couldn't bring myself to look at her and didn't want to.

"You know you can take your mask off, right?" she asked softly.

"I know," I replied, but I didn't make any attempt to do so. Tears were flowing, and the mask made it easier to hide them, but she had seen them. After a few minutes, I slyly looked at her and noticed her staring up at the ceiling, wiping her tears away. I walked up to her, hugged her, rested my head on hers while she sat up in the hospital bed and wept. Later, I knelt by the bed, held her hand, and rested my forehead on it while sobbing. I couldn't muster up words to say, and finally managed to utter, *"You know I'm crying not because I think you can't make it. I'm crying because I cannot see you go through this pain. I just can't, Maiya."*

"Yes," she agreed. *"Yes, I know."*

Later there was a knock on the door. The nurse walked in. When she saw me in such a state, she stopped and said, *"Oh, I'm sorry, I can come back."*

"No, it's ok. Please do what you got to do," I replied.

She was there to do Maya's vitals. Later, Biru and Diya came back after having a sumptuous meal and bringing some leftovers to offer. I stood there quietly while Maya laid there, half upright, staring blankly at the wall while the nurse examined her blood pressure. I could hear the nurse giving her the numbers, but I could not make sense of what she was saying. I stood looking out the window, fixing my gaze to a distant light that seemed to get bigger as my eyes refused to dry.

I didn't stay long and left after giving her a hug. She smiled softly and uttered, *"Goodnight."* I smiled back and walked backwards, slowly closing the door, looking at her from the side of the gap of the door that became narrower as I pulled it towards my side and finally closed it. I let the tears pour out of my eyes as I walked to the car. It was painful as always to see her go through this, and there was nothing I could do to ease her pain. This is the part of my life I called being helpless.

* * *

I'm no poet but I wrote this that night:

Helpless

Troubles persist in finding us,
While normalcy seems to slip away.
This role of life was not one we chose,
Feeling helpless with each passing day.

Smiles and laughter feel distant now,
As we navigate the chaos of medical ordeal.
Engulfed in negativity, we drown somehow,
Forced to tread this path, no appeal.

Yet faith and hope cling steadfastly,
Though the pain of loved ones weighs heavy.
This too shall pass, eventually,
But for now, we walk on, helplessly.

* * *

Visiting her in the hospitals had not been so difficult before. We would often share smiles and conversation, even during tough times. Sometimes, she would simply lie there while I occupied myself nearby. Every hour or so, when she woke up to use the restroom or request water, we exchanged a few words. I'd even ask her to show me some dance moves, and she would willingly oblige, despite being tethered to the IV machine. But this time, it was different.

The day I went to pick her up after she had the portal installed, which required a slight surgical procedure, to prepare for the second round for chemo, I was a wreck. Seeing her asleep in the hospital bed, I couldn't hold back my tears. I choked up several times but tried to keep it quiet so she wouldn't notice. The nurse offered me water, but I hastily asked for directions to the restroom before leaving the room. After spending some time alone, gathering my composure, I returned to her bedside.

During one of Maya's hospitalizations, Jenny wanted to visit Maya early in the morning and asked me to come along. When we arrived at Maya's room, she was on a video call with her therapist, arranged by Diya from Nepal. We were told, the therapist had a good reputation with twenty years of experience and used holistic methods to heal her patients. While we may have been skeptical before, this time we were willing to try anything to relieve Maya of her suffering and help her live a normal, healthy life. Maya had thirty more minutes with the therapist, so Jenny and I went for a short walk around the hospital. When Maya finished her session, she called us to come in. Jenny was eager to see Maya, and they exchanged smiles and hugs. I settled myself on the couch while the girls caught up.

Due to the side effect of the radiation, Maya's ears had accumulated liquid discharge, causing her to become hard of hearing. This had happened before and wasn't a major concern. I would teasingly tell her she looked cute when she was deaf. Every time she struggled to hear, she would instinctively bring her ears forward or lift the part of the head cover that was over her ears, although it didn't make any difference. When she noticed the smirk on my face, she would squint her eyes and silently utter, *"What so funny? Entertained?"*

When she experienced this for the first time, she visited Urgent Care, and with a small procedure, the liquid was drained, resolving her deafness. This time, the doctors were unsure. The discharge was yellowish, but she had no pain. As a precautionary measure, the hospital put her on antibiotics. They planned to transfer her to MSK in New York, as her surgeon wanted to examine her closely. Due to the lack of room availability, Maya was stuck in Stamford hospital for days, with hopes of being moved to MSK facility in New York gradually fading away.

As the girls bid farewell, Jenny uttered, *"Hang in there. There's light at the end of the tunnel."* To which Maya tilted her head slightly backwards and said, *"Well, I see all darkness ahead of me."* On hearing this, I was dismayed and hoarsely said, *"Can you please stop saying it? What's the use of us trying so hard if you walk around with that attitude?"*

"Yeah, please don't say that. There is hope and plenty of light awaiting you," muttered Jenny.

"Yeah, I know. I'm sorry," apologized Maya.

It's challenging to witness someone as lively and full of zest as Maya grappling with a negative outlook on her future. We can't fault her or anyone enduring such formidable trials. It takes immense courage and perseverance to continue fighting, even in the face of seemingly insurmountable obstacles.

The certainty of death, the ultimate truth of life, looms over us all, yet it's something we often push to the back of our minds. But when confronted with its imminent presence, it becomes unfathomable. What if our efforts prove futile? Maya underwent the most aggressive chemotherapy in her initial treatment, but unfortunately, it didn't yield the desired outcome. Would it be different this time? The doctors cautioned that recurrent cancer could be exceptionally challenging to treat. Nevertheless, despite the uncertainties, we clung to hope, relentlessly seeking a miracle and a cure for Maya. We remained steadfast in our belief that she would emerge victorious, no matter how many more hospital visits lay ahead.

Maya had mentioned her hair was falling out and asked me to shave it. I had promised to bring the clippers the next day. When I left the hospital the day before, Maya still had hair. But today, as she pulled off her hat, she exclaimed, "*Anupam Kher*" (Bollywood actor), with a smile. Most of her hair had fallen off. I knew she anticipated my reaction and tried to make light of the situation. It was evident by her attempt at humor, although she wasn't the best actor. Maya, couldn't lie, nor could she pretend convincingly.

Such incidents got me immensely saddened. There was a time when I had to console Diya and ask her to remain strong, and now Diya was asking me, *"Why are you so sad?"* Perhaps to cheer me up, she would say, *"I can guarantee you nothing is going to happen to di."* If only it was so easy to believe her!

* * *

DIYA'S REVISIT

UPON hearing about the recurrence of cancer, Biru and Diya had decided to visit again sometime in early February 2023. I had been living with Maya since they left last year in August. I had told Maya that even though they would be coming, I would stay with her just in case we had to make quick runs…. She hadn't waited for me to finish and said, *"Of course you are staying."* I was glad that she thought so too. As the days drew nearer to their arrival, Maya's mom called me. It had been a long time since I had spoken to her. She would always call when she needed an update about Maya or needed me to do something. So, this time I was not sure why she was calling me as I had been giving all the updates to her husband. Later, I found out that she was indirectly asking me to vacate the room that I was currently sleeping in for the visitors, Biru and Diya.

Maya's new apartment spanned a little over 1200 sq. ft. but appeared spacious despite its size. It boasted three bedrooms; the largest one was Maya's, the second was mine, where I had set up a workspace and accommodated my dog's beds without crowding the area. The third room though modest, was suitable for children but felt a bit cramped for adults. Maya's dad had occupied that room throughout his entire stay.

Maya's mom seemed to be hinting that I should relocate to the smaller room so it would be easier to keep an eye on Maya. I clarified that I hadn't faced any difficulty doing so from my current room all these months. Additionally, I pointed out that if she was suggesting I make space for Diya and Biru, she should communicate that directly to me.

I wouldn't have minded using the smaller room, but it simply wasn't feasible to accommodate my work computer setup, which consisted of three large monitors. When confronted, she defended herself, saying that she had brought it up because the smaller room was closer to Maya's, making it easier for me to keep an eye on her.

While still on the phone with her, I measured the distance from that room to Maya's and the distance from the room I was sleeping in. Both were seven steps away. It seemed like she couldn't come up with a better argument. All this time, she hadn't bothered to make things easy for me, and now all of a sudden, she cared about it.

She grew concerned when I brought up the idea of moving back to my own house and visiting Maya, as I did in the beginning. She adamantly insisted that I shouldn't even entertain the thought. *"You are the only one she has there. We find comfort solely because of your pres-*

ence. Who else would take care of her?" It was a valid point. The family relied on me when no one else was around, and now?

The next day, Maya also asked me if I would be okay with giving up the room for her sister and her husband. With a smile, I responded, *"I wish you hadn't asked, but I'll give them the room but move to Trumbull."* It made me wonder. While I trusted Maya's judgement in most situations, I couldn't shake the feeling that when it came to her sister, she sometimes overlooked practical considerations. It seemed as if her decision-making process faltered in those moments. Maya had witnessed firsthand the extent of my care and support for her, day in and day out. She knew why it made sense for me to remain in that room.

After realizing her oversight, Maya apologized and admitted she wasn't thinking clearly, urging me not to leave. As I began packing, she approached me, embraced me, and sincerely apologized once more, pleading for me to stay. Eventually, I agreed.

Karma, Maya's cousin, whom I had grown close to, was visiting Maya for a few days. He lived in Europe with his family. A few years ago, when he was transitioning to Europe from the United States, he had stayed with us for a few days in our house in Trumbull. Maya and I had also visited him in 2015 when he was still living on the West Coast. Over time, we had developed a strong bond, so I was pleased to hear he was coming. He shared a special connection with Maya, and I felt similarly close to him.

Before their arrival in the US, Diya texted me, informing that they had booked and Airbnb across the street. She asked me not to mention it to Karma so he wouldn't feel uncomfortable. Although

I knew they were doing it out of consideration for me, I suggested they simply come to the apartment, and I would go home. Diya insisted they had already made arrangements, adding, *"we'll see about that."*

Throughout their entire trip, they remained holed up in the rented apartment. Maya spent most of her time there as well. They only visited Maya's apartment during mealtimes, as I was the one responsible for preparing lunch and dinner. Initially, Diya had volunteered to prepare breakfast and lunch for Maya, but after a few days, she would call me asking for help, claiming to be busy with work. I couldn't fathom what kind of work she had, if any, that kept her occupied during those late hours in Kathmandu, especially considering the time difference.

I felt compelled to inform Maya about this and reassured her that I would never delegate her care to someone else if I were capable of doing it myself. I emphasized that she was my top priority, and everything else could wait. Maya simply smiled and replied, *"I know."* I never did but, sometimes, it was important for me to verbalize my dedication to her, even though I knew she understood it.

* * *

This incident brings back memories of our trip to Lake George when we had planned to visit the horse ranch early in the morning. However, we had to reschedule our plans to a later time because Diya claimed to have an important meeting that couldn't be postponed. She stayed in her own room while the rest of us were in a neighboring room. Biru would come into our room and speak in hushed tones, prompting me to ask Maya about his behavior. She suggested that Biru was whispering because Diya was in the adjacent room attending her meeting. I assumed it must have been a crucial and an urgent meeting for Biru to be so cautious, even though he was quite a distance away. I later discovered that it was just a weekly housewives' meeting, where they shared their domestic experiences from the previous week. I couldn't help but roll my eyes at the triviality of it all.

* * *

It was during this time that Maya was transferred to MSK in New York because of the excretion from her ears. Doctors in Stamford Hospital were unable to diagnose the issue, leading to an extended stay in Stamford hospital. Maya had to wait for a bed to become available at MSK before she could be moved. Once she was transferred, she stayed there for another week. Both Biru and Diya opted to stay in a hotel nearby, which was more convenient for them, and I had no objections.

    I went to New York every evening, bringing Maya some home-cooked food that I would prepare in her apartment. I am not a great cook, but she seemed to enjoy it. I had to improvise the dishes, so it wasn't the same thing every day. I continued to do this throughout her stay in New York, cooking for everyone so that they had something to eat.

    Maya remained in the hospital on Valentine's Day, and Diya continued to text me daily, dropping hints that she desired me to bring food. Even on Valentine's Day itself, she messaged me early, anticipating a delicious meal to be delivered later. Eagerly, I agreed, preparing a variety of dishes. As I completed cooking and headed to the hospital, I received another text from Diya, this time informing me to forego bringing anything as she and Biru had opted to dine out. Despite the change in plans, upon my arrival at the hospital, Amy was present with Maya. The three of us enjoyed the meal I had prepared, exchanging wishes for a Happy Valentine's Day!

* * *

19

TRIP TO KANSAS

ONE day while we were driving back from MSK Westchester, I overheard Diya telling Maya about a treatment plan in Kansas City Missouri. I interrupted and inquired, *"What are you guys talking about?"*

"Oh, we were going to tell you," replied Diya. They had planned an alternative healing and holistic chemotherapy in Kansas City. They had the dates scheduled and flight tickets bought. Diya further added, *"But nothing is certain, and we still need confirmation."*

I find it perplexing how some people approach planning in a vastly different manner than I do. When organizing a trip out of state, my preference is to confirm appointments and dates before purchasing flight tickets and arranging accommodations. I believe this is a common practice among most individuals. It seemed that Diya and Biru, operated differently. They wait until after buying flight tickets, booking lodging, and paying fees to confirm plans. It appears that luck always seems to favor them in these situations.

So, when the appointment which was already confirmed, was re-confirmed, Diya told me, *"You've done so much for di, so we want you to rest and that's why we are taking her."*

I would have preferred a different approach from Diya. It would have been better if she had communicated with me in a more considerate manner. For example, she could have said, *"I know you'd like to come too, but we think it's best for you to rest, so let me take her. What do you think?"* This approach would have been much more respectful. I would have agreed, and then she could have proceeded to buy the tickets. It's frustrating when decisions are made and plans are set without consulting me, only to inform me afterwards.

This was reminiscent of the time during radiation when they decided to book an apartment without consulting any of us. That's just how they operated, and so far, it seemed to work in their favor.

Before their departure, Maya expressed her discomfort with Diya traveling alone to Kansas with her. Maya voiced concerns about Diya being alone in Kansas while she herself would be at the clinic all day, deeming it unsafe. I interjected, *"What about Biru? Won't he be there?"*

Maya explained, *"Only this week, but for the next two weeks, he won't be here as he has to go back because of work."*

I responded to Maya, *"Well, if Biru is not going to be there, of course, I will come with you guys. Did you even doubt that?"*

Maya acknowledged, *"Yeah true. Thank you!"*

Diya was present during our conversation.

*   *   *

I drove them to the airport and picked them up after a week. Despite my requests for updates to Diya, I was rarely given any, so I decided to give them their space and peace. Before I knew it, a week had passed, and I found myself on my way to pick them up from LaGuardia airport.

*   *   *

Karma called me the day Maya, Diya and Biru returned from Kansas on March 3rd. I was busy and did not answer his call but messaged him saying I would call him later. He was in Europe but texted me saying he was flying to the United States the next day.

Karma had been here just a month ago. What he had made clear was that he was broke and couldn't afford the flight tickets. Initially, I had offered to chip in for his tickets the first time he was coming, but he refused, saying he would manage.

When Karma was departing after his first visit, prior to saying goodbye, I mentioned to him my hope of seeing him again soon. He responded, *"We'll see, da! It all depends on what I manage to save up. At the moment, it's paycheck to paycheck!"*

I felt a pang of sympathy for him. He already had his return tickets, the least I could do was to buy him the train tickets to the airport. I upgraded it to business class, which didn't come at a significant additional cost, but it brought him genuine joy. He hadn't packed much to take back to his family, so I offered him some clothing items, courtesy of my sister-in-law, ensuring he didn't leave empty-handed. When the time came for him to depart, emotions ran high. We shared a heartfelt hug, and I couldn't help but feel a sense of attachment. Our connection had grown strong, almost like that of siblings.

He was now coming back within a month. Something tinged in my head. Ahh! Diya must have paid for him to come and assist them in Kansas. This way, I would not go, and perhaps Diya wanted me to pack the apartment as Maya had given notice to vacate by the end of the month. This was my assumption, but it could have been different. Perhaps she really wanted me to take a break and relax, as I had been working 24/7 attending to Maya's chores. This was nice of her, but shouldn't she have at least consulted with me before the plan was made?

So, when I got the text from Karma saying he was coming back to America again, just a month after leaving, I took a wild guess and asked, *"Oh, to go to Kansas?"* He replied, *"Yes!"* Bingo, I knew it. I had already assured Maya that I would accompany them, especially when she expressed concern about Diya being alone. So, I naturally assumed I would be joining them and had started to contact my friends there and searched for the best flight deals. Since I wasn't splurging on a business class ticket, I had to make sure I found the most affordable option.

They didn't inform me about Karma's return. It wasn't a part of Maya's plan; it was solely Diya's decision. She needed someone who she could easily direct and feel comfortable doing so. I didn't fit that role. Karma was the perfect fit - he needed money, and being their cousin, he was like a little brother to them. Diya paid for his round-trip ticket from Europe, a business class ticket to Kansas for two round trips and compensated him for his assistance. While this gesture was kind, I couldn't help but feel disappointed. I wanted to be by Maya's side for every treatment she underwent. Am I unhappy about this? Yes, and I'll explain why.

Karma did not drive, and neither did Diya. Maya was left to rent a car and drive herself around during her chemo and other treatments. Later, Maya mentioned how hectic and exhausting it was for her. Karma also didn't cook, leaving Maya to handle all the household chores on top of her treatments. Perhaps Diya cooked occasionally, or they relied on takeout. Meanwhile, I was shouldering all these responsibilities and would have continued to do so if I had joined them. Furthermore, Diya had warned Maya and me to be cautious during Karma's visit in 2015. She warned Maya about Karma's slippery hands and recounted stories illustrating why she could never trust him, discouraging us from extending our invitation further. I hadn't taken the warning too seriously, knowing Diya's tendency to fabricate stories to serve her own purposes. It was during this time that I began to notice the selfishness in Diya's actions. Everything seemed to revolve around her convenience, with little consideration for those around her. This selfish trait became increasingly apparent as the days went by.

* * *

It only takes one person to voice their feelings about someone, and soon others follow suit. People began telling me, *"Glad you're noticing it, we had seen it right from the beginning."* Even Diya's friends later admitted that she had a tendency to treat everyone as her subordinates or "make-shift" servants. She didn't have many friends and mostly hung out with family members. The few friends she did have seemed more like followers. She never treated them as equals. How could she? She belonged to high society, while those around her had simple jobs. As a seemingly kind gesture, she would invite a friend, particularly one, to join them on a trip to Bangkok. Little did this person know the true intention behind it. It was already planned that she would be the babysitter while the couple ventured out for their romantic evenings.

* * *

A mutual friend of Maya and mine once confided in me, saying, *"Maya had become the slave to her little sister's happiness."* Maya hadn't stood up for what she truly wanted. Driving was the last thing she desired to do during those challenging times. On the days she was supposed to go to Kansas, she did not want to budge. To keep her busy, Diya and Karma would engage her in solving puzzles or playing cards. When I found myself alone with Maya, I would gently remark, *"I'm glad you were keeping busy playing cards."* Maya's response was always the same: "*I have no choice."*

Maya's schedule was incredibly hectic. She would spend a week in Kansas, then fly back for chemo in New York, rest briefly in Connecticut, and return to Kansas the following week. This cycle repeated for three weeks. During the short breaks between trips, they would be busy packing for their upcoming journey to Nepal, primarily packing clothes. I volunteered to handle all the other packing while they were away to alleviate their stress. I didn't want Maya to be overworked. She looked exhausted and frail, and it was heartbreaking to see her endure so much when she needed rest. Yet, I hoped it was all for her benefit, praying she wouldn't fall ill amidst the chaos.

During the final night, I noticed Karma purchasing iPads and other high-end toys for his kids, which he hadn't been able to afford previously. I felt happy for him, seeing him able to provide such gifts. Although he had confided in me about his financial struggles just a month ago, I didn't inquire about his sudden ability to splurge. I remember lending him my credit card to purchase a quality whiskey for himself. When he asked about the budget, I advised him not to exceed a certain amount. He returned with a whiskey that cost less than what I had suggested, jokingly remarking, *"See, I saved you money,"* and we shared a laugh.

* * *

20

DAY OF THE CT SCAN

EVER since Diya's visit, finding alone time with Maya became a rare occurrence. Diya never seemed to leave Maya's side, and we missed those moments we used to enjoy catching up. However, on the day of the Magnetic Resonance Imaging (MRI) and CT scan, we finally got our moment. Diya had decided to stay back, so it was just Maya and me. As I drove, we remained silent until she turned towards me from the passenger seat and softly uttered, *"I'm sorry!"*

"For what?" I asked, keeping my focus glued to the road, intentionally avoiding eye contact. I knew exactly what she was apologizing for, but I didn't want this discussion to escalate quickly, so I was searching for a distraction. Expecting the conversation to become emotional, I reached for my sunglasses to conceal any feelings. Just then, my mom called, offering a brief reprieve from the impending discussion, albeit shorter than I hoped.

After I hung up, Maya continued to express her concerns for me and apologized for unintentionally causing me distress. She admitted that with everything on her mind, she struggled to prioritize and sometimes overlooked my needs. She sensed that something was amiss and worried about my well-being. I reciprocated her concern, sharing my feelings of being taken for granted by her sister and my disappointment with their actions. I conveyed, *"I've never felt so belittled and humiliated,"* expressing my frustration over their decision-making process, especially regarding the trip to Kansas. While I usually tried to avoid stressful discussions with Maya, sometimes it felt necessary to address my discontent regarding her sister's behavior.

"You seem to turn into a different person when your sister is around," I told her.

She acknowledged that she was aware of the challenges I was facing without me having to explain them. Maya admitted that she recognized I was being overlooked and mistreated, a sentiment she agreed with. She expressed her regret and offered a sincere apology. Extending her hand towards me, she emphasized, *"You do understand that there is no one I care for so much,"* affirming the depth of her care and concern for my well-being.

Feeling overwhelmed, I struggled to find my words and remained silent as she continued to hold my hand, offering comfort through her touch. Eventually, as my emotions settled, I turned to her and expressed, *"As long as you get better, I'm willing to put up with anything."* She said, *"Yes, I'll beat this."*

Her determination was evident, and her newfound positivity was a reassuring sign. Even with the challenges ahead, I could sense that Maya was on the path to improvement, with or without my constant presence by her side.

* * *

21

SHE LEAVES FOR NEPAL

AS much as I tried to avoid dwelling on it, the day inevitably arrived when Maya would fly to Nepal. It was a bittersweet moment, compounded by Karma's departure on the same day. He left in the afternoon, and Maya's flight was scheduled for the night. Despite my efforts to push the thought away, the day had arrived, marking a significant transition in Maya's journey.

They had arrived just the day before from Kansas, late at night. As we drove back to the apartment, I noticed Maya constantly fidgeting behind her neck. Initially, I thought she was itchy, but when she continued to do it incessantly, I asked, *"What is it?"* She replied, *"I think it's a pimple and it's bothering me."*

Later, when we were in the garage, Maya asked me to check it under the light. It appeared to be a rash extending from the middle of her head to her neck. Concerned, we made several calls when we reached the apartment. Maya contacted her best friend and a doctor, Sam. After describing the symptoms and conducting a video call, the doctor confirmed it was shingles. There seemed to be no respite as Maya was being attacked by diseases from all directions. It was difficult to see her expressionless, hiding her pain beneath a stoic façade. I couldn't help but wonder about the extent of her suffering despite her efforts to conceal it.

Sam suggested a few procedures to sanitize it, while Diya reached out to a doctor in Nepal for further advice. The Nepalese doctor prescribed a few medications, prompting Diya to request a prescription from Sam as a favor. Sam declined, expressing concern that Diya was taking the situation lightly. According to Sam, doctors anywhere in the world should not prescribe medication without fully understanding Maya's situation. There was a risk of allergic reaction or adverse interactions with her existing medications, given the complexity of her medical history.

The next day, as I drove them to the airport, a heavy silence filled the car. I tried not to dwell on it too much, unsure of how the day would unfold. I couldn't shake the feeling of unease as Maya prepared to depart. A question kept lingering; why were they taking her to Nepal, leaving behind the top-notch care covered by insurance in the United States? They assured me that the treatment procedures would be the same, with Maya receiving chemotherapy in the best hospital with the best doctors in Nepal, according to Biru. So, what was my concern? What kept me up all night worrying? It made me question why Biru and Diya were so insistent on going to Thailand for the birth of their first child, citing a lack of trust in the medical team in Nepal. What had changed now?

It's not that I lack faith in the medical team in Nepal. The world chooses to come to the United States because we have the best of the best here. I was also concerned about the aftermath of chemotherapy. How would her body handle it? After every chemo session, Maya's vitals substantially depleted. Her WBC would fall below the required range of 4.5 to 11.0 × 109/L, causing her to enter a state of neutropenia. During this state, her blood count would plummet, sometimes as low as 0.1x109/L. Most of the time, this meant hospital visits and blood transfusions. In this state, one is prone to infections, and every food intake needs careful monitoring. Contact with others could be fatal, and hence the nutritionist caters special meals. I may offend people when I say this, but the best hygiene couldn't be expected in Nepal. Would Nepal be able to provide the same level of treatment she received here in America?

* * *

The atmosphere in the car was heavy as we made our way to the airport. Diya, seated quietly in the back, didn't engage in much conversation. Yet, there was a palpable sense of contentment emanating from her. She was visibly pleased that Maya was finally accompanying her home to Nepal. It was ironic to witness how, despite years of persuasion and emotional appeals, Maya's decision to return to Nepal was ultimately spurred by her battle with cancer.

During our drive to the airport, Maya once again reiterated her concern for my well-being. She urged me to take care of myself, exercise regularly, eat well, and practice mindfulness. But her words carried more weight this time. She insisted on a promise, looking at me intently as she awaited my response. I would comply, saying, *"okay,"* and promising to heed her advice. She reminded me of our earlier conversation during the drive from the CT scan, hinting at the depth of her concern. With Diya present, Maya couldn't express herself fully or openly display her care for me. Instead, she conveyed her worries subtly. *"We both can't go down together, remember that Hanchu!"* she emphasized. *"I've caused you enough pain, and I don't want you to suffer alongside me."*

Not much talking ensued after Maya's heartfelt advice. As we approached the airport, silence enveloped us more and more. The impending reality of saying our goodbyes weighed heavily on our minds. Normally congested streets seemed unusually clear for us, almost as if the universe itself had conspired to hasten our journey. I found myself silently wishing for the usual traffic jams to slow our progress, but today, even that small comfort eluded us.

When we arrived at the airport, I dropped them off at the passenger drop-off area and helped unload the suitcases. I assured Maya that I would park and return to assist with checking in the luggage. When I reached the parking lot, I realized I had to use terminal eight parking due to terminal one being closed. After waiting for the shuttle, I finally returned to terminal one, only to find that Maya had already completed the check-in process and sent off the suitcases. I asked if anyone had helped, to which she proudly responded that she had managed it herself. I couldn't help but shake my head at the thought of her handling seventy-pound suitcases alone. *"Great job!"* I remarked sarcastically.

We walked together to the security line, I stayed with Maya until the point where I couldn't accompany her any further. I hugged her tightly, feeling her beginning to tear up and hearing the hoarseness in her voice. Once again, she repeated her instructions to me, *"Remember what I told you, hai (ok)?"* I assured her, saying *"Ok Maiya, I promise."* She smiled sadly, returning the hug once more, and whispered, *"I will be back soon."*

"Really?" I responded, my voice tinged with uncertainty.

"Yes," she replied and hugged me again.

Diya clicked a few pictures of us together. When they left through the security, Maya kept turning to wave at me. I stood there, waving back, and smiling, until she disappeared into the crowd.

I was saddened to see her leave. Neither she nor I knew what the next chapter held for her. Maya remained silent, leaving her fate in her sister's hand. She had departed with the hope of being cured through her sister's efforts, disregarding the insurance coverage provided by her company, which wouldn't apply while she was out of the country. Though unspoken, uncertainty lingered on her face– a look of fear and apprehension.

* * *

The shingles proved to be a painful ordeal for Maya, but her father assured me that despite the pain, she was managing it as best as she could. With so much else to worry about, the shingles seemed like just a minor setback. Eventually, it disappeared, but not without leaving unsightly marks on her neck and skull. However, in the grand scheme of things, we didn't dwell on it too much.

Maya's father seemed to downplay her struggles while she was in Nepal, perhaps to maintain a façade of stability and positivity. In America, her health issues might have been viewed with more concern and urgency. It's likely that they couldn't afford to disclose the full extent of her health challenges in Nepal, as it might have reflected poorly on their decision to seek treatment there. So, despite the severity of Maya's experiences, her father consistently presented them in a slightly less severe light.

* * *

After her first chemo in Nepal, her blood count dropped, and she was neutropenic again. Even in the face of her health challenges, Maya maintained her sense of humor and resilience and wrote to me, *"Oh well, I am neutropenic again. It's funny how serious the doctors and nurses are about this, wearing masks all the time and telling the guests to be wearing one too. Don't touch this, don't drink that. I'm like, hello, you need to chill. I'm used to that. Lol."*

I would disagree with her and pleaded with her not to take it lightly. I urged her to listen to the medical advice and take precautions seriously. I reminded her of the measures we followed back in America, and that, even I never failed to wear a mask around her when she was neutropenic. She would say, *"I know, I know."*

It was a shocking turn of events. With all our meticulous efforts to prevent infections during her previous hospitalizations, Maya became infected during her first admission in Nepal. Fortunately, the infection wasn't severe, but it caused fluid to accumulate in her lungs, leading to significant pain and discomfort. At times, she had to be rushed to the hospital in the middle of the night to address the complications.

* * *

22

DAYS AFTER SHE WAS GONE

MAYA'S thoughts consumed my mind, keeping me awake most nights. In darkness, I found myself glued to my computer chair, checking emails, and occasionally peeking at her MSK portal for any updates from her oncologist, yet finding none. I'd send her a text now and then, worrying when I didn't hear back, though I understood she didn't check her messages frequently.

On one occasion, I opened my messenger and noticed that most of the people online were in a different time zone. The only person awake was Sudip in New York. It had been a while since I had checked on him. He was going through a similar situation, with his wife undergoing treatment for breast cancer. I had reached out to him the day Maya left, and now almost a month had passed.

"Can't sleep?" I asked him.

"No Dai[5]. You?" he inquired.

"Same here!" I replied.

It was 3 am, he was unaware that Maya's cancer had relapsed. When he found out, he called me at 3:30 am, displaying a remarkably supportive tone. His voice trembled, just like mine did while explaining our situation. Not that he did not know, but I offered him some advice on how to talk to his wife and what not to say during such challenging moments. Even though he likely knew everything I was telling him, he listened attentively. He also shared a few pieces of advice. As we were about to hang up, he generously offered me a room in his hotel in Kathmandu during my visit.

The hotel was situated in *Thamel*, the most bustling place in Nepal, often flooded with tourists. Despite kindly declining his offer, he insisted, and I eventually accepted. It was an exceedingly generous gesture, and I felt deeply touched. It always surprises and leaves a lasting impression when someone, especially someone unexpected, takes that extra step. Many whom I expected to show compassion were conspicuously absent, forcing me to grapple with this hard truth. It shattered my preconceived notions. I believed I knew people, especially my very close friends – those reserved for good times, parties, and joyous occasions. Sudip, on the other hand, was not someone I was particularly close to; we only met occasionally in someone else's homes. I had never invited him to any events of mine, and vice versa. Yet, he was among the first few to call me with consolation when Maya was first diagnosed. I was deeply moved by

---

5   Brother

his generous gesture, and after talking for about half an hour, we decided to call it a night.

*　*　*

It was a restless night for me, but the following evening, Maya called. Hearing her voice was a relief, especially because she sounded healthy and happy. We spoke for about an hour, and I could sense that she was indeed feeling good. Her little expressions while talking, or her soft giggles assured me that she was emerging from her depression. She mentioned that she had finally unpacked her luggage after a month of being in Nepal. She talked about going for long walks and mentioned that she had smiled for the first time. Maya always smiled, even in distress, but I understood what she meant. The smile was genuine, without pretense, and she did not have to force it. We ended the conversation after her mom called out for her to eat and I smiled to myself.

I asked Maya if there was anything she needed from here that I could send through Ash, who would leave on April 29th. However, I was also planning to surprise her. I had decided to leave on April 21st for two weeks. Nobody knew about this trip except her brother, and I hoped he hadn't told anyone else. It was a conversation with Kiran that convinced me to make this decision hastily.

Of course, I would take the stuff with me if she ordered on time. I kept reminding her not to wait until the last moment. Many times, I nearly spilled the beans about me coming but I was careful enough to change the topic. She didn't seem suspicious, so I knew it would be a good surprise. At the same time, I knew I had to be ready for some lectures!

* * *

Kiran called me one day to share some updates. As a brother, he was deeply pained to see Maya endure this ordeal. He described her as the *'Walking Dead'* because she never seemed fully present in the moment. Even amidst laughter and activity, Maya appeared distant, like a kid, preferring to sleep most of her time. On one occasion, there was a brief moment when Kiran got to spend time with her on the terrace, marking a rare occasion since she returned to Nepal.

He had asked her if she missed America, and she hesitantly said, *"No."* When he inquired if she missed me, the hesitation increased, and after a long pause, she replied, *"No it's not that."* When he suggested asking me to come over, she remained silent, and after contemplation, she told him not to bother me.

Kiran believed that she was indeed missing me. He said, *"Bro, I know my sister."* When I asked him if he believed my presence would help, he affirmed, saying it would make a difference. He explained that she might have been tired of being constantly surrounded by family, and my arrival would change the dynamic. He emphasized, *"No matter what happened between you two, I know that no one cares and loves her as much as you do. You are everything to her, a husband, a friend, and a confidante. You, being here is going to make a big difference. I'm sure of it."*

* * *

From the start, when Diya and Maya were planning their trip to Nepal, Kiran had insisted that I come along with them. He suggested that I could work remotely, which was feasible for me. Aware of my love for trips to the outskirts of Nepal, Kiran wanted to plan such excursions with me. He expressed his enthusiasm for these trips, knowing that Diya and Biru were not keen on exploring inner Nepal and preferred international trips instead. Kiran even brought up the idea of us renewing our vows, similar to our first marriage ceremony.

I would playfully ask him who I was renewing my vows with, and he would respond, *"My sister, of course!"* We would share a laugh, but he would stop me and stress that he was actually serious about the idea.

Earlier, while I was talking to Maya, I had expressed my intentions of coming to see her. Initially, it seemed like she wanted me to come, but then she said, *"Actually don't come coz finally you are taking care of yourself. If you come here, then it's going to hamper it."*

I responded, *"Come on Maiya, I have no intentions of coming right now but maybe later. But why do you think I will go astray? I know how to keep my word and I don't drink or whatever you think I will do there."* She said nothing but, *"I know, I know!"* and started talking about other things.

Before she left for Nepal, she made me promise that I would take care of myself and prioritize my health. Once I moved back to my house in Trumbull on April 1st, I diligently started working out, meditating, and practicing yoga.

Raj, a very good friend of mine who had undergone strict and rigorous Hatha yoga training in India, was visiting her family in the United States. She decided to stop by and teach me some Hatha practices that would help me cope with challenging moments and balance my mind. Initially hesitant, I eventually agreed, and I'm grateful I did. I've continued to take classes from her, finding that Hatha practices have helped me keep my thoughts under control to the best of my ability. Additionally, I started an intermittent diet to further support my health and well-being.

When I mentioned to Maya that I was on an intermittent diet, she playfully remarked, *"Oh well, you're always on intermittent diet."* There was some truth to her teasing, as I often went long periods without eating. *"Come on don't say that,"* I replied. *"At least I'm making an effort and learning to enjoy a variety of meals."* Intermittent diet introduced me to different menus for each meal on different days. Despite some initially complicated or unfamiliar dishes, I found that they tasted better and made me feel good.

* * *

23

THE FUNDRAISER

WHEN Maya left for Nepal, she chose to take short-term disability, resulting in receiving only one third of her salary. From the outset, she had concerns about this option. Maya was a dedicated and hardworking individual who genuinely loved her job. Even amid her battle with cancer, Maya made every effort to avoid taking any days off. The only exceptions were on days when she had chemo sessions or medical appointments, as these days would typically fill her entire schedule.

Despite her health challenges, Maya would often make an effort to open her laptop to check her work emails, driven by her passion for her job. Money was a concern for her too. She worried about whether she would be able to maintain her lifestyle if she had to rely on disability benefits. Even when we were together, she seemed to carry many concerns about our financial future. It's a common trait among humans; the more we have, the more we want.

When Maya first joined her company, she was making only a quarter of her current salary. Yet, she appeared content at that time. Simply having a job, particularly one that offered sponsorship for a green card and provided comprehensive benefits like health and life insurance, along with a positive working environment, felt like a blessing.

My approach to life was differed from Maya's. While I certainly didn't want to live in poverty and had my own dreams, I believed that money came and went, and I preferred to live in the present rather than saving at the expense of enjoying life. I encouraged Maya to treat herself to things she wanted, as long as it made sense financially. Every gift I got her, she returned if she thought it was expensive. Initially, before she had a stable job, Maya was very cautious about spending money unnecessarily, but once she secured a full-time stable job, she became a bit more relaxed with her spending habits.

Diya, on the other hand, always shared her extravagant lifestyle with Maya. She would casually mention activities like taking a helicopter for breakfast at Everest Base Camp for her in-law's fiftieth anniversary, or buying expensive jewelry and handbags as if they were everyday occurrences. Diya would boast about the lavish gifts she received from her husband and discuss the properties or land they were considering purchasing. She even talked about not needing to work, or if she did, it was within her husband's company, making it effortless to earn a handsome salary.

On certain occasions, Diya's insensitive comment to Maya and me, comparing our spending to Karma's when he visited Nepal with his family, was hurtful. She stated, *"Karma spent lavishly during his stay. Compared to him, it seems like you are very poor."* Additionally, Biru's constant reminders to his upset wife during the times they missed flights, saying, *"Babes, why are you mad? We're not poor, are we? We have enough to last seven generations,"* were tactless and unkind.

Maya listened to all of this, and despite her humility, it inevitably had an impact on her. She probably couldn't help but compare her own life to her sister's, and the comparison was stark. While Maya had a good job, she didn't have access to the luxuries that her sister enjoyed. Money wasn't an issue for Diya, but it was a constant concern for Maya, especially since she was married to someone who couldn't shower her with extravagance. Therefore, Maya couldn't help but be cautious and worried about finances.

Once, a statement made by Diya's brother-in-law, Ram, sparked a significant controversy. He highlighted the extent to which the common people in Nepal afforded foreign products in their daily lives, illustrating that it was common for a normal working Nepalese to wake up to an alarm clock made in China, have American made Kellogg's cereal for breakfast, go job hunting in a Japanese bike wearing a Levi's jeans and Bangladesh made jacket, and after a long day come home, sit in a Malaysian couch, wearing Brazilian sandals and pouring themselves an imported French wine while watching shows in a Chinese made television.

This had become the most tweeted and mocked statement in Nepal for that entire month. Everyone blamed Ram for being conceited and unaware of reality because whatever he had said did not picture the correct scenario of a 'common' Nepalese citizen. Even Biru had told me, *"He should think before he speaks in public before making stupid comments."* When we were discussing the same topic with Diya, she said, *"Why are people making such a big fuss? Ram mentioned Malaysian couch because it's cheap! We would never buy it!"*

Diya's response highlighted a common attitude among some individuals who are disconnected from the everyday struggles of ordinary citizens. While she may have meant to defend her brother-in-law, her remark inadvertently underscored the privilege and detachment from reality that some people in affluent circles exhibit. Instead of acknowledging the concerns raised by the public, she dismissed them by focusing on the affordability of certain items, missing the larger point about the impact of globalization and economic disparity on society. It's a reminder of the importance of empathy and understanding the perspectives of others, especially those who may not share the same privileges.

On hearing comments like these, Kiran would express, *"Sometimes I forget that she's my sister. She talks as if she was born into that family. She has lost touch with her integrity and our humble upbringing, totally forgetting that we grew up playing dirt. Now she mocks the same things we did as kids."*

* * *

Even with his immense ancestral wealth, Biru, and now Diya being married into wealth, people of opulence and prosperity, displayed noticeable reluctance when it came to spending on her sister. Despite their lavish lifestyles and abundance of resources, they seemed to draw a fine line when it came to extending financial generosity to Maya. For instance, she wouldn't buy an extra piece of bedsheet for Maya, but instead opted to use the same one repeatedly while Maya was not in the best state of mind to buy one for herself.

When I purchased one for Maya, allowing her to select the color, Diya would criticize the choice. While I took on the responsibility of most grocery shopping, with Diya sending me lists of items to buy, there were occasions when we shopped together. If I offered to pay, they would accept without hesitation, even though the purchase were primarily for their family. However, when it came to shopping for Maya, Diya would opt for dollar stores, while they consistently chose top brands for themselves.

Biru incessantly complained about the apartment lacking a music system, and his complaints persisted until I purchased one for Maya. He also insisted that the apartment needed a coffee machine, providing specific recommendations. While having the coffee machine and numerous items in his Amazon cart, the coffee machine never arrived until I bought one. While Diya often teased Maya for using an older iPhone 7, she never purchased a new one for her. In contrast, I gifted Maya the latest iPhone, which prompted Biru to acquire one for Diya shortly afterwards. It wasn't due to Maya's inability to afford such items; rather, they were low on her list of priorities given her circumstances.

Diya's reluctance to extend financial support to Maya, whether rooted in financial caution, unresolved grievances, or a desire to maintain a boundary between familial ties and material possessions, prompted our friends to ponder the intricacies of family dynamics and the reluctance to spend on Maya's behalf. They often approached me with questions about these complexities, seeking answers that I too, found elusive. Such motives became a daily reality for me, challenging my understanding of familial bonds and financial support.

* * *

Applying for disability was not a decision Maya took lightly. She confided with me and her dad about her concerns regarding the lack of income while in Nepal. She was worried about the substantial medical expenses she would face there, as her insurance would not cover her expenses abroad. The thought of her bank account dwindling added to her anxiety about the financial strain she would experience during her treatment.

During this challenging time, Maya's dad expressed his concerns to me, perhaps hoping I could offer some assistance to alleviate their financial burdens. Even with my own financial constraints from not working full-time for the past two years while caring for Maya, I would have willingly contributed what little savings I had to him without hesitation. Although my monetary support couldn't match Biru's resources, Maya's dad understood my unwavering commitment to doing whatever was necessary for Maya's well-being.

Once, Maya suggested that we refinance our house and take out equity. This took me by surprise, as it was out of character for her to suggest increasing debt. I was ecstatic about the idea, especially since I owed a substantial amount in taxes that year due to capital gains. While I had the funds to cover the taxes, it would deplete my account significantly. Maya proposed that we split the money obtained from refinancing, with my half going entirely towards paying the taxes. Despite her own financial concerns, she even contributed a bit more to help cover the shortfall. With her share secured, I couldn't help but wonder why she worried so much about finances when she had taken such proactive steps to address them.

* * *

When Maya's dad brought up the topic, I mentioned to him that some of my high school friends had suggested the idea of a fundraiser for Maya. Initially, I had hesitated, as I didn't believe we were in a situation that required such an effort. However, her dad expressed interest, and I informed him that, at worst, my friends could potentially raise ten to fifteen thousand dollars. Impressed, he exclaimed, *"Fifteen Thousand? Wow! That's a very good idea. So what are you waiting for?"* I clarified that this was just a suggestion from my friends and had not progressed beyond that. Seeking his approval, I asked if I could give them the green light to proceed, to which he agreed.

Upon receiving the green light, the friend who initially proposed the fundraiser believed it would be more authentic if it came from a family member. He thought that if it came from someone who wasn't familiar with my current circle of friends, it might not reach the intended audience. Reaching out to a friend and later, requesting my brother to draft something for review, he approved it after consultation with the president of our North American Society of Alumni. Subsequently, the fundraiser was launched on the GoFundMe website, and my brother shared it on his Facebook page. The fundraiser gained momentum quickly, with many people sharing and contributing. As it went live in the morning here, and with our twelve-hour time difference from Nepal, it hadn't been seen there yet.

The following morning, Biru texted my brother asking him to take it down as, according to him, *"his relatives were asking as to how much they should donate, and it was embarrassing."* This led to some exchanges between him and my brother, with my brother expressing dissatisfaction with Biru's confrontational approach. Additionally, Biru messaged me, stating that Maya wanted the fundraiser taken down as soon as possible.

When I checked with Maya, she texted me saying, *"Let's think about it if I ever come back there, but for now take it down."*

* * *

The family was embarrassed as they had people calling them and asking if they were out of cash and if they needed help for Maya's treatment. This situation was particularly uncomfortable for Biru and Diya, who had been publicly claiming responsibility for both the financial and emotional support of Maya. Despite Diya's assertions that she would cover the expenses of Maya's treatment in Nepal, I later discovered that Maya herself had diligently transferred every penny of the treatment cost to Biru's account to the extent that she had drained her bank accounts.

I initiated the fundraiser only after obtaining Maya's dad's approval, driven by Maya's concern about not having income while in Nepal. However, they portrayed me as a villain, falsely claiming that I was pursuing personal gain. It's perplexing that, while they were taking credit and boasting about supporting Maya, every expense incurred on her was systematically reimbursed through Zelle and wire transfers. This glaring hypocrisy compelled me, despite my reluctance, to share the unfiltered truth about the situation, leaving no room for sugarcoating the incidents.

The GoFundMe page discreetly communicated the challenges faced by Maya and me without explicitly mentioning the need for funds for her treatment. It suggested that, considering the extensive difficulties we had undergone, support would be appreciated. However, to divert attention and mitigate potential embarrassment, Diya and Biru devised a strategy—blame me. They spread the false narrative that I initiated the fundraiser for my personal gain. In reality, my primary intention was to channel all contributions to Maya, and while I would accept any assistance she decided to share, my main focus was her well-being. Although incurring significant personal expenses and witnessing a downturn in my real estate ventures due to the pandemic, I remained committed to supporting Maya through this challenging period.

Now I was suddenly cast as the villain in their eyes. I called up Maya's dad and asked him if he had informed them that I had consulted with him before taking this step. He simply replied, *"I didn't know it was going to be public."* They seemed more embarrassed to accept help if the world found out but were willing to do so behind closed doors.

**

During the first few days of Maya's diagnosis, her coworkers had raised some money and given it to her. I was surprised that she had accepted it. Her family and she had considered it a sign of goodwill. Additionally, some of her friends had given her money, which was also accepted graciously.

Is it just me, or is it a common association in the United States that when a fundraiser is mentioned, the first platform that comes to mind is GoFundMe or some other public fundraising company? Using such a platform makes reaching out for help easy and ensures transparency, and it has become synonymous with crowdfunding efforts. At that time, I believed it wouldn't require much explanation. In retrospect, I realize it was a mistake, and I didn't anticipate how significant it would become for the family reputation.

Maya's dad later advised me that I should have kept the fundraiser private, limited to friends only. I called out this hypocrisy, questioning if he had informed the family about his consent. Despite my repeated inquiries, he continued mumbling about the embarrassment without directly addressing the issue. I chose not to argue or put him on the spot, hoping Maya would understand my intentions. But she seemed influenced by the wealth and reputation of her sister's family, prioritizing their image over my genuine efforts.

The fundraiser came down when they told me to do so. If I had intentions of raising money for myself, I would have left it active for few more days and made excuses as to why it was taking so long.

This time, I found myself defending my actions more than ever. The family inexplicably clung to the notion that I initiated the fundraiser for personal gain. When I discussed this with Kiran, even he acknowledged that it didn't reflect well in society. His frustration peaked when one of his friends questioned if they were facing financial difficulties for Maya's treatment. Enraged, Kiran bluntly told his friend to *"Go fuck himself,"* vehemently asserting that he had sufficient funds to support his sister. In reality, this was far from the truth.

"Well then, the main concern here is you guys were worried about what others would say, right?" I asked Kiran.

"Of course, it is embarrassing when they think you are out of cash," he said. I asked him if one fundraiser that I did to help Maya out a bit should be a cause for so much animosity given that I had stood by her for more than two and a half years not leaving her side day and night, twenty-four hours a day?

I consistently stood by Maya's side every day, while the family seemed to prioritize other matters over being with her. Even while having the option to stay with her throughout the treatment in the United States, Maya's parents and Diya chose otherwise. Maya's dad insisted on leaving the day his visa expired, ignoring the approved extension Maya had requested. Disregarding my advice against making definitive statements about not returning, he insisted he would never come back to the United States. Diya too, had to return to her own family and children, citing other priorities over Maya. When leaving, she would reassure me, *"We're going back because we know you're here to take care of my sister."* Some of Maya's friends, self-proclaimed as her 'besties,' assured the parents not to worry about Maya and pledged to leave everything to be by her side. These promises turned out to be nothing more than *"second loud noise,"* as none of those who made such proclamations stayed for more than two days, something that Maya's mom herself was very critical about.

Kiran had applied for a visa but the consular decided that a letter from Maya's oncologist, stating that she was terminally ill was not enough to convince him to grant Kiran a visa. Maya had repeatedly written to the embassy to take a second look as to why he was rejected. She had accompanied her email with supporting photos of her undergoing treatment. This reason was not enough either, and they asked Kiran to reapply. The appointment date would be given for April 2023 which was about a year away. Kiran had given up and never reapplied.

At this time, nothing else mattered to me, and I found myself often neglecting my own family. When my brothers visited, they could only see me if they came to see Maya in her apartment. I had dinner with my family only twice in the entire two years. Living with Maya meant leaving my mom alone at home, but she supported my decision, urging me never to leave Maya alone. My brothers deliberately avoided sharing stressful family matters with me, taking on all responsibilities themselves, even covering my mortgages during my travels. I withdrew from social gatherings and declined party invitations, staying with Maya whenever she needed me.

What troubled me wasn't so much the smear campaign orchestrated by Diya and her family, nor the perceptions it generated among others. What truly hurt was the realization that individuals I considered family would go to such lengths to misrepresent my intentions. To this day, I find myself explaining the primary purpose of the fundraising. Although I've started returning the payments, there's still a way to go. Maya wished for all payments to be returned and for the fundraiser to be taken down. If my intention were to raise funds for myself, I wouldn't have agreed to its removal. The fundraiser was live for only twenty-four hours, and I could have let it run to garner substantial donations. I faced accusations for a crime I didn't commit, and in retrospect, I might have preferred committing it, at least giving the accusations some substance.

* * *

SECOND VISIT TO NEPAL

I had plans to visit Maya in Nepal, sooner or later, but the conversation I had with Kiran made me plan the trip earlier. Maya's dad updated me about her occasionally. Most of the time, I got the idea as to how she may have been feeling without being told. I could picture her doing certain things under certain circumstances. She would be in her own world at family gatherings. With all the noise and laughter in the room, she wouldn't partake in any conversation and decide to seclude herself.

She had confided in Kiran that she missed Trumbull. Expressing her discontent, she admitted to feeling happier before, blaming herself for 'crashing' all the good she once had. Kiran was surprised by this revelation, as Maya rarely opened up about her innermost feelings to him. He reassured her that nothing had changed. *"People still love you and Hanchu still loves you a lot,"* he told her. He also assured her that even though we were not together, the feeling, mutual self-respect and love would never cease to exist. She had agreed.

Kiran is not the kind who would have asked me for no reason or trouble me to take a trip of this kind. So, I bought my tickets via Qatar airlines on April 16th to fly on the 21st. I was excited and immediately wrote to Kiran via WhatsApp informing him about my arrival date. When a message is 'seen' in WhatsApp, the two check marks turn blue. I knew he had seen my message, but to my surprise I got no responses, not even until the day I got to Nepal.

Kiran, often viewed as the family's black sheep, seemed indifferent to family matters, a perception I always contested. When he didn't respond to my message during my visit, I chose not to press the issue. As days passed, he failed to acknowledge our earlier conversation or discuss the reason for my visit, fueling doubts about his alleged lack of concern. His apparent insensitivity frustrated me, prompting me to question why he didn't bother to respond. It made me reflect on the unrealistic expectations I had held, and I realized he wasn't someone his family took seriously, so why should I? When I eventually asked him about the lack of response, he cited my failure to confirm the date, reinforcing my initial decision not to expect much and limiting my time with him.

But, despite the complexities of our relationship, Kiran acknowledged the depth of my care for Maya. He made a candid statement at the dining table, declaring, *"Maya will never find someone who loves her as much as Hanchu does."* Uncomfortable with the spotlight, I attempted to deflect his words, dismissing them as a joke by stating, *"I'm not doing this for her, I came because I was missing my friends here."* However, Kiran remained steadfast in his assertion, responding, *"You can say what you want. Truth is the truth."* His words hung in the air, silencing the room. Maya acknowledged the sentiment with a smile, while Diya and Biru were absent at the time.

There was a lack of excitement surrounding my visit to Nepal, and I found myself grappling with introspective thoughts and wandering imaginations, overshadowing the hopes and faith I once held for the unknown. Yet, amidst this internal turmoil, I clung to my abundant reservoirs of faith and hope, recognizing their indispensable role in propelling life forward. Unyielding in my belief that a silver lining awaited us, I refused to succumb to doubt, embracing the conviction that victory was within reach. *"Faith, my dear, never give up on faith!"* became my mantra, resonating through each passing day and night.

* * *

It was already 2 am when I reached the hotel after taking the cab. Opting for caution, I decided to quarantine for three days before visiting Maya, especially with the resurgence of COVID-19 in India during those days. After settling in, I took a refreshing shower and allowed myself to relax, knowing that patience and prudence were essential in these uncertain times.

* * *

It was during Biru and Diya's recent arrival in the United States that a misunderstanding occurred regarding their quarantine period. They had mistakenly believed they could check out of the hotel a day early and come to Stamford. Maya was ok with this arrangement, I insisted they stay for the full duration of their quarantine. Diya was furious and placed blame on Maya and me for what she perceived as a lack of clarity. I had attempted to explain the situation and the necessity of following quarantine guidelines, but she hung up the phone in frustration. It was frustrating to deal with her refusal to understand the simple difference between forty-eight hours and seventy-two hours.

During this particular incident, Jamie had gone to visit Biru and Diya at their hotel. I had explicitly asked all of them to maintain a distance from each other, particularly Jamie, as she would have to return to the same apartment where Maya lived. We wanted to avoid taking any unnecessary risks. Jamie reassured us, saying, *"Oh don't worry, I'll be extra careful."*

The following day, we discovered that no social distancing had been maintained, and Jamie had spent time drinking beer with Biru and even ventured around the city in a taxi, with all of them closely cramped together. I was deeply disappointed in Biru for allowing this to happen, and when I confronted him about it, he dismissed my concerns, claiming that it was difficult to maintain distance and urged me not to worry.

Maya had asked me to find out from Jamie to see how she would explain the situation. When I encountered Jamie that day, with Maya and her dad present in the living room, I inquired, *"Jamie, how did it go? How was meeting them? Did you manage to keep your distance during your meeting with them?"*

Jamie reassured me, saying, *"Oh yeah, Hanchu da. Don't worry at all. We didn't even get close and maintained more than six feet of distance. I wouldn't risk anything that could potentially harm Maya."*

"I'm glad to hear that," I replied. Slowly, I glanced over at Maya, realizing that this incident had shattered her trust in Jamie irreparably.

* * *

Kiran hadn't checked to ensure my safe arrival in Nepal, and even after three days had passed, he hadn't called to confirm my presence. In contrast, my family and friends consistently checked in on me, eager to hear about the surprise visit and Maya's reaction.

During my stay, Pasa accompanied me every day. We enjoyed long walks towards *Thamel* and *Chettrapati,* exploring the streets and alleys of *New Road* and *Asan.* The aroma of freshly prepared *momo* tempted us, and we couldn't resist indulging in the best *momo* in town. After *momo,* we savored *paan,* a local delicacy. We also made it a point to support the rickshaw *wallas (drivers)* by taking short rides around the city. While some may pity them for pulling the weight of two passengers, we believed in providing them business to help them survive. We even sat on the pavements with street vendor, *Didi,* enjoying her street tea without bargaining. Just as we don't negotiate when dining in fine restaurants, we saw no reason to haggle with hardworking people barely making enough to support their families.

Maya and I also found joy in the simple pleasure of sitting in the streets, sipping tea, and feeding the stray dogs - a practice we shamelessly indulged in on numerous occasions. Coincidentally,

Pasa shared the same inclination. Our routine involved spending approximately an hour enjoying our tea before returning to the hotel. Pasa, on the other hand, extended his stay for an additional hour or two, heading home a bit tipsy but unfazed by the prospect of encountering the police. According to Pasa, a self-proclaimed expert in avoiding trouble, the clever cops had removed the breathalyzer tips after COVID-19, opting for a direct breath test into the device. Pasa, adept at dodging such situations, slyly blew into various directions, avoiding the device and consequently, any recorded readings.

Nepal has zero tolerance for drinking and driving. Even a slight whiff of alcohol caught by the traffic police could result in a fine or suspension of your license. Pasa only had three holes, whereas you needed five for your license to be suspended. So, he was considered safe from facing any consequences.

* * *

I went to visit Maya on the fourth day. It was a moment I had eagerly awaited, my heart pounding with excitement and nervousness as I waited for Maya to return home. When she finally walked in, her eyes widened in surprise, her face lit up with a mixture of joy and disbelief. I kept my video camera rolling, capturing every emotion, every expression that crossed her face. Her invisible tears of joy spoke volumes, reflecting her overwhelming emotions at seeing me there. As she hugged me tightly, questions lingered in her eyes, questioning why I had traveled such a distance to be by her side. It was a moment frozen in time, captured perfectly by my phone, a memory to be cherished and reminisced on for years to come.

"What are you doing here?" she exclaimed as I approached to hug her.

"What am I doing here?" I repeated with a smile. *"At least say 'good to see you.'"*

"Of course, it's good to see you," she said joyfully.

* * *

I haven't known Maya to be very expressive. When she's very surprised, she raises her eyebrows, and her eyes widen. I captured both these moments in the video, so I convinced myself, *"Yes, you managed to surprise her!"*

We caught up for a bit over lunch with the family. After a sumptuous lunch consisting of *buffalo meat, rice, daal (lentils), jack fruit* and some greens, the warm sun outside became even more inviting, tempting us to take a nap. Maya chose a small spot under the guava tree, firm enough to support her while resting. Being under it did not seem too comfortable, as a slight wrong movement of the head would have her poked with small protruding branches. I tried to put a cushion to make it comfortable, but it did not work. She had become accustomed to staying the way she was.

As we caught up on many things, it was time for her medicine, so she headed upstairs. She asked me to follow her, and we continued our conversation as we climbed the stairs adorned with old pictures of her dad and mom, which they hung proudly.

Maya opted to sleep in the same room as her parents, despite having her own room in the house. In that room, a small bed was positioned next to the wall cabinet, and the array of medicines behind her head almost served as a makeshift headrest. She told me it was mostly multivitamins, and she was right. I helped her with a few, but before I could notice, she was applying calamine on her head and neck where shingles had left a mark, occasionally causing itching. During this, her mom walked in and offered to help. Despite Maya's refusal, her mom proceeded to pour calamine on a tissue paper and began applying it to the affected area, resulting in a somewhat messy attempt. The tissue paper was tattered.

I held reservations about Maya's mom taking on the role of caretaker. I disapproved of the way she pressured Maya to do things, occasionally raising her voice. However, I recognized my place and refrained from expressing my concerns, aside from suggesting the use of cotton swabs instead of the thin sheet of toilet paper.

This visit to the house did not provide the comfort I had felt before; instead, I sensed an unwelcome atmosphere. I questioned whether Maya's family truly wanted me there. While Maya may have been excited to see me, I wondered about the sentiments of the rest of her family. It felt as if they might have preferred my absence, fearing that I would draw Maya away from them and take her back with me.

I did intend to ask Maya what her plans were and if she knew when she would return. But amidst the conversations we had, she gave me a hint that she had no intentions of returning anytime soon. She expressed her family's contentment with her being there, emphasizing a day-to-day approach with no specific plans. Nevertheless, I observed that she appeared and sounded somewhat better than the day she left for Nepal, indicating a newfound mental strength.

* * *

"Grrrrr," she would playfully imitate, frowning while conversing with the snub-nosed pug that always seemed to growl back. Though Maya didn't speak much, she showed signs of being more engaged and willing to communicate. In Stamford, she often chose silence or rest, but here she seemed a bit more active. She wasn't sleeping as frequently and even joined her dad for long walks. With a nurse assigned to her daily, I felt reassured about her medication regimen. The nurse was well-informed about Maya's schedule and ensured she didn't miss any doses.

As the sun began to take its toll on Maya, she expressed a desire to rest, and I encouraged her to do so before taking my leave. Maya's mother was persistent with her invitation to stay for dinner which I politely declined, changing the subject, and bidding them farewell with a hug, promising to return soon.

Leaving Maya's place, I couldn't shake off the feeling of anguish seeing her so frail and vulnerable. Witnessing someone's struggle against time is a profound experience that words can hardly capture. Despite my own emotional turmoil, I kept my composure, concealing my pain behind a façade of strength. It's a burden I carry alone, unable to convey the depth of my emotions to others. With each passing moment, I clung to the hope that Maya would find relief from her suffering, offering silent prayers for her recovery, the only solace in the midst of uncertainty.

* * *

25

THE DIVORCE

RAJ had asked me to visit the *Linga Bhairavi* temple in Nepal. Her suggestion to visit the *Linga Bhairavi* temple resonated with my inclination toward spirituality rather than religious practices. *Linga Bhairavi*, consecrated by Sadhguru, symbolized not merely a deity but an embodiment of profound energy and positive vibrations. Even though I had my reservations about traditional religious beliefs, I was open to experiencing the spiritual essence that emanated from such sacred places. Moreover, the testimonials from friends like Nina and Jess, particularly Jess's transformative experiences, added credibility to the temple's aura and its potential to influence one's life positively.

Setting aside my skepticism, I embraced the opportunity to participate in the *Klesaya Nasana Kriya*, a body cleansing ritual involving fire. This ancient practice, believed to purge impurities and obstacles from one's life, intrigued me with its promise of spiritual renewal. For three consecutive days in May, I made my way to the temple, a mere fifteen-minute walk from Maya's house, immersing myself in this transformative experience.

At the temple, I was struck by the diverse congregation of devotees gathered there. People from Europe, Asia, and various walks of life had converged, united in their shared pursuit of inner cleansing and renewal. The atmosphere buzzed with energy, as chants and prayers filled the air, punctuated by moments of silent contemplation and fervent cries of release. It was a palpable sense of collective devotion, infused with a profound spiritual energy that transcended cultural and linguistic boundaries.

On the first day following the ceremony, I joined Maya for breakfast at her house. Afterwards, Maya asked me to come up to her room. I got momentarily distracted downstairs. When I finally went up, I found the nurse present as well. Maya politely asked the nurse to excuse herself, indicating that she wished to speak with me privately.

"Uh oh," I quipped to departing nurse, who smiled and left the room. *"It's never a good sign when Maya says that,"* I added jokingly.

After the nurse left, I asked, *"So what's up?"*

"I want a divorce," demanded Maya.

Taken aback by Maya's sudden declaration, I struggled to process her words. *"A divorce?"* I echoed, disbelief coloring my tone. As Maya's words sank in, a wave of confusion and bewilderment washed over me. *"I didn't know what to make of it,"* I admitted to myself. *"Why would she ask for it now?"* With so many pressing concerns weighing on us, the request for a divorce seemed incongruous and perplexing. Yet, Maya's insistence left little room for negotiation. *"It wouldn't mean a thing whether we went forward with it or not,"* I reasoned internally. But she wanted it.

"Is that what you're thinking about right now? A divorce? Of all the things that you should be worrying about, a divorce is what's stressing you out?" I asked, my voice tinged with a mix of surprise and concern. *"Why?"* I pressed, hoping to understand the underlying reasons behind her sudden declaration.

"I know Hanchu, there's nothing that's going to change between us, but this has been stressing me out. People may think I am a bitch for doing this. But at least they won't think I am using you. At least they would know that we are not together even though we mean so much to each other," she replied, her words carrying a mixture of resignation and frustration.

"Is someone asking you to do this or is it something else?" I probed, trying to understand the source of her distress.

"No, neither," she responded, her voice tinged with uncertainty. *"I just think it's the right thing to do. Why? Don't you want it?"* she inquired; her words laden with a hint of desperation.

As she spoke, I couldn't shake the feeling that external influences were at play, particularly her sister's, which seemed to loom over our conversation like a shadow.

"I know who's behind this, your sister I'm sure of it," I asserted, voicing the suspicion that had been brewing in my mind. It seemed all too convenient that Maya had suddenly decided on divorce just two months after arriving in Nepal, a decision that contradicted the perception others had of our relationship. It begged the question:

who had planted this idea in her head? And why was she so easily swayed.

I assured Maya that my hesitation wasn't due to a lack of desire to comply. Rather, I was simply bewildered by the suddenness of her decision. Her dad had asked me to get back together but had shrugged him off. Her brother was encouraging me to renew our vows, and Maya herself had made plans for the two of us once she returned. I recounted such instances, where her family members had expressed hopes of reconciliation between us, only for me to rebuff their advances.

Expressing my frustration, I reminded her of my previous advice not to stress over trivial matters, yet here she was, fixating on the idea of divorce. With a heavy heart, I relented and told her to proceed with the necessary paperwork, promising to be there to sign the papers whenever she wanted and dashed out.

As I hurried downstairs, a sense of sadness weighed heavily on me. I couldn't bear to leave her in such a state. Turning back, I climbed the stairs once more and enveloped her in a hug, assuring her that everything would be alright. Even with my outward reassurances, I couldn't shake the feeling of unease that lingered within me.

As I made my excuses to leave, Maya's family seemed puzzled by my sudden departure. Deep down, I knew that this breakup marked the end of our relationship, with no hopes or desires to reignite the love that had never truly existed from her side. With this realization, a sharp pang of pain pierced through me. This was the final goodbye, and the weight of that reality was heavy.

Anger surged within me, directed not only at Maya but also at her family. However, upon reflection, I questioned the necessity of this anger. Did it serve any purpose in this moment of finality? As I grappled with these conflicting emotions, I couldn't help but feel a sense of resignation, accepting that this was the end of a chapter in my life that I had held onto for so long.

When I got to the hotel, I reached out to Kiran, to discuss the situation. To my surprise, there was no shock or concern in his response. The same individual who had encouraged me to remarry his sister showed no courtesy to console me or engage in a conversation about the situation. It left me wondering about his true intentions.

Rumors circulated that Kiran and the family had orchestrated my visit to Nepal under false pretenses, intending to pressure Maya and me into divorcing. However, I lacked concrete evidence to substantiate these claims, leaving me grappling with uncertainty and unanswered questions.

The next day, Maya sent me a text saying that the divorce proceedings were scheduled for the following day at 2 pm in the district court. It was such short notice that I didn't even have time to comprehend the situation. Later, Kiran texted me to confirm the time, but he didn't bother to call and offer any comfort. The whole family remained indifferent, and naturally, I didn't expect anything different from them.

For all those times when people told me that I was just being used and that I was a fool to not see it, it seemed true. My actions were driven solely by my commitment to Maya, and I paid little heed to the judgments and opinions of those around me. Some hailed me as a saint for my efforts in supporting someone who had seemingly abandoned me in my darkest moments. Conversely, others labeled me a fool for aiding someone who had left me during a challenging period of my life. The opinions of others held minimal importance to me. I followed my heart, and I would repeat the same actions a hundred times over for Maya. Some cynics had warned me that, *"Once the family no longer needed me, they would discard me like a fly off their drink!"* The allegation appeared to hold weight. After bringing Maya to Nepal, the family seemed intent on pushing me aside.

In an attempt to overcome the pain, I sought solace in pain itself. I decided to get a tattoo—specifically, a painful one. The process lasted two hours on the first day and four hours on the second, causing excruciating pain throughout. While it wasn't my first tattoo, this time, the pain was tangible. The experience, however agonizing, served to make the painful contemplation of divorce a bit more bearable by comparison.

* * *

THE COURT HOUSE

PASA and I met Maya and Mala at the courthouse. Kiran showed up after finding a parking spot, which is always a challenging endeavor in Kathmandu. It seemed that Kiran was quite familiar with the ins and outs of the courthouse. He led us upstairs to an attorney's office.

The attorney was seated sipping his tea which he seemed to have just ordered as the steam coming out of it made it look tempting. The weather outside was dull and it was beginning to drizzle. It was unusual for Kathmandu to be so cold at this time of the year, but it was chilly this time. I had no complaints of the weather. I preferred rain, snow and cold instead of the hotness and the humidity in the air. After taking a sip with a *"surrrp,"* he acknowledged us with a *Namaste*.

"Namaste," we all replied. The office was small, barely 10 x10 sq. ft. with just two chairs across his seat but he was kind enough to offer us to be seated even though there were no chairs, as if he wanted us to figure out who would sit and who preferred to stand. Later Maya and I sat as instructed by his interns as we were the plaintiff and the defendant. The attorney then shifted his focus from the tea to Kiran who went and sat right beside him in a makeshift seat, and both got into a conversation like long-lost friends. They were indeed friends. They used words like '*tă*' as used among old friends in Nepal. The choice of words otherwise, for elders and for dignitaries or anyone holding government position would be '*tápai*' instead of '*tă*' or even '*hajoor*' instead of '*tápai*.' It all means 'you' but delegated in a more respectful way to the elders.

While the two were engrossed in their conversations, the attorney, skinny in appearance and attired in *daura suruwal*, traditional Nepalese attire, with the traditional hat, '*topi*,' rather big for his head, did not fail to keep his interns busy. He compelled them to rush to the court to organize the papers or collect numerous signatures before the paperwork could be sent to the judge. While we waited in silence, listening to the never-ending conversation among two friends, I was overwhelmed by the odor wafting in from the nearby bathroom in our cramped office. Unable to tolerate it any longer, I stepped out to shut the bathroom door. I'm not sure if it was my actions that made the attorney realize the smell was bad, but he suggested that we move to a bigger conference room. After we settled in the new room, to my delight, the attorney asked if any of us wanted anything to drink.

"*Tea, coffee, anyone?*" he asked.

"*Yes tea,*" was my immediate response but later I felt awkward and said never mind. The poor intern would have to run down again to fetch the tea. I'd rather have this thing taken care of and leave. Later, to break the silence, everyone engaged in conversations. Even Pasa got in a conversation with the attorney. They both seemed to know each other so started enquiring about each other's acquaintances.

"*Do you know Ajay from Bhainsipati?*"
"*Is he the one who has a shop in New Road?*"
"*Yeah.*"
"*Do you know Samir from Kumaripati?*"
"*Is he a little chubby?*"
"*Yeah, he used to be but now has lost weight.*"
"*He's also called Puntey, right?*"
"*Yeah, ha ha.*"
"*Ah, there you go, now I know who you are.*"

This went on between the two and I can't recall who was asking what as I was lost in my own thoughts, keeping my gaze fixed on the floor. Maya was sitting across from me, and I could see her looking up to me sympathetically. I kept my gaze down as I did not want eye contact with her.

After Kiran and the attorney exited, an uncomfortable silence pervaded the room. I had no inclination to engage in conversation. Thankfully, the interns arrived, breaking the tension with a stack of paperwork requiring Maya's and my signatures and fingerprints. They provided clear instructions, guiding us through the process as we took turns signing and fingerprinting, the pages seemingly endless. I mechanically completed the documents without bothering to read them; attempting to decipher the complexity of the Nepalese language would have been futile after so long.

As we neared the end of office hours, the interns exchanged glances and suggested finishing the remaining work in court, expressing concern that the judge might leave. Reluctantly, we followed them out into the rain. They directed Pasa and me to enter via the main entrance, while they escorted Maya through a special entrance at the back.

Following a security check, we stepped into the main courthouse, a structure I found to be quite expansive. Rising to about six stories, the center of the building was left open, offering a view of the floors above and showcasing a constant stream of people entering and exiting various rooms throughout the building.

There were pickpockets and other minor offenders being ushered in, all handcuffed together. Sometimes it was two, other times six or even eight individuals bound by handcuffs, guided to a room where they were made to sit on the floor. I felt a twinge of sympathy, not for the handcuffed, but for the comedic challenge they faced when attempting to sit cross-legged with their hands bound to each other. Coordination was lacking, leading to some falling while others struggled to sit. It provided a brief moment of amusement for the onlookers, all present for reasons unknown. I had never witnessed so many people shackled together, and upon inquiry, I learned that it made escape more difficult. A few months prior, two individuals managed to run out of the court in a well-coordinated escape, prompting authorities to avoid taking any more chances.

After a short wait, the interns collected more of our signatures and fingerprints. Once the signing was completed, I was instructed to approach a counter for a payment related to file preparation. Following that, we were informed that we had to go to the adjacent building to meet the judge in Room 28. Kiran had returned by then, and we all hurriedly crossed the rain-soaked street, facing the challenge of getting the traffic to halt in the pouring rain.

"*Where's room 28?*" we all uttered.

"*Ah there it is,*" someone pointed out.

We entered the room. It was yet another small room rather unsuitable for a building of that size, let alone call it a courtroom. It was an unfamiliar setup, where hearings were conducted. The judge was already seated and was engaged in conversation with his freehand typists who were seated right under his nose.

The judge did not make any eye contact with me. After reading the document, he turned to Maya and asked, "*Are you sure you want to go through this divorce?*"

"*Yes,*" she replied.

"*And you're aware you are not demanding anything for settlement,*" the judge asked her.

Maya nodded and said, "*No.*" The judge then quickly reviewed the paperwork and signed off on it, considering the divorce valid. However, it later became apparent that, in his haste to expedite the process, he had failed to scrutinize the fraudulent reasons involved to validate the divorce.

After completing all the procedures, Kiran took me aside, expressing his desire to discuss the situation. He began by stating his intention to dissuade Maya and conveyed that they were not pleased with the decision. I stopped him, sparing myself from receiving his sympathies. I informed him that it was over and requested not to dwell on the matter. If we needed to talk, I suggested doing so at a later time.

Maya wore a similar expression of helplessness. At that moment, I couldn't shake the feeling that it wasn't her decision to seek a divorce but rather a result of family pressure, particularly from her sister. She repeatedly apologized, making me promise that nothing would change between us. I reassured her that things would remain unchanged, and I'd always be there for her. As I uttered those words, a chill ran through me, a sentiment she might have also sensed.

Pasa was my only consolation, encouraging me to stay strong. When I confided in a friend, Kamli, about the situation, she remarked that it was about time we had taken such a step, and contrary to how others would feel, she believed it was inevitable. Maya's dad would write to me, assuring me that I was still like a son to him, expressing his love for me. Diya also reached out, writing, *"Don't worry Hanchu da, we are still family, and we will always be there for you."*

Just like so many thoughts raced through my mind, I'm sure Maya's mind was equally active. I saw the divorce as the final straw that kept us together in name only, but now it was settled. Maya continued to check on me and she'd ask how I was doing and whether I was alone or spending time with friends. I knew she wanted me to be around people. If I was alone, she would worry, but I'd reassure her that friends were coming over soon and that I was okay. I made sure to reassure her that she needn't worry about me.

Deep down, I felt the family that once cherished my presence had cast me aside. The reasons behind this change could be myriad misunderstandings, shifting priorities, or perhaps an intentional decision to sever ties. Whatever the cause, the shift from a once indispensable role to a dispensable one was a stark and disheartening transformation, leaving me to grapple with the reality that I was no longer of use to them and lost my former significance.

During my trip to Nepal, I had intended to spend more time with Maya and her family than I did during my last visit. However, things turned out differently, and my stay was brief. I couldn't help but wonder if Maya's family suspected that I was there to take Maya away. Everyone seemed to want Maya to be there, and Maya herself expressed her desire to stay. Yet, her words lingered in my mind when she said, *"I'd rather spend the last few days of my life in Nepal to make it easy for everyone."* It's a statement that continues to haunt me. While I didn't mind Maya being there, the thought of her not making it out of Nepal weighed heavily on me.

The day, the only day, we finalized the divorce, I was with my friends in my hotel room. Suddenly I received a text from Maya expressing her apologies for any negative statements included in the divorce papers, despite their explicit instructions to the attorney not to write anything disparaging about me. *"Negative?"* I questioned, but before waiting for her reply, I assured her that it didn't matter to me. Curiosity got the best of me, and I decided to read the documents with the help of my friends, something I had never considered before. What we found within them left me utterly shocked.

Everything written about me was false and was demeaning. It painted a distorted picture of my character, tarnishing my reputation despite the praise I had received for my unwavering dedication to Maya throughout this ordeal.

In summary, the documents falsely claimed that upon learning of Maya's cancer diagnosis, I neglected to care for her, spent time away from home, and showed no concern for her well-being. These fabrications alleged that Maya found it difficult to live with me as a result. Additionally, they falsely asserted that I forcefully demanded the divorce, coinciding with the time I was excited about surprising Maya with a visit.

I was informed that the reason for presenting the case in a certain way was to expedite the divorce proceedings, which otherwise might have been delayed for months or even years. During my subsequent visit to the courthouse, I raised this issue with a different attorney, and he concurred. I confronted them, stating that they were then resorting to deception and using a lie as the basis for their case. They remained silent and later responded saying, *"This is how it is in Nepal."*

Moreover, this divorce was fraudulent from the outset. Maya and I were both American citizens, but in the divorce documents, they falsely identified Maya as a Nepalese citizen to fast-track the process. Filing for divorce as American citizens abroad would have entailed a lengthier procedure or even beyond the jurisdiction of the government. I went along with it because it was what Maya desired, or perhaps her sister had pressured her to do so. Given her existing state of distress, I didn't want to cause her more duress.

Biru and Diya always had the desire to secretly own a house or an apartment in the United States. They were planning to buy alongside Maya once she moved to Texas after her treatment. This would help them evade certain financial obligations they had in Nepal. They perceived my continued presence as a potential threat to their investment—what if I had a change of heart? To dispel this misconception, it was crucial to clarify that my actions were never motivated by financial gain. I had already assigned my brokerage account to Maya, and even the house I diligently worked to purchase had its deed transferred to her name. This decision was grounded in trust, a sentiment that persists. Any assumption by the two conspirators that I would ever demand what isn't rightfully mine is fundamentally mistaken.

* * *

VISITING MAYA BEFORE LEAVING NEPAL

A day before my departure from Nepal, Samir, Nina, and Pasa visited my hotel. We spent the time catching up on various aspects of life. Having introduced the trio during my previous visit, it felt like reuniting with long-lost friends. The atmosphere was filled with nonstop laughter, especially when a bit of alcohol was involved.

Nina and Pasa's infectious laughter made everything I said seem nonsensical to Nina, prompting her to repeatedly exclaim, *"What nonsense?"* after every sentence. Pasa and Samir, anticipating her response, would playfully join in, saying *"What nonsense,"* before Nina could utter it, resulting in fits of laughter. Amidst the enjoyable moments, a twinge of guilt lingered, reminding me that I should be spending time with Maya. Sensing my contemplation, the three friends insisted I go visit her while they waited in the car, considering it was my last day in Nepal.

"Bro, you're not going to have time tomorrow. Might as well get done with it now and then start packing," they suggested. They had a point. I had considered stopping by later that day, but then it wouldn't be easy to leave without having dinner and then lingering for more chit chat. I also dreaded the goodbye I had to bid to Maya.

I did have a few things to pick up from my apartment before returning my keys to Neera aunty. It made sense to go there first and then stop by Maya's for a quick goodbye. Having friends waiting outside would provide an excuse for not staying too long as well. Additionally, Maya wasn't in a good state to be meeting people. We set off after gobbling down a plate of *momo,* which the hotel owner had kindly sent up to our rooms.

As we reached *Ring Road*, we encountered a flat tire. Back in America, we'd usually take the car to reputable dealerships like Town Fair Tire, where the wait time could be anywhere from an hour to a whole day depending on their workload. Just as I was dreading the wait and considering taking a cab to Maya's while the guys got the tire fixed, Samir spotted a small, shabby shack which he identified as the *'mechanic.'* It was unmistakable, with heaps of tires stacked high enough to catch the eye of passerby, serving as makeshift signage!

Samir rolled out his windows and shouted, *"Brother, we need air."*

I got out of the car followed by others. A short, stout, older gentleman emerged and grinned, exposing his stained teeth from years of tobacco use. His clothes were dirty, with grimy grease stains accumulated over time. Though his eyes looked tired and watery, the toned muscles in his tanned body suggested he was ever ready to take on more work. He barely made eye contact and began examining the wheel. Curiously, I tried to observe what he saw. In a minute, he pointed out the problem, *"There's a cut caused by a wire."*

I didn't see any wires. I wondered how he knew without seeing it. Perhaps the monotony of the trade had made him perfect, I thought. Before I could ask him anything, he dashed in and brought out the jack and hauled up the car. Quickly, he started unscrewing the wheel with no power tools. He took off the tire from the rim and dipped it into a puddle of water stored inside another huge tire from some larger vehicle. Finding out where the cut was, he immediately started working on it.

He burned something, sealed the hole, dipped it in the water, took it off, hammered it with some makeshift stone used as a tool, smelled it, dipped it again, hammered it, and replaced it in the rim. Voila! It was fixed. He finally made eye contact when I asked him how much I owed. *"Rs. 200,"* he grinned. *"What? 200?"* I exclaimed, looking at Pasa. Nina quickly took out Rs.500 and gave it to him. He rushed inside and came out with change, but before he handed her the change, she told him to keep it as a tip.

Nina looked at me and remarked, *"It's ok, no? He did a good job."* Samir and Pasa looked at us blanky, perhaps trying to figure out my surprise. I was surprised because I perceived it to be very cheap. Considering the conversion, it would have cost $1.65 back in the United States. However, when gauged against the per capita income of the country, the expenses for an average person in Nepal could be twice as much as in the USA. Yet, for someone earning in the United States and living in Nepal, life would undoubtedly prove luxurious.

* * *

Heading towards Grande Apartments, we quickly cleaned up and gathered the things I needed to take with me. When we arrived at Maya's place, I requested to be dropped off inconspicuously, instructing the guys to park discreetly. After a few minutes of ringing the doorbell, the maid greeted me at the door and confirmed that everyone was upstairs. I rushed up and met Maya in the hallway. As we chatted, I made my way to her parents' room. Both Maya's dad and mom appeared pleasantly surprised to see me, perhaps growing accustomed to my unannounced visits. I felt it was better that way, or else they might have prepared a feast, or so I thought.

Maya's mom was playing *'marriage'* (a popular card game in Nepal) with Mala and a visiting neighbor whom I did not recognize. I told them I had come to say goodbye. Her dad seemed surprised, expressing his discontent, *"Why? Aren't you coming for dinner tonight?"*

"Yes Uncle," I replied, forcing a smile. *"If time allows and I manage to wrap everything up by 8 pm, I'll definitely be there."* It was a blatant lie, but I couldn't bring myself to admit it. I had made up my mind that I wasn't coming back. I still felt unwelcome, and I hoped it was just my feeling, but I would never know. Maya looked at me, and I knew she knew I wasn't coming later. She made small talks about my flight and asked how I was getting to the airport. She said she wanted to come out and say hello to the guys, but I stopped her. I explained, *"I told them that you were not feeling well, so not to mind if*

you didn't come out." She hesitated but later agreed. We hugged each other. I was choking and so was she. With a battered voice, I said, *"You take care of yourself, and I'll see you when I see you!"* She looked at me blankly and asked, *"I'll see you when I see you?"*

I nodded, mustering a reluctant smile, and silently walked out. I could sense her gaze lingering on me as I moved away, yet I couldn't muster the strength to turn back. It was a painful farewell. Would our paths cross again soon? How would she be when we met next? When would that day arrive? How would she cope without my support and care? Would her family provide the same level of attention to her well-being? With a heavy heart, I headed towards the car, parked more discreetly than I had instructed. I slipped on my sunglasses, hiding any emotions that threatened to surface.

As I settled into the car, the inevitable question came from everyone: *"How did it go?"*

"Fine," I responded tersely. The conversation died down after that, with no one pressing for further details.

* * *

Maya called me that night and expressed her hurt over the way I had said, *"See you when I see you."* To her, it sounded like I was hinting that I would never see her again. She believed I was angry about the divorce. She sought assurance that I would be there for her when she needed me, confident that she would heal, but wanting me by her side just in case. She missed my care and support, urging me to visit her more often. She made it clear she would have asked me to stay longer if I didn't have other responsibilities. Maya emphasized the importance of taking care of myself, not wanting me to suffer alongside her but rather to be there for her.

This conversation with Maya was one of the most emotionally challenging I've ever had. Tears accompanied every word, leaving both of us unable to hang up. I promised her I would return sooner than she expected, and if she needed me even after a week of my departure, she should let me know so I could come back. She agreed. Before ending the call, I asked her to smile, and she gave me the impression that she did. With heavy hearts, we said our goodbyes and hung up.

*　*　*

It had been over a month since my return from Nepal, and Maya hadn't bothered to call. Our interactions were limited to just three conversations, and her texts only touched on superficial topics or requests for things she needed to be sent.

June 16[th,] she wrote mentioning she had a lung infection during the time she was neutropenic. Despite her suffering, she assured me not to worry too much, as it wasn't as painful as the first time. In the following days, she seldom picked up my calls. Whenever I texted her to inquire about her well-being, her responses were brief and curt, usually just a simple *"Super."* I couldn't help but wonder why she wasn't answering my calls. Perhaps she knew she would be caught if she was lying, and lying wasn't something she could do easily.

Throughout this challenging time, I discovered that Diya and her family had gone on a family vacation to South Korea, with plans to head to Bangkok just a few days later for another vacation. It baffled me how Diya could indulge in such leisure when she had a sister back home requiring medical attention and facing an uncertain future. I received such information without them informing me directly, likely knowing how I would react. When I spoke to Maya's dad and feigned ignorance, asking about Diya's whereabouts, he hesitated before reluctantly revealing that they were in South Korea for a family vacation.

"Vacation? At a time like this?" I would counter. He explained that he and his wife were there to care for Maya, and Kiran was also present. However, this rationale failed to convince me, as Maya's parents might not be very helpful if she needed to be taken to the hospital. Kiran had his own concerns, and there could be times when no one was available when Maya required immediate attention.

* * *

THE THIRD VISIT TO NEPAL

DAYS would pass without any messages from Maya. Occasionally, she would send a brief update on her health, but none of them sounded reassuring. She faced challenges but Maya remained hopeful and resilient, never painting her situation in too dire a light. Behind her brave façade, she endured excruciating episodes of pain, often necessitating emergency trips to the hospital and prolonged admissions. Witnessing their daughter's suffering must have been unbearable for her parents. In moments of overwhelming grief, Maya's dad would reach out to me, his voice choked with emotion as he sought solace and release for the tears he had long kept hidden.

I often encouraged him to let his emotions flow in front of Maya, assuring him that it was perfectly natural and could even provide comfort to her. By showing his vulnerabilities, he might create a space for Maya to express her own fears and concern more openly, but he remained steadfast in his resolve not to break down in front of her. He couldn't bear the thought of his daughter seeing him in such a vulnerable state, wanting to maintain a strong disguise for her sake.

The moment that struck genuine fear into everyone, particularly Maya's father, occurred after midnight on a specific day when Maya endured intense pain, necessitating an urgent trip to the hospital. It was during this time that Diya and her family were once again away, enjoying another vacation, this time in France.

* * *

Returning from their vacations in Bangkok and South Korea, I learned that Diya was arranging another trip, this time to France, with Maya, despite Maya's frequent hospital visits. *"Are they out of their minds?"* I pondered. Who in their right mind would plan a trip far from medical assistance when anything could happen? I expressed my concern to Maya's dad, who shared his discontent but hesitated to speak up about the matter.

I wrote to Maya expressing my concern, hoping she would reconsider taking the trip, while also encouraging her to think clearly about the risks involved. She acknowledged the risks but expressed her desire to seize the opportunity to travel while she still could, recognizing the uncertainty of her future. What could I say to that? She was right; it was a now-or-never situation. I advised her to do whatever brought her peace.

Maya's health showed no signs of improvement leading up to the day they were supposed to depart for France. Predictably, the doctors advised against Maya traveling. Nevertheless, Diya and her family proceeded with their trip, leaving behind Maya once again. Not even Maya's fragile condition was enough to deter them.

*　*　*

Few days had passed, and Maya remained in the hospital as the pain persisted. To manage it, the doctors administered multiple doses of morphine along with smaller doses of painkillers. A PET scan was scheduled for the following day, and we awaited the results anxiously.

During this time, Maya's dad would call me even more distraught, his voice filled with anguish as he shared his concerns. He often cried helplessly, expressing the agony of witnessing his daughter, who was once so full of life, slowly losing vitality with each passing day.

When the PET scan results were disclosed, her dad conveyed the dreaded news we all feared. The cancer had aggressively spread in her abdominal region, and the doctors admitted the severity of the situation. Unfortunately, they acknowledged their inability to save her or halt the relentless progression of the cancer. The only option left was to hope for a miracle, even though it appeared highly improbable. Their primary focus was on alleviating her pain.

As he shared this heartbreaking information, he struggled to contain his emotions. Through choked words, he expressed, *"My poor daughter is suffering, my daughter is in pain, and there is nothing I can do,"* breaking into loud fits of weeping. After regaining his composure, I inquired if I should come. Despite acknowledging that my presence wouldn't usher in a miracle, he believed it brought Maya some comfort, even if unexpressed. Sensing the urgency, I assured him that I would book the next available tickets and be by their side in a few days.

When I got my tickets, I wanted to travel to Nepal without anyone knowing. Knowing Maya would need some items from the United States, I had to come up with an excuse to get her to give me a list of things she might need. I told her that a friend was coming to Nepal and was willing to bring a whole suitcase for her. Excitedly, she said she would even order a few items from Amazon. If there were items that wouldn't arrive on time, I would go pick them up from the stores no matter how far. She expressed her gratitude, and the few items she initially requested quickly multiplied, filling up a suitcase. I found myself having to rearrange my other suitcase to accommodate the additional belongings. When I mentioned this to her, she'd respond with a playful *"Oops!"* accompanied by a mischievous smiley emoji!

* * *

I arrived in Nepal on the evening of Wednesday, July 27th. After being picked up by the driver Neera aunty sent, I headed straight to the hotel I had booked in *Thamel*, the same one I had stayed at before. After freshening up, I called Maya's dad to inform him of my arrival. He was excited and wanted me to come over right away, but I requested to rest for the remainder of the day. Although I was eager to see Maya, I knew I needed to take it easy. Quarantining was not required by this time, so I skipped that process.

That night, Pasa came over to take me out for dinner. We took a leisurely walk around *Thamel* and then found a cozy little restaurant that served delicious *momo*. After dinner, we called it an early night as jet lag had caught up with me, and I struggled to stay awake. Once Pasa left, I fell asleep.

* * *

VISITING MAYA AT THE HOSPITAL

THE next day, after dropping off the suitcase at Maya's and having a quick lunch with her ever-insisting family, I left for the hospital along with Kiran and his newly wed, pregnant wife Mala. We didn't talk much on our way to the hospital as I was dozing on and off.

When we arrived at the hospital, I was the last one to enter Maya's room. Diya was already there, seated in the corner on the couch and engrossed in her phone. I approached her and gave her a hug, which she returned somewhat reluctantly while remaining seated. I sensed a certain coldness in her demeanor, but my focus was on Maya, so I quickly turned towards her. Maya's eyes were closed, but upon hearing the commotion, she opened them and looked around. When she spotted me, her face lit up with joy, and she exclaimed,

"Lau, when did you come? Another surprise, is it?" I asked her if she was happy to see me, and she replied, *"Yes of course."*

Diya left as her shift at the hospital was over, likely in a hurry to attend to other matters. Her departure without a word left me puzzled. I couldn't comprehend her coldness towards me. I wasn't there to cause any trouble and wondered if I had inadvertently done something to offend her. Though she was the least of my concerns, her demeanor still bothered me, so I decided to review all our chat conversations since my last visit just to be sure. The last message she had sent was the day after the divorce, reassuring me that nothing had changed between us and that I was still considered part of the family. In response, I had thanked her for her kind words and apologized for not responding promptly. There seemed to be nothing amiss in our interactions.

Maya appeared to conserve her energy solely to greet me with a warm smile and a hug. Thereafter, she drifted in and out of sleep, occasionally making an effort to smile even with closed eyes, signaling her engagement in the conversation. Sometimes, she squinted her eyes intensely, prompting us to call the nurses to adjust her painkiller dosage. Throughout the hours, Maya remained mostly silent, while the three of us engaged in light chatter. Kiran, in his usual manner, dominated the conversation, often rousing Maya with his hearty laughter.

When mealtime arrived and Maya opened her eyes, Mala and Kiran would subtly hint that I should be the one to feed her. It was evident that the portion sizes of her meals had dwindled, and Maya persistently refused to eat. Yet, I knew precisely how to coax her into finishing her meals. Once she managed to finish, I'd receive approving smiles from the others, while Maya often wore a slightly sullen expression. I'd tenderly stroke her forehead and say, *"Good job, Maiya!"*

Around 7 pm, a nurse hired by Diya arrived, accompanied by Maya's housemaid. They were to spend the night while everyone else went back home for a break. I wanted to stay overnight, as I always did when she was hospitalized in America. Here, it didn't feel comfortable to insist, especially since they already had designated caregivers. It was strange; the family, who had relied on me to take care of Maya and had seemed at ease when I was with her, now appeared to have a different attitude. Perhaps they were afraid to leave me alone with her. Maybe they feared that Maya would have a change of heart after finally adhering to the family's rules. At the same time, I was content that there was a nurse, someone more knowledgeable than me, to stay by her side all night.

After bidding farewell to Maya and the others, I left with Kiran and Mala who were heading home. I asked to be dropped off in *Thamel*, which was enroute. In the car, amidst the quiet hum of the engine, I was enveloped in a storm of thoughts and emotions. Maya's condition weighed heavily on my mind, and the gravity of the situation left me speechless. As we drove through the familiar streets of Kathmandu, I found solace in the stillness, allowing myself to process the whirlwind of emotions in my own time.

Witnessing Maya's health decline was heart-wrenching, and each day seemed to weigh heavier than the last. Despite her frail appearance and the immense physical and emotional pain she endured, Maya's resilience remained unwavering. Even in her silence, she found ways to communicate, often with a simple smile that spoke volumes. Though she struggled to articulate her thoughts and feelings, her spirit shone through, illuminating the room with its quiet strength.

* * *

Before falling ill, Maya relished the outdoors, especially on bright, sunny days. She thrived on activities like gardening that allowed her to bask in the warmth of the sun. Her mood seemed to sync with the weather, as she emanated boundless energy during the vibrant days of summer. Conversely, in the cold embrace of winter, her vitality waned, resembling the dormant trees patiently awaiting the return of spring's rejuvenating touch.

It was the middle of summer, yet Maya seemed trapped in the depths of winter. I made a conscious effort to steer clear of memories of her healthier days, keeping my thoughts rooted in the present. Dwelling on the past only stirred up sorrow, echoing Maya's own exhaustion with her current situation. She longed for semblance of normalcy, to live without the burden of constant care. The uncertainty of her prognosis and the duration of her bedridden state loomed heavily on her mind, casting a shadow over her already burdened spirit.

These thoughts continued to swirl in my mind until I found myself dropped off in the heart of *Thamel*. The streets pulsed with energy, where sex workers prowled the corners, enticing potential clients with honeyed words. It was a revelation to witness ladyboys strolling the streets, their attempts at blending in betrayed by their deep, husky voices. Though once a novelty, they now blended seamlessly into the backdrop of *Thamel's* nightlife. The environment was vastly different in the nineties when I left for the United States. Women rarely walked the streets at night, and it was uncommon to see girls in bars or clubs on their own, except those accompanied by male companions.

* * *

After navigating the chaotic flow of vehicles and motorbikes in the narrow streets, I arrived back at my hotel. Ignoring my hunger, I took a quick shower and slipped into bed. I was awake for some time, but my mind was blank, and exhaustion quickly overtook me. My sleep was often disrupted by sudden jerks and frantic sleep talking, a recurring phenomenon that had plagued me for a while. Initially dismissing it, I had begun to notice these episodes more frequently, especially since my time in Stamford caring for Maya. Now, they were becoming increasingly severe, signaling a deeper issue at play. Although friends had warned me about the toll my situation was taking on my health, I stubbornly ignored their advice. It wasn't until now, with my body exhibiting clear signs of distress, that I began to acknowledge the gravity of my condition.

The following day, I deliberately planned my visit to Maya for later in the day to avoid encountering Diya. After confirming Kiran's visiting hours, which he mentioned would be around noon, I scheduled my arrival for 4 pm. When I reached the hospital, Kiran was nowhere to be found as he had also decided to take some rest.

Surprisingly, no other family members were present except for the maid. When I asked about their whereabouts, the maid informed me that Diya had dropped in for a few minutes that morning but had to leave for some chores. She explained that with Biru's birthday approaching that Sunday, Diya was busy arranging a surprise party for him.

Feeling concerned about Maya being left alone during such crucial moments despite having family around, I couldn't help but reflect on the difference in the United States. There, I never left her unaccompanied in the hospital and stayed for as long as the visiting hours permitted.

Kiran showed up around an hour after I arrived. Maya appeared even weaker than she did the day before, drifting in and out of consciousness under the heavy influence of painkillers. Additionally, her family had begun administering a high dosage of Cannabidiol (CBD) oil to help her relax and sleep better. The doctors noticed that the dosage exceeded what was appropriate and advised against it. Maya's dad vehemently disagreed with the doctors, insisting that she continue receiving the CBD oil regardless of their instructions. He was adamant, saying, *"No, I disagree. Make sure you give it to her no matter what the doctor says. They don't know what they are talking about."*

The doctor too had joked, *"Every time I come to see my patient, she is always high, and I don't even get a chance to talk to her properly."* I shared a similar sentiment. I hadn't been able to spend any quality time with Maya while she was conscious. I began to wonder if this was why she always complained about not being able to think clearly.

Sometimes, your mind becomes your enemy, conjuring up unthinkable scenarios as reality. I couldn't shake off the nagging thought of why they persisted in keeping her so heavily medicated despite the doctor's objections and the hospital already administering morphine for her pain. Maya had herself expressed her dislike for the way she felt after taking the CBD. To Maya's father's dismay, they refrained from giving her any CBD that night, and her medication dosage was reduced, with the option to administer it if necessary.

The following day, Maya's parents picked me up in *Thamel*. When we reached the hospital, it was a pleasant sight to see Maya up and conversing. She looked healthy that day and had also regained some of her appetite. It seemed like she had flushed out all the medication that made her feel drowsy, and her face glowed with vitality.

Interestingly, Biru's grandmother was also admitted at the same hospital, a few rooms away from Maya's. The room buzzed with people dropping by and engaging in continuous conversations with Maya. Even Diya joined later, amplifying the noise in the room. She discussed various topics with everyone but chose not to acknowledge my presence. The room was frequently occupied by more than ten people at a time. On one side, Kiran shared his views on the recent political situation in Nepal with a friend, while Diya, perched on the edge of Maya's bed, simultaneously planned Biru's birthday party. Amidst party planning, she ensured to consult Maya, who responded weakly before closing her eyes.

I sat quietly on the couch. Maya would occasionally glance at me as if to ask me if I was okay. I would nod and smile at her.

One of Biru's aunts entered the room and engaged in conversation with Maya. Unfortunately, like some others, she overlooked the cues indicating Maya's fatigue and the need for rest. The conversation persisted for a lengthy forty-two minutes before she finally left. Maya's dad and mom were also getting ready to leave and I asked if I could catch a ride with them. Later, Biru wanted them to drop his mom off too. I was not getting in the same car with her.

* * *

Despite Biru's family having visited us in 2015 and his parents staying in my house in the United States, they never communicated with me properly whenever they saw me in Nepal. Only Biru's dad would approach me, engaging in conversation as if genuinely concerned. He would discuss hydroelectricity, a topic I had previously shown interest in and sought his expertise on. Even eight years later, or each subsequent year since 2015, he would still bring up the same topic. On the other hand, Biru's brother never spoke to me. His wife, with whom I had bonded at some parties where we shared greetings and laughter, never bothered to acknowledge me in public. Whether it was the influence of alcohol or sheer indifference at the moment, their recognition still held little importance to me.

Years ago, when I mentioned feeling ignored to Maya and hence my discomfort in visiting that family, she would become upset and discuss the matter with her sister in my defense. I urged her not to bother, as their opinions were based solely on the impression Diya portrayed of me. Regardless, I knew it wouldn't be anything positive.

I thought, like Biru, the entire family might be a group of affluent, conceited individuals.

Once in Maya's apartment, I was preparing whiskey and wine for all the guests as per their preference. Ryan, Diya's son, was watching me do so. He asked if I had poured one for myself and I replied, *"No kid, I don't drink!"* To which he replied, *"But you used to, a lot."* If a child could remember such a delicate matter, why would I even be surprised by anything else she talked about.

A friend of mine from India, called me once to share something important. He revealed that he had met Biru and Diya, along with Biru's brother, Ram, at a mutual friend's wedding in India. During a conversation where someone inquired about Maya, Biru had claimed that she was alone in the United States with no one taking care of her. According to Biru, now that she was back in Nepal, they were there for her, and she was doing much better. Unhappy with this misinformation, Ram defended me, asserting, *"That's not true. Her husband was taking care of her full time."*

I've been informed that Ram stood up for me once again when Biru spread a similar story during a family gathering. Ram's steadfast support in defending the truth about Maya's situation was deeply appreciated, particularly in light of false narratives propagated by Biru. Reflecting on his actions, I recognized the significance of advocating for honesty and integrity, even in casual conversations. Although I hadn't yet had the chance to thank Ram for his defense, I held onto the hope of expressing my gratitude to him someday.

* * *

Maya's dad seemed a little puzzled when I mentioned that I would stay a little longer and that my friend would pick me up. Whether he understood my intentions or not remained uncertain. As they left, Diya promptly suggested to Maya that they should go for a walk. Maya, albeit reluctantly, slowly got off the bed, and without a word, Diya took her hand and they both left the room. There was no indication of whether they would return soon or if I was invited to join them. I anticipated Maya giving me a glance or a signal of acknowledgement, but that didn't happen either. Left with no clear indication of their return, I decided to call *Pathau,* the Nepalese version of Uber, and quietly exited the room.

About two hours after returning to my hotel room, I received a text from Maya, *"You left? Sorry didn't know it would take time."* I replied, *"That's ok. I didn't know where you guys had gone so I left."* I reassured myself that Maya might not have been thinking clearly. After all, it was the first time in a while she was feeling a bit better.

The next day's visit wasn't very productive either. Maya drifted in and out of her sleep but appeared better overall. Not having taken the CBD oil the previous night made her look more alert, but with someone always present in the room, I didn't get to spend any quality time with her. There were certain things I wanted to discuss with her. I always had something to share, whether it was something witty or a funny anecdote that would bring a smile to her face.

The doctor had visited her in the morning and after checking her vitals, decided that she could be discharged. Maya needed assurance that the pain wouldn't return like the last time, as she didn't want to make the late-night runs to the hospital. Now that she was feeling better, Diya was excited that Maya could attend Biru's birthday party scheduled for the next day. Upon being asked by Diya, Maya reluctantly obliged. I couldn't believe it; Maya could hardly move without being helped, and here she was being encouraged by her sister to dance the next day. I thought it was foolish to suggest stress and exertion instead of a restful evening.

As usual, I began convincing Maya, explaining to her that attending the party was a bad idea given that her WBC and platelet levels had dropped to the minimum. Anything lower could jeopardize her health. Her dad and brother agreed, and Maya frowned before reluctantly nodding in agreement. I wasn't sure what heated discussion may have followed after Diya found out that Maya wasn't going, but I imagine they may have heard a mouthful, especially if they mentioned that it was my idea for Maya not to attend.

Maya was discharged the next day. Diya had organized the surprise birthday party for Biru the same evening. I had no intentions of attending the party if I was invited and assumed none of Maya's family members would go either, choosing instead to stay by Maya's side. Around 7 pm Maya's dad called me and asked if I was going. I said I couldn't party with so much going on. He insisted that I should come for a bit, but I refused. He mentioned he was on his way. Kiran and his wife had already left for the party. When I asked who was with Maya, he replied, *"Everyone is there."*

"Everyone who?" I asked.

"Her mom and the nurse," he replied.

The following day, more guests visited Maya at home. Unfortunately, her pain persisted without improvement, despite the continued administration of morphine and CBD oil as insisted by the family.

*　*　*

These thoughts and the multitude of questions bombarded my brain, desperately searching for answers. Was I overreacting? In America, I seized every opportunity to be with Maya, fearing the worst. Yet, the situation felt different here. Maya's sister seemed to have different priorities, even when they were in the States. They didn't hesitate to have date nights every Friday, spending the night at a hotel. When they needed to go, they went without reservation.

At times when Maya was exceptionally weak during the nights Diya and Biru were away, they would assure me they'd return early. Consequently, I would go home for the night. The following morning, I'd receive a call from Maya's mother, seemingly complaining and indirectly suggesting that Maya was being stubborn and not heeding her advice to rest. When I inquired why, her mother would mention that, despite not feeling well, Maya had gone to CVS to buy eggs and bread, for breakfast, for the kids the day after her chemo.

Her mother would then imply that Diya and Biru hadn't returned from their date night, even though it was already past noon. She would subtly suggest that I come over early just in case there were tasks to be done. I would hurry over, ensuring Maya rested, and even prepare lunch for the family, understanding the purpose behind her mother's call.

When the couple returned, rejuvenated from their night of intimacy, they would inquire about Maya's well-being. When I informed them that Maya had thrown up and couldn't eat much the previous night, Diya would respond with, *"Oh no, maybe because I wasn't there to feed her."* She would then rush to make some juice or a snack, while I discreetly stepped aside to avoid confrontation. This was Diya's approach.

Expressing my discontent about this, the parents would side with me, intensifying my dissatisfaction. However, they never confronted Diya and Biru about it. Maya was a bit afraid and more concerned of hurting her sister's feelings, given all they were doing for her. At times, I wondered if Diya perceived me as competition and went to great lengths to prove she loved Maya more than I did. I wasn't competing, nor was I attempting to reconcile with Maya. My sole purpose was to help Maya get better in any way possible.

When Maya's parents occasionally confronted Diya, she would burst out with anger, *"Oh God, why can't people see how much I am doing for my sister? Why can't anyone appreciate it?"* I would just ignore her when she got into such fits. She didn't bother me much and I never stepped on her toes unless she crossed the line. This gave her even more reason to dislike me, as I was one of the very few in her circle who would tell her like it was to her face and didn't take her nonsense!

* * *

One day, while I was standing by her side in the hospital, Maya mustered the strength to share with me that she was aware the recent PET scan hadn't yielded favorable results. No one had informed Maya about the spreading, and I had played along, pretending not to know, asking her why she felt this way. She revealed that when she inquired about the report, the doctor informed her that he would discuss it with Diya and decide on a new chemotherapy program.

Unaware that there were no new alternative procedures in line for her, Maya remained hopeful. The medical team had already communicated that the best they could do was manage her pain with painkillers, and there were no other treatment plans awaiting her. My heart sank, when she said, *"But I don't care. I'm going to fight this and get healed."* I admired her resilience and determination to stay strong, taking each day as it came. I didn't want her to give up, especially considering she had already emerged from depression, and the fear of her relapsing into it loomed large.

Her health was deteriorating and witnessing her decline was heartbreaking. The uncertainty of the future weighed heavily on everyone's minds. While I tried to hold onto hope, there was a nagging fear lingering in the corner of my heart. Some friends had gently advised me to prepare for the worst, but I resisted such thoughts. Instead, I held on to the vision of Maya stepping off that hospital bed, regaining her strength, and returning to the United States, where her vibrant career and promising future awaited her.

I had plans to step back from Maya's life once she returned, intending to maintain our friendship and offer support if she needed it in Texas. I had also anticipated helping her settle into a new apartment in Houston, as she had expressed excitement about the prospect. Additionally, Maya had invited me to accompany her to Norway for work-related seminars after her return to Texas, a much-needed break for just the two of us, a plan that once felt exhilarating but now seemed distant and uncertain. Amidst these thoughts, I hesitated to contemplate the future, preferring to focus on the present, even though I was unhappy with how things were unfolding.

I couldn't shake the thought, *"What if her treatment had continued in the States?"* The United States was renowned for cancer treatment, attracting celebrities, politicians, and those who could afford it. Yet, Maya's family remained determined that she would recover in Nepal. Did Diya already know that Maya couldn't be saved? Despite assurances that the treatment was coordinated with her oncologist at MSK, it felt akin to a doctor instructing a nurse to perform surgery over the phone or a chef guiding a sous chef to replicate a secret recipe.

It's often said that it was Maya's decision to return to Nepal. She had expressed it herself to me. But were those truly her words? When exploring options, we even visited a different oncologist in Boston to gather opinions about clinical trials. The doctor had reviewed Maya's report and mentioned, *"Seems like your chemotherapy is working. God forbid, if anything changes, then we could consider the clinical trial."* However, when the treatment didn't yield the desired results, nobody mentioned the trial. Even with my numerous pleas to Maya's dad, urging him to convince Diya, who seemed to have taken charge, Maya's father never acted on my messages. It felt futile, leaving me feeling helpless.

Maya believed that returning home would ease the burden on her family, particularly her sister, allowing her to be with her kids without having to stay away for extended periods. She also feared that Diya's frequent visits might strain her relationship with Biru and her in-laws. It was unfortunate that Kiran couldn't join Maya, even with his futile pleas to the United States embassy to grant him a visa.

Maya expressed her desire for her family to share meaningful moments with her, recognizing the complexity of the decision. While I empathized with her motivations, I encouraged her to approach the relocation positively, hoping for a recovery rather than viewing it solely as spending her final days with her parents. Diya assumed control of the decision-making process, asserting that the move would aid Maya in battling depression. Although I agreed with the potential benefits, the decision seemed premeditated, as Diya had prompted Maya to inquire about conducting chemotherapy in Nepal, days before she learned about the cancer's recurrence. Despite my disagreement when Maya had asked the oncologist about such possibility, Maya had insisted, saying, *"She just wants me to be informed."*

Maya, usually outspoken and independent, now found herself in a delicate state, weakened by illness unable to think clearly. The strong-willed individual she once was had become fragile, and a sense of fear seemed to permeate her interactions and decision-making, particularly in her relationship with her sister, Diya.

Maya used to speak up to her sister and offer advice or express herself when she believed her sister was wrong. However, while battling cancer, Maya seemed to have lost her assertiveness. She was once strongly opinionated about things, but now, if her sister opposed her opinions, Maya remained silent, fearing she might hurt her sister's feelings. The dynamic between them appeared to shift from love to fear, with Maya feeling helpless, while Diya seemed to have taken control. Even my words held no weight in front of Diya's dominance.

With me temporarily sidelined, Diya assumed the role of decision-maker. Maya, aware of her vulnerable state and perhaps feeling dependent on Diya for care, refrained from voicing dissent. It marked a noticeable shift. Maya, once assertive and vocal, now seemed hesitant to challenge Diya's decisions. Diya, sensing this power dynamic, seized the opportunity to assert control, subtly reinforcing her authority. Maya's fear of disagreement and Diya's opportunistic assertion of authority created a complex and uneasy scenario, not just for me, but also for friends who wished to visit Maya. Everyone sought moments to connect with Maya discreetly, away from Diya's influence.

I needed a break. If Maya had been alone, I wouldn't have thought twice about it. But now with so many around, it was difficult to find a moment alone with her. I couldn't even get the chance to ask her how she was feeling and hear it directly from her. I needed to get out of Kathmandu, away from all this negativity and to recharge. I told Pasa that we should get out for a few days. He agreed that I needed to take time off and he adjusted his own hectic schedule and we set off to Barahi Jungle Lodge the next day.

* * *

BARAHI JUNGLE LODGE

PASA and I boarded the tourist bus early in the morning, embarking on our journey to Chitwan. The anticipated travel time was five hours, but with the ongoing monsoon season and daily rainfall since my arrival, concerns of potential landslides loomed over us. Navigating the narrow roads, scarcely wider than a single lane in the United States, presented challenges, especially with the added risk of being stranded for hours or even days in the event of a landslide.

For locals like us, accustomed to traversing these roads since childhood, the familiarity bred a certain resilience. We had navigated these paths routinely, shuttling to and from boarding schools and returning for holidays—a ritual performed three to four times annually for nearly a decade. However, for foreigners, every twist and turn might evoke fear. The two-lane road seemed terrifyingly small, and the stakes were raised by the potential consequence of a slight driver error—sending the vehicle tumbling down the hill into the swollen river ready to engulf anything in its path. The river, once formidable and populated with rafters embracing its currents, now flowed calmly, yet it seemed restless. Even the most daring thrill-seekers hesitated to challenge the might of Mother Nature in this season of unpredictable weather.

We were fortunate, encountering no landslides along the way. After occasional stops for lunch and restroom breaks, we arrived in Chitwan. We had coordinated to meet an old friend whom I hadn't seen for decades. He came to receive us from the bus stop, and after stopping for refreshments at his house, he drove us to our hotel, which was about forty-five minutes away, far from the maddening crowd. We were eager to settle in and enjoy a relaxing time for the next couple of days.

It felt as though the hotel staff were attuned to my needs. They spared no effort in delivering the finest hospitality I had ever encountered. When we arrived, they allowed us to freshen up in our room, nestled within individual huts designed with architectural elements that reflected jungle living while offering all the luxuries for our comfort. Then, we were treated to a lavish meal, truly fit for royalty.

As the weather cooled down, we embarked on a village walk guided by friendly locals who eagerly shared insights into village life. They explained the reasons behind the unique architecture of the houses, the significance of the tattoos worn by older women, and the simple yet fulfilling lifestyle embraced by the villagers. Although having little in material wealth, everyone appeared genuinely content. They seemed to possess a richness of happiness, grateful for the simplicity of their lives.

While I couldn't help but envy their contentment, I knew deep down that I wouldn't be able to adapt to their way of life. My reliance on modern conveniences had become ingrained, sparing me from the concerns of fetching drinking water from afar or gathering firewood for cooking.

The children in the villages were oblivious to iPads, and televisions were a rarity in many homes. Instead, they found joy in simple pleasures, playing with whatever came their way. They chased ducks, frolicked with dogs, built stone houses, and dashed around trees and bushes, their laughter echoing through the air. As we passed by, they greeted us with radiant smiles, eagerly shouting, *"Hello!"* while waving their tiny hands.

Some children assisted their mothers in feeding the ducks, herding them back into their coops or coaxing them out to be fed. Their innocence was palpable, and their contentment with their surroundings was evident. It was truly remarkable.

Guiding us through this enchanting scene were two young women in their twenties, their hair neatly styled in buns and their English flawless. As they shared further insights, I couldn't help but be filled with an unshakeable smile. It was a stark contrast from the tears I shed just days prior. I found solace in this simplicity, even though I knew it was temporary. The pain I faced still awaited me, but in that moment, I was willing to immerse myself in this bliss forever.

It felt as though nature and the wilderness had conspired to bestow upon us a remarkable experience. The following morning, we embarked on a jungle safari, setting out in the dim hours before dawn. As we delved into the depths of the jungle, we were greeted by the sight of a majestic leopard, countless deer, and imposing rhinos. Our luck peaked when we caught a glimpse of a tiger, stealthily trailing a baby rhino who steadfastly remained by its mother's side. While I acknowledged the cycle of nature, I couldn't help but hope that the tiger would refrain from harming the vulnerable calf.

Returning to the hotel after the safari, we indulged in a refreshing dip in the pool. Suddenly, a wave of commotion swept through the area, accompanied by the urgent instructions of the manager directing the staff to rush to the riverbank in search of the floating baby rhino.

The manager received a call from another hotel located a few yards upriver, prompting me to rush to the riverbank to offer assistance in spotting the missing rhino calf. Within minutes, army rafts arrived with individuals engaged in the search effort. As they approached, I anxiously inquired about their progress, only to be met with the distressing news that the calf was suspected dead, seen floating belly up.

Struggling to process the grim possibility, I retreated to the shallow end of the pool, seeking solace in meditation. Immersing myself in the water, I found a sense of weightlessness that transported me to a serene state of mind. Despite the somber news, I remained focused on the present moment, allowing meditation to ease my troubled thoughts.

Thankfully, the outcome was far more hopeful than anticipated. The rhino calf was miraculously rescued alive and reunited with its mother, evoking a wave of gratitude among all who witnessed the heartwarming reunion, me included.

Later that evening, the sunset safari was a breathtaking experience, reminiscent of the earlier jungle excursion but culminating in a unique setting where the *Narayani* and *Rapti* rivers merged. The hotel had thoughtfully arranged a lavish food stall on the riverbank, complete with chefs and waiters ready to cater to our every need. Underneath a tent facing the setting sun, we were treated to an array of delectable snacks, including pork bellies, barbecued pineapple, *momo*, roasted chicken, peanuts, and our choice of beverages.

As we savored the flavors and soaked in the tranquil ambiance, the sky transformed into a kaleidoscope of colors, transitioning from bright red to soothing hues as the sun dipped below the horizon. It was a moment of pure bliss, a stark contrast to the hustle and bustle of city life in the United States, where opportunities to connect with nature are often scarce.

Reflecting on these moments, I couldn't help but appreciate the healing effect nature had on my soul. While living in the city confines us, I often find solace in waking early to witness the sunrise. The sight of my backyard bathed in morning hues, especially during winter, never fails to take my breath away, leaving me yearning for the perpetual beauty of snow-covered landscapes.

* * *

As per our original plan, we were due to depart the following day, but I found myself yearning for more time in this oasis of nature. Tentatively, I broached the idea of extending our stay with Pasa, hoping he might share my sentiment. To my relief, he was open to the idea, and we agreed to linger for another night, departing on Saturday instead.

Opting for a more leisurely pace on our final day, we decided to forgo strenuous activities and simply bask in the tranquility of our surroundings. We spent the day lounging by the pool, taking leisurely strolls, and indulging in much-needed naps. It was a rejuvenating experience, allowing us to fully appreciate the luxury of our lodge and the serenity it offered.

* * *

As the time to leave approached, our car was set to arrive precisely at 7 am. We missed breakfast but the manager kindly packed our lunch boxes for the journey ahead. After exchanging traditional goodbyes, he bid us farewell, inviting us to visit again soon. *"Of course, I'll see you soon,"* I replied. Though I've uttered this line many times before, this time I meant it wholeheartedly, knowing that I would indeed return very soon.

After our arrival in Kathmandu around 1:30 pm on a Saturday afternoon, my intention was to unwind and relax. I headed straight to the hotel, took a refreshing shower, and settled into the couch. Initially, I had planned to visit Maya the following day, a Sunday, partly because I was hesitant about visiting on a Saturday. Saturdays were typically when Biru and Diya would come by and stay late.

With Maya now in the picture, I found myself uncertain about their schedule. Knowing Biru and Diya's tendency to disregard conventional schedules and create their own, I couldn't predict their plans this time.

Despite my reservations, a nagging feeling persisted, urging me to go and see Maya. There was something pulling me towards her, compelling me to push aside my uncertainties and take the leap.

After sending a message to Maya's dad inquiring about her condition, he responded indicating that she was feeling very down. Prompted by concern, I immediately placed a call to him, seeking further clarification.

"So, who's with her right now?" I asked.

"We're all here," he replied solemnly.

Hoping I wouldn't need to explicitly ask about Biru and Diya's presence, I felt a wave of relief when Maya's dad informed me, *"Diya is sick and down with a cold."* Without hesitation, I expressed my intention to visit, and he sounded genuinely pleased by the prospect.

After ending the call, I wasted no time. I quickly arranged for a bike ride with *Pathao* and headed straight to Maya's place, eager to offer whatever support and comfort I could.

As the driver navigated through the streets, I couldn't help but feel frustrated by their apparent lack of reliance on the map in their app. Instead of following the digital guide, they opted to ask for directions, leaving me feeling helpless in guiding them through the bustling streets of Kathmandu.

The sudden surge in population and rapid development of real estate only added to the confusion, making it even more challenging to navigate the maze-like streets. Even with my best efforts to provide guidance, the ever-changing landscape of the city left me feeling disoriented and uncertain.

We had barely reached halfway when there was a sudden downpour. Ignoring the rain, the driver kept going, hoping it would subside soon. Eventually, we had to pull over and take out the rain cape. I didn't have one myself, but fortunately, all *Pathao* bike drivers carried capes large enough to cover both the rider and the passenger. It felt a bit odd to share the same cape with a stranger, but it served its purpose well. Although we were both soaked, it at least prevented us from getting even wetter.

* * *

MAYA'S HOUSE VISIT

AS I rang the doorbell and helplessly stood outside the gate, hoping that the maid would increase the pace of her footsteps, I was drenched again by the pouring rain. She finally got to the door, let me in, and handed me the umbrella she had brought for me. I looked at her, then at myself, and back at her. I saw her smiling, understanding my silent grievance. I ran inside and met Maya's dad, who got me a towel and asked if I wanted to change into something of his. I declined and headed upstairs to see Maya.

Maya was lying in bed, with an oxygen mask attached to her and receiving painkillers via IV. The newly hired nurse was seated by the bedside, and Maya's mother occupied a seat next to her head. When Maya's mother saw me, she greeted me and instructed me to come in wearing a mask as per the doctor's instructions. Maya's dad had asked the maid to fetch a mask for me, but she seemed to have forgotten and never returned. I informed them that I wouldn't come in but only wanted to catch a glimpse.

Maya was fast asleep, and every breath she took seemed like a struggle. Her body shook with each exhale, indicating the severity of her condition. Her potassium levels had dropped significantly, and maintaining her oxygen levels was crucial. She seemed asleep but was likely aware of everything happening around her. Sensing her awareness, I chose not to disturb her and quietly left the room.

* * *

Seeing Maya in this fragile state stirred memories of our time together in America. During such days, she often sought me out for massages, indicating whether she desired a head, shoulder, or full-body massage. After each session, she would express feelings of relaxation and rejuvenation.

One evening, as I worked in my room and Maya was engrossed in a TV show, I sensed her program was coming to an end, and she was getting ready to go to bed. Wanting to make tea, I headed to the kitchen. Maya noticed me and asked if I had come to watch TV. I replied that I would stay for a bit, and she insisted on joining me. Taking her usual spot on the couch, Maya gradually drew closer, eventually resting her head on my lap and intertwining her fingers with mine. It was a simple yet intimate moment, one that spoke volumes about the bond we shared.

Her actions always caught me off guard, and this particular gesture touched my heart deeply. Tears welled up in my eyes, but I couldn't wipe them away as she held my hand. A tear rolled down her cheek, and when I looked down, I saw tears streaming down her face as well. It was a heartbreaking moment, simultaneously sad and beautiful. Though separated, our care for each other was unselfish and profound. Our connection transcended the typical dynamics of a husband and wife, making it something more precious than words could express. I couldn't have asked for anything more.

Seeing Maya in such a vulnerable state, I longed to comfort her, to hold her close and soothe her with gentle strokes on her back. However, with so many people surrounding her, it was impossible to do so. It might have been just my perception, but it seemed that everyone attending to her was lacking the gentleness and care that I had always provided her with. In that moment, I yearned for us to be together again, to shield her from the rough handling and ensure that things were done according to her preferences.

Yet, I had to face the harsh reality. The mere signature on a piece of paper that declared us no longer husband and wife, bounded us to respect it, even though it was deemed void. The legalities dictated our separation, but my heart still longed to care for Maya in the way she was accustomed to, to provide her with the comfort and tenderness she deserved.

* * *

Leaving everyone with Maya, her dad and I retreated to adjacent room, which was once Maya and my own, but now belonged to him. There we sipped tea and nibbled on the cookies the maid had brought us. Our conversation revolved mostly around Maya and the updates from the doctors. He tried to remain composed, but sadness lingered on his face, and I could tell he was struggling to hold back his tears. If we had been on the phone, I'm certain we both would have succumbed to our emotions. But here, in person, we did our best to keep it together, perhaps both influenced by the notion ingrained in us from childhood: *"Boys don't cry."*

As I moved about the house, I overheard Maya's mom engage in conversation with her. Concerned, I approached the maid to inquire if Maya was awake. She informed me that Maya had just managed to eat the smallest bite, more out of obligation than appetite. Feeling a rush of urgency, I hurried to Maya's room, informing her dad that I would only be a moment.

Maya had already closed her eyes when I entered. I softly whispered, *"Hello Maiya!"* She made an effort to look at me from the top of her eyes, tilting her head slightly and managing a smile. She tried to raise her hand to wave, reaching out for mine, but I gently told her to rest up, explaining that I was in the other room conversing with her dad. She smiled in understanding and murmured *'okay'* before closing her eyes again.

Maya's dad and I extended our conversation, finding a certain comfort in each other's company. To maintain privacy, we closed the door to prevent eavesdropping, especially since Maya's mom had a knack for it. At one point, Kiran peeked into the room, seemingly surprised to find me there. He smiled and nodded, explaining that he had been taking a nap, which accounted for his absence over the past three hours. I reassured him that I wasn't bored and enjoyed talking with his dad. Kiran excused himself, promising to return shortly.

Later, I could hear a slight commotion from the adjacent room where Maya was resting, but I didn't think much of it, considering Maya's family's tendency to be boisterous. Whenever Kiran and Diya conversed, it sounded like they were almost yelling, likely a way to assert dominance. Disregarding the noise, I continued my discussion with Maya's dad. We delved into the surprising aspect of Maya seeking a divorce while facing such challenges. He offered an explanation that I found hard to accept. According to him, Maya wanted a divorce to ensure that I didn't feel tethered to her during her difficult times. She aimed for me to find someone else and move forward with my life, as per her father's perspective.

Maya and I shared a unique bond, characterized by our ability to engage in lighthearted conversation and reminisce about our past without any expectations of reconciliation. Even with this mutual understanding, Maya's decision to pursue a divorce amidst her ordeal remained a source of perplexity for me. I often found myself questioning the reasoning behind her choice, pondering, *"Why? Why was removing me from her life deemed more crucial than focusing on her own well-being?"*

Nevertheless, I harbored no ill will towards Maya for her decision. It was a reality I had come to accept, albeit with lingering questions. I couldn't help but wonder why she hadn't broached this topic earlier, particularly when I first began caring for her at her apartment. Perhaps there were underlying factors at play that I was yet to comprehend.

* * *

During our younger days, we both worked hard with the shared goal of buying a house. Whenever I brought up the topic, Maya didn't delve deeper as it seemed implausible. One day, when I mentioned having saved up enough for a down payment, her eyes had sparkled with excitement. The revelation that I had saved a substantial amount for a house had taken her by surprise, and she was genuinely pleased. At that time, Maya didn't have a permanent job, and she was cautious about spending. I encouraged her to save, and when we decided to sublet our rented house, I let her keep all the rent and utilities paid by the renters. She never questioned me about it. I was happy to be the provider, having worked hard since my arrival in the United States. Buying a house brought us one step closer to our American dream. I took pride in depositing extra money into her account after she moved to Stamford. Despite deeming it unnecessary, I explained that it was to make up for the mortgage payments she had made during times when I couldn't contribute. Her happiness was my priority, and I always wanted her to be content.

* * *

Later Kiran entered the room, his expression conveyed a sense of urgency. He stood there silently, his gaze fixed on me, before finally speaking up. *"I think I need your help, and I believe you're the only one who can assist us."*

Curious and concerned, I inquired, *"What is it?"*

"We're running low on oxygen, and I'm not sure where we can find more, especially on a Saturday," Kiran explained urgently, subtly suggesting that I should reach out to Arya.

Without hesitation, I assured him, *"Of course. You don't even have to think twice about asking. Arya and her mom inquire about Maya every day, and they would be more than willing to help."*

* * *

Arya, a dear friend of mine, was in charge of her family's oxygen company. Knowing the severity of Maya's situation and my urgent requirement for oxygen, I immediately contacted Arya. Our families shared a strong bond, with Arya's mother, Neera Aunty, being best friends with my mom. As a result, they frequently checked in on Maya's well-being through my mom.

As I explained the critical situation to Arya, she immediately empathized, expressing similar concerns to Kiran's. Arya reassured me that Kiran could contact her directly if a similar issue arose in the future. She promptly arranged for Kiran to retrieve as many oxygen cylinders as necessary from her factory. Despite the logistical challenge of delivering them on a Saturday, Arya coordinated with her team to ensure Kiran encountered no obstacles. Unfortunately, her general manager had suffered a heart attack that morning, further complicating matters. Arya's commitment to assisting Kiran during this crisis was evident as she mobilized resources and communicated with various staff members to ensure a smooth process.

* * *

The noise in the room grew louder as Biru peeked in, engaged in a phone call. He flashed a smile upon seeing me, to which I reciprocated, but our interaction was brief. Diya's voice could also be heard from the adjacent room. Sensing urgency, I approached to investigate and learned that Maya's oxygen levels had plummeted. Biru had brought another tank, but they encountered difficulty changing it due to a broken knob on the old one. I stood at the doorway, feeling powerless, as they deliberated on the next course of action.

As I raised my hand to wave at Diya when our eyes met, I received no acknowledgment. Perhaps she didn't see me amidst the panic in the room. After everyone had left, I caught a glance of the oxygen tank and noticed what it was missing. Realizing what was needed to open it, I went downstairs in search of the right wrench. While I was rummaging for the tool, I received word that Biru had successfully opened the tank and connected the new one. Maya's gasping for breath added urgency to the situation. With the nurse's assistance, Maya was helped to sit upright, providing her with support. As Maya's breathing gradually eased, the nurse gently guided her back to a reclined position. With a subtle signal, Maya indicated that she felt some relief from the distressing episode.

They decided to take Maya to the hospital and called for an ambulance. When Maya's dad heard this, I could see him worried. He would utter, *"They said they were taking her tomorrow. Why are they taking her now?"* He did not know what was going on. I felt sorry for him.

He seemed lost, and to compound the situation, he was experiencing memory lapses. Events from just three days ago would escape him, such as the day when I hadn't taken a ride with him from the hospital upon their return, or the incident when he gave a ride to Biru's mom. When I reminded him of these occurrences, he would respond with a puzzled, *"Did I?"* and slowly avert his gaze, staring blankly from one corner of the room to another. He expressed his growing forgetfulness, making it challenging for him to recall recent events. Initiating conversations about people required providing detailed introductions, including where he had met them, before delving into the discussion. While his struggle with remembering names and faces was apparent, to my surprise, he retained recollection of our deep talks back in the States. The difficulty lay in remembering people and their associated details, prompting me to describe them to him for clarity.

"Uncle, remember the tall guy with the beard?" This is how I had to start a conversation rather than just stating the name which he wouldn't remember even though he had good quality time with them when he had met them.

I conveyed to him the importance of Maya receiving medical attention at the hospital, emphasizing the superior care she would receive there compared to remaining where she was. While he acknowledged the rationale behind my explanation, something appeared to trouble him. He maintained a blank expression, frequently closing his eyes for extended periods before offering any response.

When the ambulance arrived, Biru took charge, announcing his intention to carry Maya to the vehicle. He tasked me with handling the oxygen cylinder, although he felt compelled to provide an explanation. It was evident to me that the girls wouldn't be able to manage the heavy cylinder themselves, which is why he was asking me to take charge of it. I stood there silently, not eager to take the lead in anything. I believed in handling things calmly, all the while observing the commotion in the room. I anticipated that the paramedics would bring a stretcher and transport Maya down without unnecessary fuss.

Fortunately, the paramedic arrived with a stretcher, but surprisingly, he seemed confused and unsure of what to do. I had to instruct him to position the stretcher next to Maya. As Biru lifted her, against my advice, I directed others to slide the stretcher beneath Maya. While step one was completed, the *strongman* was already out of breath. Biru then requested my assistance, as he mentioned having a bad back, to carry one side of the stretcher.

*　*　**

I thought to myself, *'Of course asshole! Of course, I know you have a bad back. How could I forget? You made me carry all the furniture for your daughter's party three story down while the elevators had chosen to fail on the same day while you sought your wife's approval whether you should have breakfast before you left. We were already late; couldn't you see that people had started to come and we were the hosts? I remember, when I was done loading all the heavy stuff, after making thirteen trips up and down three floors, it was then you decided to walk down with your arms around your wife while you carried a small bag with the other. I remember every detail asshole. I also remember that Maya had paid for all the food, and I had bought the drinks for YOUR daughter's birthday party as you guys were contemplating whether to spend so much on people you didn't know.'*

'I know you have a bad back when you made me carry sixteen suitcases from Maya's apartment, helping me only to wheel it but leaving

everything for me to carry it down the stairs and then lift it and load it in my car so I could drop you off to the airport. Of course, I know you have a bad back when you still decided to take jujitsu classes just for the heck of it and then later coming back to the apartment tired as if you had just fought a real fight in the octagon! Of course, I remember because even then you had asked me to massage your back and help you stretch your arms. Of course, I remember every detail, asshole.'

* * *

When I took hold of the stretcher, I directed everyone to step back and assigned two people to the other side, managing the top part of the stretcher myself. I ensured Maya's well-being by checking in, *"Maiya, you ok?"* She nodded in approval, reassuring she was hanging in, eliciting a brave attempt at a smile. While I held the top portion of the stretcher, Kiran and the paramedic managed the bottom part as we descended the stairs. I provided instructions to keep it straight, ensuring no tilting. Staying calm, I asked Maya to maintain her composure during the challenging moment.

When we reached the first floor, we carefully placed Maya on the main stretcher. As we pushed it toward the ambulance, a light drizzle began. While whispering something to Maya and trying to discern her response, a raindrop fell on her face, causing a startle that turned into a meek smile. Swiftly, I wiped her face and shielded it from further rain until she was safely pushed into the ambulance. Diya and the maid had already boarded, and I could hear Biru asking Kiran if he wanted to ride with him. Kiran declined, opting to drive his own car. While Biru inquired others, there was no mention of me joining the ride.

Later when the ambulance was gone, Maya's dad and I sat in the front yard of the house. I tried to calm him down while the mother seemed to pace back and forth with heavy breathing. I was once again reassuring that everything would be fine and that it was best that Maya was in the hospital. At least we wouldn't be worried about the oxygen running out. He sat there quietly. When I told him I too should get going he replied, *"No, you're staying, and we are having dinner and are going to continue our conversation."* I slowly put it out there that I too was tired as I had just come back from Chitwan the very same day. He would mumble something and look away.

Later Kiran, his wife, and brother-in-law along with the maid came downstairs. The constant talking over each other was not something new in that family so if you ignored what they were talking about, it probably would go unnoticed. Maya's dad and I were still seated at the front yard while those ready, got in the car. Kiran rolled out the window and asked me, *"You'll be here for another two hours, right? I'll see you then and we will catch up."*

I thought he was inquiring if I wanted to accompany them to the hospital. How I wished to be by Maya's side at that moment. I could have made the request or gone on my own, but the circumstances felt inappropriate for such demands. With a multitude of people already heading to the hospital, I trusted that Maya was in good hands. Although I didn't voice anything, I abruptly stood up, bid farewell to Maya's dad, and asked Kiran if I could join him, planning to get off in *Thamel* if that was his route. Confirming that it was, I hopped into the car. After leaving, in the car, Mala expressed that I should have stayed a bit longer. I inquired why and she said so that I could give company to the old couple! *"Seriously?"* I thought.

After they dropped me off, I wandered through the streets of *Thamel* and headed to the hotel. I didn't know what to do. I wasn't hungry so I tried to sleep. However, I kept waking up in the middle of the night. Around 1 am, I messaged Maya's dad, observing that he was still active. It concerned me to see him up at such late hours. I wondered if there was a specific reason for him being awake or if, like me, he couldn't find any sleep.

"Everything okay?" I inquired.

"Yes, she is resting and seems to be catching up on her sleep," he replied. I breathed a sigh of relief and attempted to sleep once more.

* * *

The next day, I visited *Swayambhunath* temple along with Pasa. It was a place where I found solace and tranquility. My intention was to light some butter lamps for Maya, praying for her speedy recovery. In a somewhat lighthearted manner, I even tried to "bribe" the Gods, promising that if they healed Maya, I would dedicate the rest of my life to social service, helping the poor and needy in any way I could.

Upon reaching *Swayambhu*, the temple appeared more like a gathering place for *'Tik Tokers'* than pilgrims. It seemed everyone was engaged in dance moves or strutting down a catwalk. Many held cameras with lenses so long that I had only seen them on National Geographic channels capturing pictures of wildlife. Yet, here they were, used to capture shots of young individuals with bright red or blue hair, some in wildly baggy pants and others in skinny jeans. Despite appearing undernourished, everyone managed to strike a perfect pose for their Instagram or Facebook profile pictures. The noise of young kids and a crowd unsuitable for a temple was a turn-off. After spending about ten minutes enjoying the view of the hills, Pasa and I decided to head back.

I wished to visit Maya alone, so I texted her father, asking for the room number she was assigned in the hospital. He responded, but instead of providing the room number, he suggested that I relax or take care of my health. Since he didn't address my initial request, I asked again. Ignored twice, on the third attempt, without responding to his inquiry about my well-being, I directly texted, *"So I guess you don't know the room number?"*

He replied, *"Same floor same room."* Why was it so difficult for him to give it to me? This too, as if, he wanted me to guess, but I knew it well. Sixth floor, room number 602.

* * *

HOSPITAL VISIT WITH KAMLI

MY good friend, Kamli, and I had been postponing our lunch plans for the longest time. We finally scheduled a meeting on Tuesday, just two days after Maya was hospitalized. Kamli had lost her father a few months ago to sarcoma. After a year-long battle with cancer, her father had succumbed to the disease. Both of us understood the traumatic experience of being a caretaker and the overwhelming feeling of helplessness. The agony of not being able to do anything while our loved ones suffered in front of our eyes was unbearable. Kamli was distraught and completely broken. I wanted to visit her, but she asked me not to come and to give them some time. I respected her request and was finally meeting her when she felt ready.

We went to *Decheling*, a restaurant popular for its Bhutanese cuisine. We ordered our share of food and caught up on our journey. Kamli had not been able to express herself and I was one of the few people she could open up to. The passing of her father had created a void, and she would share her stories of her struggle of how she was coping with her loss.

When we were nearly done with lunch, she insisted that we go see Maya. I was a little hesitant as I knew that everyone probably would be there that day, and Kamli herself wasn't very comfortable with Diya and Biru. Noticing my hesitation, she said, *"Who cares about those two? I want to see Maya and that's what matters."* I agreed. She was eager to meet her and so was I. Excited, we couldn't even finish the food and after taking care of the check, headed straight to the taxi stand.

Had Maya's dad not sent me the room number, I would have had to go to the reception and follow the protocol of the hospital, but now that I knew: I led Kamli straight to Maya's room.

The door to the room was slightly open, allowing me to catch a glimpse of who was inside. Diya was seated in one corner of the couch, while her dad occupied another corner. Kiran sat by Maya's foot, gently massaging her, while Biru seemed preoccupied, focusing on the monitor to track her oxygen levels and blood pressure. From time to time he would exclaim, *"It's maintaining and it's good."*

When we entered, there was a feeling of awkwardness. I greeted everyone upon entering, but Diya seemed unfazed, occupying her corner of the couch. Maya's dad and Kiran acknowledged Kamli and me with nods and smiles, inviting her to take a seat. Biru was in and out of the room and would ask, *"Do you need anything? Tea, coffee?"* Despite his offers, Diya's whispered interactions with him seemed to halt his hospitality gestures. He would intermittently leave the room, attending to other matters, including visiting his grandmother who was in a room nearby.

Maya was seated upright with an oxygen mask aiding her breathing. Her eyes remained closed as Kiran tenderly massaged her foot. A heavy silence filled the room as Kamli engaged in quiet conversation with Maya's dad. Meanwhile, Kiran occasionally provided brief updates on Maya's condition, keeping me informed with a few words.

At that moment, when Maya likely caught the sound of my voice, she opened her eyes, surveying the room from right to left, her head was tilted slightly in that direction. I stood by her side, on her left, near her feet. As her gaze met mine, her face lit up with a radiant smile, one of the most beautiful smiles I had ever seen. It was a smile filled with joy at my presence, tinged with a hint of curiosity about my whereabouts. It was a smile untouched by the disturbances around her, simply grateful for my company. With a contended sigh, she closed her eyes. Sensing her intention to rest, I gently interjected, *"Wait, before you close your eyes, see who else is here?"* She turned her head towards Kamli and smiled. Although her expression hinted at a desire to speak further, she chose to remain silent. Later, in the days that followed, Kamli and I found ourselves speculating about what Maya might have said if given a chance. Surprisingly, we both arrived at the same conclusion: *"I'm sorry for your loss!"* The synchronicity of our guesses left us both astonished, pondering the mysterious ways of human intuition.

Maya eventually closed her eyes, and Kiran gestured me to take a seat. There was a small mat on the floor where Kiran had been sitting. He pointed it out to me, and as soon as I settled down, Diya abruptly stood up and addressed her dad, *"Why don't you take the 'guests' downstairs and entertain them with tea or coffee?"* Her gaze then shifted towards Kamli and her dad, indicating towards the exit. Kamli promptly rose and headed towards the door. Finally, Diya made eye contact with me and firmly instructed me to leave as well. It was the first direct address and eye contact I had received from her since my arrival in Kathmandu.

"Don't do this Diya, please don't! I came here to see Maya, not to get entertained," I pleaded.

"No, there are too many people here," she responded firmly.

"I came here to see Maya. You know how much I care for her," I insisted, hoping to convey the depth of my concern for Maya's well-being.

She then uttered some things that I couldn't quite comprehend. Was she under stress? In our last conversation, she had assured me that I was still considered a part of the family. Since then, we hadn't communicated, and I hadn't made any remarks, direct or indirect, that could have offended her. In the three encounters we had before this day, there were no conversations or exchanges. What could have triggered her sudden change in demeanor? I had no intention of creating conflict; my sole purpose was to be there for Maya. I hadn't inserted myself into their family affairs and had maintained a discreet presence.

"Oh yeah, I know all the shit that you've been saying behind my back," Diya remarked suddenly.

"What shit? What did I say?" I asked, genuinely puzzled by her accusation.

"You just said it," she retorted.

"Just said it? What did I say? Tell me what I said because I don't remember," I insisted, feeling confused and caught off guard.

"There, you can't even remember what you said a minute ago," Diya fired back.

Feeling bewildered, I turned to Kamli and then to Kiran, seeking clarity, "What did I say?" I implored them.

But Diya wasn't finished. "I know what you have been doing behind my back. You think I don't know?" She continued her frustration evident in her voice.

Later I confronted Diya, saying, "Don't start a war with me, Diya. If you do, I'll destroy you. You know how much I love your sister so why do this?"

Her response was immediate and challenging. "Oh yeah, Oh yeah? You love my sister? Prove it. Write it down," she demanded, her tone accusatory.

Turning to Maya, she raised her voice and exclaimed, "Heard what he said? He said he's going to destroy me. Destroy me?" as if to underline the audacity of my words towards her, Maya's sister.

Then with a defiant air, she turned back to me and issued a blunt invitation: "Let's go out and start the war."

Certainly, I refrained from going out, but she brought up the fundraiser once more, attempting to gain Maya's sympathy after orchestrating the entire show. The incident seemed to have damaged their reputation significantly, as they continued to mention it months after it had been removed. She seemed fixated on it, holding onto an opportunity that allowed her to tarnish my reputation, and she showed no signs of letting it go easily.

"I did it after I got permission from your dad who's standing right here in front of you, ask him." I asserted, pointing towards her dad, caught between conflicting emotions.

"My dad would never accept a dollar from you," she retorted. Despite knowing otherwise, I chose to stay quiet, unwilling to put the old man on the spot by revealing that he had been accepting money from me.

* * *

This was a moment of immense sadness. Instead of acknowledging the sincerity of my feelings, Diya, whom I had regarded as nothing less than a younger sister, and for whom I had fervently prayed during her brief illness, was demanding tangible proof of my love. It felt like a betrayal of the unspoken bond that had bound me and Maya for so long. The emotional depth of shared experiences and genuine care was now overshadowed by doubt and skepticism.

Her request to document my love not only clouded the sincerity of my emotions but also served as a painful reminder of the fractures that had developed in our relationship amidst Maya's illness. It was a moment that burdened me with the unexpected task of proving the authenticity of my feelings to someone who should have inherently understood them. This was a sadness stemming from a love that felt unacknowledged and doubted, a love that should have provided solace amidst the turmoil of Maya's illness. It seemed to undermine the very essence of the deep connection I shared with Maya for twenty-eight years, leaving me to navigate the turbulent waters of doubt and sorrow alone.

* * *

Given Diya's unscrupulous and conniving nature, I should have anticipated such a demand and guarded myself against being affected by it. While I have never disclosed this to anyone, each time I returned to Nepal, I provided financial support to Maya's dad. I even did so when he visited Maya here in the United States. Aware of his financial needs, he always accepted the assistance. Occasionally, I also extended some financial help to Maya's mom. While Maya's dad was aware of my support to his wife, my contributions to him were kept confidential. During the COVID-19 pandemic, I transferred money when I realized their income was affected. Although he indirectly hinted at financial concerns, I should be clear that he never directly asked for help, and I would have willingly assisted if he had.

As I talked to him on the phone, I swiftly arranged for cash to be sent through Western Union. I assured him that he needn't feel uncomfortable asking for help, emphasizing that he should consider me as a son, as he had always referred to me. Later, he sent me a note expressing his gratitude after picking up the money. This was a secret I had kept, but today, I decided to break that promise. It was time to embrace the role of the "bad guy" for a change, the character Diya so eagerly portrayed me to be. Diya is also unaware that during her wedding, it was me who contributed all my savings to Maya, so she didn't leave any stones unturned to have the décor that she desired for her sister as, Maya herself was crunched with cash at that moment.

One day, during a casual conversation with Maya, I inadvertently mentioned that I had sent some money to her dad. Her immediate question was, *"Did you tell anyone about this?"* I replied, *"No, I promised him I wouldn't and that you wouldn't know about this either, but it slipped. Why? Does it matter?"* She cautioned against sharing it with any of our friends, as it might not reflect well. Then, with a smile, she remarked, *"Daddy is so sly,"* and smiled. Reflecting on it now, I realize that she too, didn't want anyone to know that her father had accepted help from me, concerned about their reputation.

* * *

Quietly, I upheld the promise I had made, choosing silence amidst the storm of accusations being hurled at me. As this person continued to level accusations, alleging perceived wrongs, I found myself speechless. The trivial allegation of raising money for myself seemed insignificant compared to the outrageous claim that I was somehow responsible for Maya's cancer. Despite my fervent hope and willingness to bear the burden of cancer myself to spare Maya from pain, I now confronted the absurdity of being accused as its cause.

Diya's insistence that I had somehow caused Maya's illness through stress ignored the true extent of the emotional burden Maya carried.

Unaware of the strain Maya endured from her sister's calls, where Diya often complained about family matters, Diya failed to comprehend the toll it took on Maya's well-being. Maya frequently confided in me about these conversations, recounting how her sister would call from Nepal in tears, expressing her disappointment at not having Maya by her side when she needed her big sister. These intimate details and Maya's innermost feelings were documented in a personal diary entrusted to my care. Despite its presence with me, I refrain from reading it out of respect for Maya's privacy. I've always maintained this trust, never reading her texts or emails without her knowledge.

Accusing me maybe the easy path, given that I spent most of Maya's adult life by her side. It's convenient to point fingers and lay blame on me for her cancer, conveniently ignoring the family's role in causing her pain. Maya confided in me with certain childhood traumas she had endured, a secret I felt the family needed to be aware of. Shockingly, when I revealed these traumas, I was met with indifference; no one took any action. Maya, already traumatized, was left in dismay. When she battled depression, her mother dismissively remarked, *"She's always been depressed. She's been depressed since childhood."* But do they truly understand why? Do they comprehend the emotional scars left when her parents abandoned her in her grandaunt's house at the tender age of three, as she gazed out the window, yearning to be rescued from a place that only offered pain and torment?

Once, when a close friend of mine was getting married, Diya invited me to her room for a conversation. She inquired, *"How are you feeling about her getting married?"*

"I'm genuinely happy for her," I replied.

"Are you sure? Will you be able to live with that? It seems like you guys would have made a great couple!" Diya queried further; her tone thoughtful yet probing.

People were already pointing fingers at her for breaking up her brother's first marriage, and now she seemed to be planting seeds of doubt and temptation, perhaps aiming to sow discord between Maya and me. Was she subtly suggesting that I should pursue someone else while still being married to her sister? This incident, among many others orchestrated behind my back, was a rift that Maya was deeply hurt to learn about when I confided in her years later.

Similar to how Maya had attributed her decision to walk away from me to my drinking, now it was the family accusing me of embezzlement to drive me away—especially her conniving sister, adept at using people and discarding them when deemed unnecessary. When Maya blamed me for our breakup, she propagated the narrative among her friends. I had to intervene, clarifying that the alcohol wasn't the root cause; rather, she had never been fully committed to the relationship and sought an excuse to end it.

Even with my frustration, I never gave up on Maya, even though our years together lacked intimacy. While she was battling to find the answers to her unhappiness, I stood by her and supported her. I questioned whether her personal problems were my fault—there's only so much one can do to influence free will. Unable to make her love me, I ceased trying. Maya had expressed unhappiness before and after our marriage, yet she initiated it, chose the date with her family, and kept me hanging on despite her discontent. I went with the flow. We were already living together, and I had thought, and hoped marriage would heal the relationship. I desired to have children, but she didn't, so I pretended to share her sentiment to spare her feelings. Even though secretly wishing for a daughter, whenever I proposed the topic, she coldly deferred the discussion, leaving it unresolved.

* * *

Diya's loud and obnoxious behavior continued, despite my pleas for her to stop, especially in front of Maya. When I glanced at Maya, I saw the sadness in her expression, and she managed to say, *"It's tensing me out."* I hated that this situation had been created. Kiran remained silent, not uttering a word.

As I prepared to leave, addressing Kiran, *"In times like these, the husband holds the authority to make decisions, correct?"* He nodded, and I continued, *"So the divorce you compelled us to undergo is inconsequential; all the information is null and void, and I've verified it."* Turning to Diya, I asserted that I would set things right and would eject her from the room the next time she came, just as she was expelling me now without cause. Although, having uttered those words in the heat of the moment, I would never be able to bring myself to carry out such an act. I would never separate Maya's loved ones from her, especially in times like these. My journey had brought me this far with the sole purpose of being with Maya, and nothing else.

Despite my attempts to mend relationships during family disagreements—be it the discontent with Kiran's choice of a bride, dissatisfaction with Biru's treatment of Kiran as a subordinate, or even friends in the United States questioning Diya's intentions—here they were, destroying the very bridge that Maya had built between me and her family.

* * *

I went downstairs and bumped into Maya's dad. I told him, *"Did you see what your daughter did?"* As usual he agreed and said that such an action was inappropriate in front of Maya. I asked him as to why he hadn't stopped her and needed to point out the right from wrong. He seemed confused and said, *"I don't know what happened to Diya. Maybe she's still mad about the fundraiser."*

Later Kamli walked by us, and she had a question for him too. She said, *"I know right now we are here for Maya but what about him? Why is he being treated this way?"* Before I heard his answer, I saw Kiran coming out. I told him we needed to talk and went to the parking lot together. I expressed my discontent towards Kiran for not having said anything and letting her get away with such childishness. He looked at me and said, *"That's what I just did. I told her she did a great job by provoking you and walked away from her."* He had no idea as to what her problem was with me and said this was probably riled up since the time we had that scuffle in the States.

We lost track of time until Kamli came looking for me after about an hour. She asked him the same question she had posed to Maya's dad, and Kiran agreed that what Diya did was wrong. I proceeded to express all my discontent. I inquired about the details written in the divorce papers, to which he replied that he hadn't seen them except during our time at the courthouse. I conveyed my dissatisfaction about why he allowed it to happen, knowing it was not right. He explained that in Nepal, they had to come up with a false narrative, portraying one party as the 'bad guy,' and in the process, it didn't matter how negatively they depicted the person.

Kiran tried to convince me that it was okay and that it was only on paper. I countered by emphasizing that it mattered to me. I had kept the divorce a secret from my mom and brothers, knowing it would hurt them. I planned to tell them eventually but hadn't found the right moment. Mom discovered the divorce papers the day I was coming to Kathmandu, in a suitcase that I had so carefully hidden that I too, had forgotten to check. My mom had cried. I told Kiran, *"Of course, it matters what was written. You made my mom cry."*

He looked up at me without saying a word, quickly taking another drag of the cigarette. I despised the fact that we were having these discussions, and I'm sure he didn't like it either. I don't know how it came up, but he brought up the topic that it was better for Maya to have come to Nepal for her treatment. He shared that when he first saw her upon arriving from the United States and during the days she spent at home, she looked like a corpse.

I had heard enough, so I said, *"Well, nothing's changed since she's been here, has it?"* He was upset that I had said that, but I told him, *"It's the fact and you know it. It may have helped with her depression but what's the proof that it was Nepal that got her out of it? You guys had prevented her from taking the antidepressants because of your own beliefs when she was in Connecticut. It was you who told me to discourage her from taking the antidepressants. Before she could address the issue,* you guys brought her here. The entire world comes to the United States for their treatment and you guys brought her here. Am I not saying the truth?"

He listened, acknowledging the truth in my words agreeing to most of what I said. I then pleaded with him, *"Kiran, I beg of you that you not let this happen. I don't want to be pushed away. God forbid if these were the last few days of Maya."* He assured me it wouldn't and said he saw all the faults in Diya and had never doubted my intentions. He understood that I was there because I genuinely cared. He also expressed how saddened he was upon hearing that Maya and I were separating and that he had tried his best to prevent it from happening.

After he finished expressing his thoughts, he suggested that it might be a good idea for me to visit Maya when Diya was not around. I agreed, explaining that it was my intention, but I wasn't getting much communication from anyone. The only person I could rely on for updates was his dad, but even he wasn't the best source for all the details. He assured me he would keep me informed moving forward.

When we finished our conversation and walked towards the hospital, I conveyed to him that while I wasn't surprised that Diya had nothing good to say about me, it didn't justify her spreading false information. Reluctantly, I went on to share with Kiran what Diya had thought about his wife and how strongly she opposed the idea of getting her married to her brother. She believed Kiran's wife lacked class and even expressed that introducing her to family members would be embarrassing. I chose to end the discussion there, realizing it could become too painful to delve deeper. Since Diya had falsely accused me of spreading rumors about her, I decided to give her the benefit of the doubt, except, this was the truth.

* * *

When Mala and Kiran had just started to date, Diya expressed her curiosity about Mala's mysterious source of income, referring to her ability to afford a well-attired appearance and even hinting that she might have a 'secret' source of income. Diya would draw the conclusion as Mala co-owned a bar in the heart of Thamel. She always judged people and had expressed to Maya how hard it would be to teach Mala societal norms and introduce her to family members. Maya and I tried to challenge her narrow perspective, emphasizing that a person's character is more important than appearances. However, Diya stuck to her shallow arguments, stating, *"Gu lai jatti safa garey pani ganauncha!"* which translates to, *"No matter how much you clean the poop, it will always stink!"* Maya and I exchanged incredulous glances, with Maya dismissing the topic, saying, *"Whatever,"* and changed the subject. Diya wouldn't like to lose a discussion and Maya didn't want to agree with her when she knew her sister was wrong.

The entire family opposed Kiran's relationship with Mala, except for Maya and me. I admired Mala for her strong will and entrepreneurial spirit, having opened a bar in *Thamel*. I viewed this as an accomplishment, while the family considered it shameful due to societal expectations. They held a negative opinion about a girl owning a bar, period! Once again, I was the one who initially persuaded

Maya's dad to acknowledge Mala and engage in conversation with her during her visits. Otherwise, he would ignore her. The rest, as they say, is history. Although he still harbored suspicions about her motives, we will leave it to time to reveal the truth.

* * *

Kiran kept listening in disbelief. I had sparked a splinter and knew this would give rise to animosity among the siblings. I did not feel-good doing this, and it was against my conscience, but I had to. Diya said I was backbiting. I am exposing the truth now, and I don't care what comes of it. I further added, *"Why do you think Mala isn't invited to all the family events in Diya's house?"* and before he said anything I added, *"It's because she's ashamed to call her sister-in-law."* I felt bad to see Kiran quietly listen to all this about his pregnant wife, but I knew that he knew his sister very well.

* * *

Once Kiran had shared with me an incident that had upset him. It was one of the Saturdays that Biru and Diya along with the kids had come to his house. On that day, Kiran had a guest who had stayed on for a couple of hours and then left. When he left, Diya came up to Kiran and told him she didn't like 'such' people coming to the house and that she would rather have him meet them outside. Kiran was offended and had retaliated, *"This is my house, and I can have anyone come to this house and this should not concern you."*

A few months later, Biru found himself in trouble with the law and was arrested for undisclosed reasons. When this happened, Diya called Kiran and sought his help to see if he knew anyone in the police force who could help. Kiran had made a few calls to his contacts, and after pulling a few strings, Biru was released. Kiran had then called Diya and told her, *"Remember the guy who you said you didn't want to see in the house? Well, he was the one who got your husband out of jail."* Despite Kiran's effort and revelation, Diya's responded dismissively saying, *"Whoever, I don't care!"* This interaction left Kiran disheartened and used this as an example of his sister's arrogance.

* * *

I hugged Kiran goodbye and asked him to call me with updates. Kamli and I got into the cab. On our way back, in the cab, Kamli looked at me and asked, *"Is this how you've been fighting your battle? All alone? One versus the rest of Maya's family?"*

I looked at her and after comprehending what she had asked, I smiled and said, *"Yes! That's how it's been all along."* I was so glad that someone got to witness this. Someone I could call a friend or else it was always my words against theirs like how it had always been. After all, the family would always stick together. Unlike them, I chose not to divulge family matters to everyone and opted to keep my grievances to myself. Perhaps my silence was the reason why others were inclined to believe them over me. No one saw what I was going through, and it was the first time I had someone unbiased to witness it. It made me think and also relieved.

Having Kamli by my side, witnessing the dynamics within Maya's family, was a revelation. For so long, I had been fighting this battle alone, against the tide of Maya's family's opinions and actions.

Kamli's observation brought this reality into sharp focus. It was indeed one person against the collective force of Maya's family. Their unity, while admirable, often felt like an impenetrable barrier. My struggles, my efforts, and my intentions were often overshadowed or misunderstood.

Having Kamli there, an unbiased observer, gave me a sense of validation. Finally, someone understood the complexities of the situation, someone who saw the truth behind the façade. It was a relief to have someone I could confide in, someone who could empathize with my plight. For the first time, I didn't feel like I was fighting alone. Kamli's presence provided a glimmer of hope amidst the chaos, reminding me that I wasn't as isolated as I had once believed.

* * *

Earlier that week, Chaya's parents had visited Maya in the hospital and stayed for about an hour. Diya was furious and would call her mom, telling her, *"Why are people so inconsiderate? They come to the hospital and stay for hours. I couldn't even have my lunch."* Her mother, having no filter, shared this with me. Diya had further gone on to yell at her mom saying, *"Don't give the room number to everyone, I don't want everyone coming. I don't care even if it's Chaya's parents."* It seemed like Diya was angry at everyone.

* * *

Maya stood by my side through thick and thin, driven by care and perhaps, the love she felt for me—though she might not have consciously realized it, and I'll give her the benefit of the doubt. We never kept track of each other's contributions, as it flowed naturally in the context of marital harmony. However, Diya kept a meticulous count. She consistently believed I didn't do enough and likely filled Maya's ears and others with such sentiments. It seemed like an excessive interference from her sister that hindered Maya from expressing her true feelings. Despite everything suggesting otherwise, Diya had convinced herself that I wasn't the right person for Maya.

* * *

One day, Maya confided in me, expressing concern that people might view her as a 'bitch' for leaving someone as nice as me. I laughed it off, assuring her, *"If anyone's being cursed, it's probably me. I doubt anyone would think that of you."* She disagreed. Curious, I asked her, *"Okay, be honest. I see so many of our friends who seem to have lost their spark once they got married and had kids. Do you agree that I never let that happen until the time we were…?"* Before I could finish my sentence, she quickly interjected, *"Yes, that's for sure!"*

"Doesn't it feel good to talk about all these things even when we have gone our separate ways?" I asked.

"Yes, very," she replied, *"and I hope we are this way until forever."*

I would assure her by saying, *"Of course, until the time I will be changing your diapers."*

"My diapers?" She'd reply and add, *"What makes you so sure that you will be fit enough to change mine? Perhaps I will be changing yours."*

I had even joked and told her that if anyone asked her as to why we separated even though we were in such great terms, to tell them that she had become my mother!

"What do you mean?" she asked.

"It's because you've become just like my mom. You're always telling me to eat this, do this, don't do that, sleep on time etc." I replied.

We both laughed. We were driving back from one of her appointments and then she wanted to hear a song by *X-Ambassadors*, a band she was trying to familiarize with as we were attending their concert in a few days in Stamford. Increasing the volume to the level we hardly heard each other; she sang along, slapping her thighs slightly to coordinate with the beats in the song. I would drive along smiling and happy to see the healthy Maya.

* * *

33

THE DREADED DAY

AFTER dropping Kamli off, I took the same cab back to the hotel, seeking solace once again in the art of getting a tattoo to ease my pain. As I finished, Pasa came to visit, and we made plans to grab dinner together. Just as we were about to head out, my phone rang, and Kiran's distressed voice filled the line.

"Is everything okay?" I asked, a knot of worry forming in my stomach.

"No, bro. It's not," Kiran replied, his tone heavy with concern.

"What's wrong? Is Maya okay? Why don't you talk to me?" I pressed, my mind racing with apprehension.

There was a pause. I then realized that he was crying and needed to gather his composure.

"*Hanchu, you should go and see her. They shifted her to a different Intensive Care Unit (ICU) ward on the 5th floor. Just go and ask to see her and they will let you,*" he finally managed to say amidst his tears.

My heart started to race. I was relieved it wasn't the worst news, but I couldn't comprehend why she had been moved. Would the entire family be gathered there too? I didn't care. I asked Pasa if he could take me. *"Of course,"* he replied and off we set. I didn't know what to expect and I didn't know what was going on. On our way there, I didn't hear half the things Pasa was telling me. He understood and just kept quiet.

I hurried to the designated ward as soon as I got to the hospital. It was an ICU unit and only one visitor was allowed. Pasa said he would wait outside for me. The security guided me to the ward, and I was permitted entry. As I entered, I saw Maya's bed in a corner, and she appeared to be fast asleep. She was on a ventilator and her blood pressure was being maintained by a machine. I stood there, gazing at her condition. She seemed to gasp with every breath she took. Life was attempting to squeeze out every breath she had. Tears welled up in my eyes, and I began to cry uncontrollably.

I had a few questions for the nurse, but sensing that she preferred I ask the doctor, she called for her. The doctor entered and introduced herself. She inquired about my relationship with Maya, and I informed her that I was her husband. She seemed to wonder where I had been during the family briefing. Observing my distressed state, she offered me a seat, but I declined, insisting I was fine. I then asked her directly, *"Doctor, please be honest with me. Will she make it through tonight?"*

She looked at me and said, *"Very unlikely, sorry!"*

Her candid response hit me like a ton of bricks. My worst fears were realized in that moment. I braced myself for the worst, but hearing those words from the doctor was devastating. I struggled to maintain my composure, feeling a surge of emotions overwhelming me. My mind raced with thoughts and memories of Maya, and the gravity of the situation weighed heavily upon me.

I found myself crying even more, my shoulders jerking with the force of my sobs. I wanted to say something to the doctor, but words wouldn't come out. She stood there, her eyes filled with sympathy, and later fetched a chair for me to sit on. I lowered myself into it and drew closer to Maya's bed. Gently, I took her hand in mine, feeling the weight of her fingers, swollen from the illness. Her nails still bore the nail polish she had applied a few days prior. Her skin appeared flawless, perhaps enhanced by the expensive 'celebrity' cream she had recently purchased. Maya had shared this with me during one of my visits to the hospital, and I had complimented her, telling her she was glowing.

Her eyes were closed, but I still spoke to her. I apologized to her if I had hurt her in any way, assuring her that it was never my intention to cause her pain. I wished desperately that I could take away her suffering and restore her to health. I expressed my longing to be by her side during the days when I wasn't permitted to visit.

I may have stayed there for about two hours, but time seemed to lose its meaning. Throughout that time, I spoke to her, pouring out my heart even though she seemed unresponsive, trapped in a seemingly endless slumber. I tenderly caressed her hands and pressed gentle kisses upon them, pleading with her to return to us, to be the vibrant and lively person she once was. I begged her telling her of the adventures we still had to share, the places we had yet to explore together. How could she leave without experiencing all the joys that awaited her? It was a question that lingered in my mind, filled with a mixture of sadness and bewilderment.

* * *

As the clock struck ten, signaling the end of visiting hours, I was engrossed in my conversation with Maya, unwilling to let go. It was then that the guard gently tapped me on the shoulder, a reminder that it was time to leave. Reluctantly, I rose from my seat, still hopeful that there might be some way I could stay with her through the night. I pleaded with the doctors and nurses, begging them to allow me to stay with Maya throughout the night, even though I knew it went against hospital protocol. Sadly, despite my heartfelt appeals, they couldn't grant my request.

At 10:15 pm, I asked the nurse to keep me informed of any developments, assuring her that I would be right outside. They suggested that I wait in the lobby, but I insisted on waiting in the small waiting room just outside the ICU. The room had a bench for three, and I informed the guard that I would wait there all night. Although initially hesitant, he eventually agreed, and I settled into the uncomfortable seat. Throughout the night, I remained glued to my seat, with only a few trips to the hospital cafeteria, which stayed open, to grab some coffee. To pass the time, I engaged in research, stared at my hands, stared at my nails, and anxiously awaited the early morning visiting hours. It seemed like an eternity, but it was just 11:30 pm, I still had about seven hours to go.

As I waited, nurses would frequently enter and exit the ICU, some taking the elevator down for coffee or snacks. Both the doctor and the nurse I interacted with in the ICU noticed me waiting there. They might have considered my decision to stay in the waiting room rather than using the lounge's soft seats or the carpeted floor, where others rested, a bit unusual. I hoped that they would take pity on me and allow me to be with Maya, it didn't happen.

Realizing my phone was dying and not having brought a charger, I grew concerned about missing any important calls from the doctors. What if they were to call me and my phone was dead? It was already 1:30 am but I decided to call a cab to quickly retrieve my charger from the hotel. Before leaving, I gave the guard some money, urging him to call me if anything happened before reaching out to anyone else. Although hesitant, he agreed. During the forty-five minutes I was gone, there were no calls. As the clock ticked closer to 6 am, I realized I had only half an hour left. Just as it was about to hit 6:30 am, I approached the guard and requested to be let in.

Maya still had her eyes closed. The chair I had sat on last night was still there, so I went to sit on it. Maya was neatly tucked into a bed that seemed untouched. Perhaps the nurses had cleaned her and changed the bedsheets and blankets, or Maya had remained in the same position since last night. Slowly, I lifted the blanket and reached out to find her hand. When I did, I held it and took it out of the blanket. I kept looking at her hand, which appeared a little more swollen. When I looked up, I saw Maya's eyes open and blinking, but she was looking in the other direction. She seemed dazed, as if trying to figure things out.

I said, *"Hey Maiya, it's me."* She tried to turn her head towards me, but I rushed to the other side. The moment our eyes met, her expression transformed, revealing a sense of relief and happiness that someone was there besides her. It was as if seeing me brought comfort and a flood of unsaid words she longed to share. She may have come to senses many times that night and may have been disappointed in not having anyone there.

With a tenderness that filled the room, I asked Maya, *"You know I love you, right Maiya?"* In response, a subtle, affirmative nod emerged from her weakened form, a silent acknowledgment that transcended the limitations of spoken words. Encouraged by this connection, I took a deep breath and gently inquired, *"You love me too, right? Maybe just a little?"* In that moment, Maya's response was not just a nod; it was a more vigorous affirmation, a gesture that spoke volumes. I apologized to her for the minor scuffle the day before with her sister and promised her I wouldn't fight with her ever again. She kept listening to me. She wasn't able to talk but I know she would have said, *'That's ok.'*

It became clear that Maya, despite her physical limitations, was attempting to convey a message. The intensity of her nod seemed to carry a weight of unspoken emotions, a silent confession of deep affection and regret. In that intimate exchange, it felt as though Maya wanted to apologize, not just for the circumstances that had unfolded, but for the pain and heartache that her illness had inadvertently caused me. Her struggle to communicate became a heartbreaking expression of love, remorse, and the complexity of emotions that accompany saying goodbye.

She made an effort to speak, but the words wouldn't come out. Sensing her struggle, I gently inquired if there was something she wished to convey, and she nodded in response. I asked the nurse if it was possible to facilitate communication, but she explained that it would only be feasible once the tube was removed.

Maya was breathing with the assistance of a ventilator, rendering her unable to utter a word. I felt a deep sense of sorrow and helplessness witnessing her suffering. Gently, I placed my hands on her cheeks and kissed her forehead. Despite the tears in her eyes, there was a faint smile as she held onto my hand. In that moment, our silent exchange conveyed volumes, it was a heartbreaking realization that she couldn't speak to me or convey those final sentiments. If I were to imagine her last words, they would likely be, *"I'm sorry I have to leave you behind, but please take care of yourself."*

I had been there for just about fifteen minutes when the security guard came and informed me that Diya had arrived and needed to enter. Initially, I responded sharply, *"Tell them they have to wait,"* forgetting that Maya could hear me. Quickly, I softened my tone and politely repeated the sentence, addressing Maya directly. *"I have to go now, Maiya. Your sister is here,"* I told her gently, noticing the longing in her eyes. She held onto me as if asking me to stay a little longer. Promising to return that night to stay with her, I kissed her and said goodbye. As I left, her eyes followed me, and it would be the last time I would see her alive. Tears streamed down my face as I made my way out, the pain of parting overshadowed by the precious time I had spent with her.

As I stepped out, I noticed Biru and Diya waiting on the bench where I had spent the night. Biru acknowledged me, but Diya, made no gesture, instead, she walked in with her head turned to the other side. They proceeded to enter the hospital. Reflecting on the situation, I realized how fortunate I was to have stayed by Maya's side all night. Had I been even slightly delayed, Diya might not have allowed me that precious moment with her.

I had just a fleeting fifteen minutes with Maya, but it brought me immense joy. It marked the first time since my arrival in Kathmandu two weeks ago that we had the chance to be alone, to communicate face-to-face. Even with her inability to speak, Maya's silent language spoke volumes. Her eyes, even with the constraints of medical equipment, conveyed a profound depth of emotion, offering solace and a poignant reminder of our enduring love, despite the physical barriers that separated us. It was clear she had much on her mind, a wealth of thoughts and feelings yearning to be expressed. Her repeated insistence on my self-care underscored her unwavering concern for me. I assured her repeatedly that I would heed her advice. Learning later that this would be our final meeting while she was alive, I couldn't help but feel as though Maya had waited for this moment, a moment of closure and acceptance before embracing the liberation that awaited her beyond this life.

The following day, I learned that Maya's prognosis upon her transfer to the ICU was exceedingly grim. The doctors had conveyed to the family that her chances of survival were a mere one percent, casting a shadow of uncertainty over the possibility of her waking to greet the dawn. Reflecting on the situation, I couldn't help but question why the entire family had chosen to depart from the hospital at 7 pm, knowing full well that Maya's condition was dire and that they might not have the opportunity to see her again. I had anticipated their presence, yet once again, Maya found herself alone, isolated in that corner of the hospital without a single family member by her side—not even the maid. The realization ignited a surge of anger within me. I had expressed to Maya's father my willingness to stay with her throughout the night, offering her the solace of companionship during her darkest hours.

After leaving the hospital, I made my way back to the hotel, hoping to catch some much-needed sleep after staying up all night. But sleep proved elusive as I was plagued by frightful dreams that jolted me awake repeatedly. The frequency of these nightmares was increasing, disrupting any chance of rest. Frustrated and exhausted, I decided to seek solace in getting another tattoo. Conveniently, the tattoo studio was just across the street, and the artists, a friendly couple, provided a welcoming atmosphere. Getting tattoos became my way of escaping the mental anguish I was experiencing. During this visit, I ended up getting six tattoos, finding some relief in the physical pain that distracted me from the turmoil within.

Arya and Neera aunty had arranged a family dinner for that evening and insisted that I join them. I told Arya that I may be in the hospital. She asked, *"But you still need to eat right? We will make it a quick one."* Agreeing to their invitation, I informed Kiran of my plans and inquired if it would be acceptable for me to spend the night with Maya.

To my surprise, Kiran informed me that Maya had been transferred to a different isolation ICU where visitors were not permitted. However, upon further inquiry, I discovered that the family members were indeed allowed to stay with her. It perplexed me why Maya was left alone, once again, with only a hired nurse, especially when I was willing to be there for her. If someone was allowed to stay, how come no family members stayed with her? Wouldn't Maya have preferred the comfort of a loved one during such a critical time instead of a nurse? If left me questioning why my presence was not welcomed when anyone would desire the support of family members during their final moments.

I sensed that I wasn't being given the full truth but opted to set aside my doubts and await further developments until morning. The dinner was brief, and I returned to my room by 8:30 pm, settling in front of my laptop, intending to catch up on some writing. At 10:40 pm, my phone rang, displaying Diya's number on the screen. My hand trembled as I answered, knowing that it was Biru on the other end. Biru wouldn't call me without a significant reason, and I braced myself for potentially distressing news.

"Hanchu da, I'm sorry to say that di passed away peacefully today. We are at the hospital, and they are ready to take her body to prepare for cremation. If you want to, sorry I meant I know you want to come. I can tell them to wait for you. Should I?"

"Thank you, Biru, for letting me do this. I will never forget," I choked out, my voice thick with emotions.

An immense emptiness had engulfed me. I inquired about Diya, and he informed me that she had collapsed and was disoriented. Urging him to take good care of her, as she would undoubtedly be equally shaken, I couldn't help but feel a genuine sense of sorrow for her. Biru told me he would wait for me to come, but if Diya's condition worsened, they would go home. I told him he didn't need to wait and urged him to return home, but to ensure that the nurses waited until I arrived. He reassured me, stating he had already informed the nurse and that they would await my arrival.

I was going to take the cab but decided to call Arya to send me her car. Her driver came within ten minutes and took me to the hospital. I rushed to the unit, and they directed me to the room where Maya was kept. Biru and Diya had already left by then. When I saw her lifeless body, I froze for a moment, and I burst into large spurts of crying. I couldn't stop myself. I let myself out. Her body was cold and looked like she was fast asleep, but I knew she couldn't hear me cry or call out her name. I was there for about two hours or so. This entire time I cried and finally before leaving I prayed and kissed her goodbye for one last time. As I walked out, I whispered, *"Rest in peace, Maiya and I will see you when I see you."* I felt light, perhaps I had accepted that she was gone, free from all the suffering.

When I was leaving, I bumped into Kamli in the corridor, who had insisted she would come. When she saw me, she too went in to bid Maya farewell and we left. We cried our hearts out again in the hospital parking lot. We silently sat across each other and didn't utter a word except during times I would stand up to put my head in her lap and burst out crying. She would caress and comfort me while she too needed comforting. By the time she dropped me off, it was nearly three in the morning. I went into my room and threw myself in the shower and don't remember how long I was there for. I tried calling Diya and Biru later, but they wouldn't answer.

I couldn't sleep that night. I was getting a few calls from concerned friends, but I didn't answer. I was being selective as to with whom I wanted to talk. I was still trying to digest everything that had happened. It was still hard for me to believe that she was gone. Had she really waited for me? She had said yes when I had asked her and now, she was gone. The day we got to spend what little time we had; she had decided to leave us the same day.

As I closed my eyes, I would see only her. Her images were like falling dominos in my head but this time it was an infinite array of dominos that did not stop. I remembered her smile and the times we had spent together. The nurses in MSK had called her their *'happiest patient.'* Ironically, she took her last breath at 10:14 pm. She chose a time when even the clock was smiling. But she had left me crying and that's what I did for many nights to follow.

I tossed and turned but trying to sleep wasn't an option. There would be rituals the next day and I hadn't been filled in about it. I needed to call Kiran the first thing the next morning and find out the next steps. I made myself a coffee and sat on the couch remembering the good times we had shared. We had made a promise. Until death do us apart. It was death, indeed, that separated us!

* * *

THE FINAL GOODBYE

I called Kiran early in the morning to inquire about the timing of the planned ritual. He advised me to be there at the site around 11 am and informed me that they had opted for an electric crematorium. I considered this a more suitable choice than the traditional one. Pasa and Samir expressed their desire to accompany me to the ritual. My friends, Arya and Anju also came along and met me there.

Upon arrival, I found Maya's body resting on a small platform, and everyone was observing traditional Nepalese funeral rituals. Witnessing her in that state was overwhelming, and I couldn't hold back my tears. Arya and Anju were by my side, providing comfort and support. These four friends stood unwaveringly with me during this difficult time. Despite the presence of many acquaintances, none seemed inclined to offer consolation or engage in conversation.

When I saw Maya's dad, I approached him and hugged him, but the embrace felt distant, almost rejecting. This wasn't just a feeling; it was palpable. I knew how that man hugged, and this time it was evident that he did not want to be seen with me. I wondered if anyone out there even knew if Maya and I were married. Even if they did, they probably went with the picture of what the family drew of me. Regardless, I cared little about people's perceptions. Fueled by anger, I was prepared to confront anyone attempting to interfere with the funeral rites.

Biru's dad approached me, offering a comforting pat on my shoulders, while Biru's brother, Ram, handed me water. Even his mom presented me with a garland to place on Maya's body. The rest of the attendees seemed reluctant to step forward and express their condolences.

Neera aunty and Arya had advised me to remain calm despite my anger at being denied the rites. They suggested letting them proceed with it their way, assuring me that we knew what Maya would have wanted, and we could bid her farewell in our own way. Following their counsel, I refrained from interfering with the rituals as they unfolded according to Maya's family's preferences. I ensured that I was there to lift Maya's body during the transition to the crematorium and then to place it on a different platform before it entered the burning chamber.

Watching the plank carrying Maya being pulled toward the chamber was emotionally challenging, marking the final sight of her body. I broke down again but managed to regain my composure. As everyone walked outside, I observed some treating this solemn moment as a casual get-together, with laughter and chatter. While I didn't expect everyone to cry, witnessing such casual behavior was difficult. The four supportive individuals by my side noticed this too, providing comfort without needing to say a word.

After spending about an hour outside, I noticed the crowd gradually diminishing, although no one appeared to be visibly leaving. Later, Arya informed me that everyone had moved to the riverbank to participate in a specific part of the remaining ritual. Unfortunately, we were left out as we were unaware of the ongoing events. When we reached the riverbank, I witnessed Maya's dad conducting a ritual under the guidance of one of the company's employees. Surprisingly, there was no designated priest or qualified individual to officiate a ceremony of this magnitude. Although I felt it was my rightful role, I refrained from demanding it, as I had promised not to argue or create a scene during the proceedings.

It turns out that I had never previously given much thought or importance to rituals, but when the time came, I wanted to be the one performing them for Maya. It felt significant. Witnessing her being bid farewell, as an unmarried woman, seemed somewhat lacking, and though it's challenging to articulate, it mattered to me.

The necessary rituals were completed. Throughout this entire time, no one spoke to me. Later, as one acquaintance was leaving, he spotted me and expressed surprise, having failed to recognize me due to my newly grown beard. When he learned of my mourning for my wife's death and that Maya and I were married, he apologized for not knowing.

Similar to him, it seemed that nobody knew or cared. Most attendees were there not for Maya but merely out of formality, fulfilling the obligation to support other family members. This somber day would soon be forgotten, and despite the sorrowful appearances, life would resume as usual for everyone the next day. If they knew Maya, she would become a memory, someone's daughter, a sister, a friend whose time had come. People would begin posting stories of their vibrant lives on social media. After all, many that were there had never reached out to Maya, even during her treatment, to express their sentiments.

After everything was concluded, I planned to have lunch with Arya and Anju at their place. Unfortunately, Pasa and Samir had to leave, so they couldn't join us. We exchanged our goodbyes, and while walking towards our car, we noticed everyone forming a circle as someone had slipped and fallen on the steep walkway. To my surprise, it was Maya's dad. Without altering my pace, I continued walking towards the car. Once seated, I observed people helping him up, and he walked with a limp. Initially, I felt relieved, assuming it wasn't too serious, but later, I learned that his injury had swollen and left him bedridden for a few days.

After lunch, I returned to my hotel for some rest. Later that day, I called Kiran and expressed my desire to come over to spend some time and discuss a few matters with his family. He mentioned that he would call me back to arrange a suitable time, but that call never came. When he did eventually call, it was to apologize, explaining that people were continuously visiting to offer their condolences during the thirteen days of mourning. I didn't understand as to why it wouldn't be okay for me to visit despite the visitors. Traditionally, I should have been invited for that ceremony, but it didn't happen, and it didn't surprise me. I had decided to be present for the thirteen-day mourning ritual, but it seemed unimportant to include me, despite the significance it held for me. I believed I deserved to be a part of it, considering I had given my all to take care of Maya and stood by her until her last moments. It felt unjust to be excluded, and deep down, they knew it too. Only time would reveal the true sentiments.

* * *

That night, a few friends visited and took me out to dinner to lift my spirits. The following day, I spent the entire day in solitude. Taking a solitary walk to *Swayambhunath* temple, I embraced the rain as it provided the perfect cover for my tears. I spent about three hours in silent contemplation, allowing the rain to soak me. Though I had a small umbrella, it was insufficient for the task. The rain served as a refreshing release, washing away some of the grief and offering solace in its gentle embrace.

Deciding to take a longer route back to my hotel, I attempted to locate the childhood house where I had grown up. Even though, I knew its general location, the numerous buildings that had sprung up in the twenty-five years since I left for the States made it challenging. Even the landmark bridge proved elusive. After inquiring with locals, I eventually found my way. Although the area had undergone significant changes, it still evoked memories of carefree days. It transported me back to a time when I played and ran freely through those streets, recalling instances of running away from approaching cows and the misadventure of riding a motorbike right into a neighbor's house when I was just learning. Each corner held a piece of my past, a fragment of my childhood that seemed both distant and vivid in my memory.

Reflecting on it all made me nostalgic for my childhood. I was taught to make the best of it, and now, recalling certain experiences brings a smile to my face. Life back then was carefree, but now, with numerous responsibilities and challenges, it's a different story. Nevertheless, as I walked in the rain, a smile graced my face, providing a brief respite from the sorrow that had recently entered my life. In those moments, amidst the rain and the memories, I found solace and a sense of peace.

Later that evening, I headed to *Durbar Marg* for dinner, revisiting the places I cherished as a teenager – *Nanglos* and *Nirulas*, situated next to each other. *Nanglos*, unfortunately, was no longer there, but in its place stood *Sam's One Tree*. The ambiance remained unchanged, with one notable improvement: a commendable step toward inclusivity.

Sam's had employed individuals without a voice, providing them an opportunity to work. Unlike the United States, where server errors might annoy us, here at Sam's, most servers, despite their limitations, took orders by us pointing to the menu. They noted down our preferences, mumbled a few words, and served our meals. Even when mistakes happened, patrons displayed remarkable patience, recognizing the efforts and challenges face by these employees.

As I sat enjoying my usual order of *momo*, I was oblivious to the fact that tears were streaming down my face. Not in response to the servers' challenges but as a manifestation of my own sorrows. A server approached, signaling if everything was okay. I gave him a thumbs up and wiped away my tears. Did he realize I was grappling with inner pain, or did he assume I cried due to dissatisfaction with the food?

There were instances when thoughts of Maya or memories of our visits to the same restaurant triggered unintentional tears. We had celebrated her seventeenth birthday there, and I vividly recalled gifting her a watch I had saved for months to buy. She had loved it. As more memories flooded back, becoming overwhelming, I decided to leave. The rain continued, and this time, I had no umbrella. I walked back to the hotel, immersed in the downpour.

* * *

35

THE REVELATION

THE first few nights after Maya passed away were the toughest. I found myself crying out for her at nights, wailing, *"Maiya, please come back."* I would have never known this if I wasn't using the sleep and snore tracker on my phone. The app recorded any noise in the surroundings after I fell asleep. I was surprised to hear the things I would say unconsciously when I checked it in the morning, like I always did.

Many have spoken of the phenomenon where the deceased visit them in the first night or so after passing. I am still a skeptic, but I experienced something similar. I recognize it as a hallucination, a creation of my mind to bring comfort, yet I find it noteworthy as it prompted me to reconsider aspects I had previously overlooked.

On the first night, my room was filled with imaginary figures, akin to scenes from movies. Despite my attempts to convince myself it was a dream by pinching and opening my eyes wide, the figures persisted. Children were running around, and as I grasped the concept of deceased loved ones visiting, I focused on filtering the images to find Maya. Finally spotting her, I questioned aloud if it was truly her and reached out. I inquired about her well-being, and she whispered back, *"Yes Hanchu, but you don't seem fine. You need to take care of yourself."* Overwhelmed with emotion, I confessed how much I missed her and promised not to bother her if she didn't want me around. She responded, *"Don't be stupid. I am sorry to leave you so suddenly."*

The next night, I caught another glimpse of her. However, this time it was very hazy, and I found myself questioning whether it was really her. She seemed to be running around with a group of kids, playfully teasing me. I couldn't understand how she could be so cheerful while I was consumed by sorrow. She insisted that I should understand from her demeanor that she was genuinely happy and in a better place. Gesturing to the laughing children around her, she emphasized the joy she felt. Yet, every time I tried to communicate with her, the images would fade away. In desperation, I pleaded with her to stay a little longer and spend more time with me.

I felt like I was losing my mind and eagerly awaited the next visit from Maya. The nights that followed brought fewer sightings of her. The figures became less distinct, and Maya seemed to disappear altogether. When the children appeared, I would plead with them to tell me where she was, but they didn't seem to understand. Frustration consumed me, and I would fall to my knees, begging them to bring her back to me. In moments of despair, I would pinch and slap myself, hoping to wake from what felt like a nightmare. Even staring into the bathroom mirror and pinching myself failed to dispel the hallucinations when I returned to the room.

* * *

I had to leave Nepal. Kiran would call me nearly every other day, informing me they were still too busy to entertain me. It felt as though they never wanted to see me again. I wasn't ready to return home, not yet. But where else could I go? Raj suggested I spend a few days at her place in Monzuno, Italy. It was precisely the kind of place I needed – a countryside retreat, far away from everything. Without hesitation, I purchased the next available tickets and departed the following day.

Raj was one of the few people who provided solace during this entire ordeal. She lived in Italy and had travelled to the United States a few times to visit Maya. They had bonded well, and Raj had spent a few days at Maya's place, taking care of her, teaching her Hatha Yoga practices, and often giving her body massages.

The flight was challenging. I had become quite emotional. While that wasn't embarrassing, what did embarrass me was when I started talking in my sleep, only to be awakened by the fellow passengers looking at me with confusion. When I opened my eyes, thinking I was talking to them, they would respond, *"I'm sorry but I don't understand what you are saying."* I would then awkwardly explain, *"No, I'm talking on the phone."* This likely added to the confusion, especially considering there was no actual phone in my hand while cruising thirty thousand feet above the ground. My journey involved a layover in Doha before reaching Rome and then continuing on to Bologna. However, the flight to Rome had even more interesting moments.

Seated in the aisle, as I usually preferred, I found myself next to a younger couple, presumably Italian. Throughout the flight, I involuntarily talked in my sleep and experienced sudden, frightening jolts that caused my legs to jerk, inadvertently hitting the seat in front and perhaps the person seated beside me. Upon realizing this, I would open my eyes to find the couple staring at me. Apologizing, I explained that I often suffered from cramps. To emphasize, I even pretended to massage my feet, hoping I hadn't accidentally struck them in my sleep. The male beside me seemed apprehensive, and every time I opened my eyes, I could sense his curious gaze fixed on me.

I even put my hands through the seat belts, as if to tie myself, so as not to swing my arms around when I fell asleep. Had I been wearing shoes instead of the flip flop, I would have tied my laces to keep my legs bound together as well. The couple perhaps were more eager to get out of the plane and not be seated next to me. The flight from Rome to Bologna was a short flight lasting just under an hour. Luckily, there was no one seated next to me. I stayed up, afraid of disturbing anyone if I happened to yell in my sleep. I didn't know what else I did when I dozed off.

Raj was kind enough to pick me up when I arrived in Bologna. However, that night took an unexpected turn. I woke up to find her standing next to the door, in tears. Raj had come to check on me upon hearing my shouts in my sleep. To her astonishment, she discovered me engaged in a romantic conversation with a pillow. She recounted instances when she observed me with my head pressed against the mattress, legs raised and pointing backward, as if attempting a headstand while digging into the bed—reminiscent of the behavior of my dogs. There were moments when I woke up in the middle of the night, reaching for my wallet and standing with a five-dollar bill in my hand, with no recollection of why I had done so.

Raj witnessed several peculiar incidents, including my interactions with unseen figures and talking to plants. Looking out the window, I perceived the plants and trees drawing close, staring at me, and engaging in conversations. Raj grew increasingly concerned, and I, in turn, felt a sense of fear. The notion of *"Love leads to madness"* crossed my mind. Was I going crazy? Did this indicate schizophrenia? Would I spend the rest of my life in a mental asylum? These thoughts troubled me, especially as my actions seemed reminiscent of Russell Crowe's portrayal of Professor Nash in the movie *"A Beautiful Mind."* The resemblance intensified my anxiety.

I had lost in love, but I did not want to lose again to life. I didn't want people sympathizing. I did not want people to be looking at me as if I was some kind of crazy and assuming that the loss of Maya had made me so vulnerable. I had to do something about it. With Raj's guidance, I started meditating and hydrating more often. She is a professional Classical Hatha Yoga teacher who had undergone rigorous training of seventeen hundred and fifty hours before she got certified. I believed and relied on her and was ready to show her my vulnerabilities, willing to follow her instructions to learn to accept and cope with my loss.

Slowly, the figures disappeared. I never saw them again. Perhaps my body was beginning to heal and there were no more hallucinations. Raj kept me busy and took me on drives. I tried not to dwell on situation and instructed my mind to do the same. I started meditating more, and very soon, I stopped experiencing anything unusual. Looking back, it's almost amusing to think that I was once glad to be experiencing such a phenomenon, as I thought I had gained a unique ability to see dead people. I'm relieved I didn't acquire that.

Coping with the situation would have been impossible without the support of my friends and family. Some advised me that the easiest path to healing was to let go. They emphasized that it was time for Maya to move on, and I should come to terms with it. The more I clung to the idea, the more difficult it became. Missing her for our own selfish reasons complicates the grieving process. We often cry when someone dies because we miss them, and this could be a selfish act. We struggle to accept the reality that the person who passed away is gone, taking away all their sufferings. It's challenging to acknowledge this truth and resist the temptation to wish they were still with us simply because they made a significant impact on our lives.

Maya had already released me even when she was alive. She desired a different life, one without me. Our paths crossed for a while to share each other's company, and for me to stand by her side during her most challenging days. Regardless of whether others perceive it or not, I am indifferent because I know she genuinely cared. The healing process might seem endless, but I must embark on it. It is now my turn to let her go. Approaching it with this mindset makes the process much more manageable. Her memories will endure, and I am aware they always will. I feel a closer connection to her now and comprehend her better after her departure. I clung to the past for too long, my love for her, obscuring the positive things that quietly slipped away.

She used to point out that I had a tendency to go to extremes in everything. According to her, if I loved someone, I would go to great lengths for that person, and if someone displeased me, they ceased to exist in my world, and I had a penchant for cutting them off completely. She often advised me to find a balance. Perhaps she was urging me to apply the same to our relationship. It's a lesson learned rather late than never, and I understand that now. While achieving that balance might have lessened the pain, I harbor no regrets.

Reflecting on it now, I realize I gave it my all. I spared no effort in making her feel loved and attending to her needs, especially during the most challenging moments of her life. I am now at peace, and her memories will forever be a cherished treasure, guiding me through life's toughest challenges. I have become a better person, and I owe it to her. I harbor no ill feelings toward her family. I believe she is smiling down on me for acknowledging my shortcomings and speaking the truth. I had asked her to read this book when I finished it. Her response was, *"Oh my God! I'm scared,"* accompanied by a smile. I never envisioned concluding this book without her presence amongst us.

It's a beautiful feeling to love and to care for someone so much selflessly, where you give in your hundred percent and expect nothing in return. I never knew I was capable of that but I'm sure everyone has that ability waiting for the right person to activate it.

She decided to free herself from all the chaos of the world before I could. We all have to perish one day; she chose to do it now. Her soul now breathes, and I can finally take care of mine. She may not be with us physically but will always remain in our hearts. I know she is with me and will continue to do so forever!

I will see you when I see you. Until then, rest well Maiya!

* * *

ABOUT THE AUTHOR:

Born and raised in Nepal, Parinaya relocated to the United States at the age of twenty to pursue higher education, ultimately earning an MBA. He always had a passion for writing, but when the recent tragedy struck, it became necessary for him to channel his feelings into his writing. His interests span business, finance, spirituality, and self-discovery.

A yoga and meditation enthusiast, he finds tranquility in these practices. His love for nature is evident in his passion for hiking and trekking every time he visits Nepal. Parinaya cherishes family and maintains close ties with his mother and two younger brothers. His life is a testament to his pursuit of purpose, growth, and appreciation for life's beauty.

His experiences and insights shape his writing, making his book, "Chasing Shadows," a compelling read.

ACKNOWLEDGEMENTS.

To all those who offered comforting words or a listening ear during my moments of doubt or difficulty, your kindness has meant the world to me. Your support has been a beacon of light, guiding me through the challenges of this endeavor.

To the readers who have welcomed my story into their homes and hearts, I am deeply touched by your embrace. Your willingness to engage with these pages is a testament to the power of storytelling, and I am humbled by your presence on this journey.

As we navigate the twists and turns of life, let us remember the preciousness of each moment. Let us choose love over resentment, kindness over bitterness. Life is fleeting, and it is our responsibility to make the most of every opportunity, to cherish the connections we share, and to spread love wherever we go.

Thank you all for being a part of this beautiful journey.

I'd love to share a cherished poem by David L. Weatherford that has profoundly impacted my approach to life:

SLOW DANCE

Have you ever watched kids on a merry-go-round,
Or listened to rain slapping the ground?

Ever followed a butterfly's erratic flight, or
gazed at the sun fading into the night?

You better slow down, don't dance so fast,
Time is short, the music won't last.

Do you run through each day on the fly?
When you ask: "How are you?" Do you hear the reply?

When the day is done, do you lie in your bed,
With the next hundred chores running through your head?

You better slow down, don't dance so fast,
Time is short, the music won't last.

Ever told your child, we'll do it tomorrow?
And in your haste, not see his sorrow?

Ever lost touch, let a friendship die,
Cause you never had time to call and say hi?

You better slow down, don't dance so fast,
Time is short, the music won't last.

When you run so fast to get somewhere,
You miss half the fun of getting there.

When you worry and hurry through your day,
It's like an unopened gift thrown away.

Life isn't a race, do take it slower,
Hear the music before the song is over.

Milton Keynes UK
Ingram Content Group UK Ltd.
UKHW052102300624
444882UK00004B/250